State Parties in India

State Parties in India:
Parliamentary Presence & Performance

Manisha Madhava

GYAN

Published, 2020

Published by

Gyan Publishing House
5, Ansari Road
Daryaganj, New Delhi-110002
Phone: 011-47034999, 9811692060
www.gyanbooks.com
E-mail: books@gyanbooks.com

Printed at: Gyan Press, Delhi.

Cataloging in Publication Data—DK
Courtesy: D.K. Agencies (P) Ltd. <docinfo@dkagencies.com>

Madhava, Manisha, 1970- **author.**
State parties in India : parliamentary presence & performance / Manisha Madhava.
pages cm
Includes bibliographical references and index.
ISBN 9788121220132

1. Political parties—India. 2. Representative government and representation—India. 3. India—Politics and government. 4. India. Parliament. Lok Sabha. I. Title.

LCC JQ298.A1M33 2020 | DDC 324.20954084 23

Dedicated to My Mother

Shanta

She gave me wings to fly

Contents

Preface

State Parties have significantly altered the contours of Indian politics in the post-Congress polity. They have been the vehicles of political mobilisation and democratisation, often carrying the aspiration of the new and emerging forces in Indian society. The consolidation of State Parties and their growing influence on the political process is both interesting and important phenomena in Indian politics. It is indicative of the changing contours of Indian democracy and the role that parties have come to play in it.

The desire to work on this area emerged out of my previous interest in the study of the parliamentary membership and its functioning. As I poured into the changing profile of Members of Parliament (MPs), I began to wonder if the change in the party composition of the Parliament, with large presence of MPs from regional political parties, has also led to change in the nature of the political elite. Who are these new political elite? Are they different from MPs of national parties? What changes have they brought to the functioning of the Parliament? How do they carry out their functions as MPs? How do they reconcile the interests of their constituencies with their roles as representatives of national Parliament?

The fourteenth Lok Sabha, which had a large presence of State Parties (173 MPs) made the task comparison even more interesting. It provided a reasonable basis for assessment of the relationship between voters, State Parties and Parliament. However, these questions would have remained unanswered, had it not been funded. The ICSSR funding of the project and the support of CSDS- Lokniti Programme, with its large data base of National Election Study made the task feasible. Thus, was conceptualised this work.

The year 2014 saw a new party system and dramatic changes in the composition of the Parliament with the BJP emerging as the single dominant party in the Lok Sabha. The Congress Party has been reduced to its lowest numbers ever in the Parliament and the strength of regional parties in the Parliament has also reduced considerably. The challenge to this government comes from State Parties, some of which sometimes support the ruling party, as in case of abolition of Article 375, but oppose it in the Rajya Sabha or in the GST council meetings. Some State Parties, such as the Shiv Sena, Telugu Desam Party and Shromani Akali Dal have also walked out of the National Democratic Alliance to assert their independence.

What does the future hold for State Parties? Will the opposition to the ruling party come from these State Parties? Will they again gain prominence? This, as the study shows, would depend upon two factors; their ability to retain and expand their support base; and the role that they imagine for themselves in the national politics. And in this, the State Parties and scholars of the subject will have much to learn from their experience in the past.

Acknowledgements

Research on State Parties is an ambitious exercise, not just because of the large amount of literature available on the matter, but also because of the diversities among the parties themselves. To expand the horizon of the study to the Parliament is fraught with danger of over simplification. This book is the result of a project that was carried out for Indian Council of Social Science Research, (ICSSR) New Delhi. I am thankful to ICSSR for funding a project. A research of this magnitude, which involves data collection and interviews from all across the country, could not have been undertaken without adequate funding and support. The ICSSR through Research Project Scheme made this work possible.

The data required for the work is humanly impossible to collect by an individual researcher. It requires collective effort and institutional support. For this, I am thankful to Lokniti- CSDS for providing me access to the National Election Study 2004 and 2009 data. I am deeply indebted to Prof Sanjay Kumar, Director CSDS for readily providing with all data and guiding and mentoring me in conceptualising the research work.

Prof Sandeep Shastri, Pro Vice Chancellor, Jain University and CERSSE, Jain University gave me the ambience and the advice to complete this work. A project of this nature requires focused effort over a period of time for its completion. Jain University gave me the space and the facilities which went a long way in completing this work. Prof Shastri's invaluable advice helped me shape its many drafts.

I sincerely appreciate the efforts of Prof Vasundhara Mohan, Retired. Professor of Mumbai University, who read the draft several times and made valuable suggestions. She also stood by me at all times to encourage and guide me through this work

Many thanks are also due to my mentors. Prof. Suhas Palshikar of Pune University and Prof. K.C. Suri of Hyderabad University who gave valuable inputs that helped in conceptualising and organising the entire work. They spared their valuable time and gave detailed suggestions that gave a new dimension to the work.

I sincerely appreciate the efforts of my young and enthusiastic team of research assistants who helped me in putting together this work. Srimanti Sarkar and Sudeshana Chatterjee in data collection, Vedika Nair, Nayantara Kurpad, Monica Chauhan, Divya Gangadhar in copy editing and Sumedha for analysis of data. Their enthusiasm was infectious and helped in overcoming the fatigue of data collection and proof reading.

My thanks are also due to my team of field investigators, Suman Damera, Harpreet Kaur, K. Manjunath, Sudeshna Chatterjee, Baba Mayaram without whom so many interviews and survey would not have been possible.

Thanks are also due to my colleagues Reetika Syal of Jain University, who taught me how to use statistical data effectively. Also the Lokniti team of Jyoti Pant and Vibha Agarwal who readily provided me with all help. Also, I would like to put my appreciation on record for Gyan Books, especially Mr.Javed & Mr. Imran to bring out this volume of time.

Last but not the least, I am thankful to my family; my husband Subramayam Gorti, who stood behind me at every step, providing encouragement, advice and information. But for his support not only would this research have been possible, my research career itself would have come to a standstill; brother Rajsekhar who from the beginning to the end has encouraged all my academic endeavors. He has been by severest critique and best friend- all at once.

Most of all, I remember with love and gratitude my mother, to whom I dedicate this work. She passed away in course of completion of this work. She was my friend, philosopher and guide and whatever I am is because of endless energy, love and enthusiasm with which she supported me. She taught me to think independently, to dream and soar high, higher than I could ever imagine which she could dream for me. *Thank you Mummy, wherever you are......*

Abbreviations

AC	:	Arunachal Congress
AIADMK	:	All India Anna Dravida Munnetra Kazhagam
AGP	:	Asom Gana Parishad
AIFB	:	All India Forward Bloc
AITC	:	All India Trinamool Congress
BJD	:	Biju Janata Dal
CPI (ML)	:	Communist Party of India (Marxist- Leninist)
DMK	:	Dravida Munnetra Kazhagam
ECI	:	Election Commission of India
FPM	:	Federal Party of Manipur
INLD	:	Indian National Lok Dal
JD(S)	:	Janata Dal (Secular)
JD(U)	:	Janata Dal (United)
J&KNC	:	Jammu & Kashmir National Conference
J&KNPP	:	Jammu & Kashmir National Panthers Party
J&KPDP	:	Jammu & Kashmir Peoples Democratic Party
JMM	:	Jharkhand Mukti Morcha
KEC	:	Kerala Congress
KEC(M)	:	Kerala Congress (M)
LNJP	:	Lok Jan Shakti Party
MGP	:	Maharashtrawadi Gomantak Party
MDMK	:	Marumalarchi Dravida Munnetra Kazhagam
MNF	:	Mizo National Front
MP	:	Member of Parliament
MPP	:	Manipur Peoples Party
NPF	:	Nagaland Peoples Front
OBC	:	Other Backward Class

PMK	:	Pattali Makkal Katchi
RJD	:	Rashtriya Janata Dal
RLD	:	Rashtriya Lok Dal
RSP	:	Revolutionary Socialist Party
SAD	:	Shiromani Akali Dal
SAD(M)	:	Shiromani Akali Dal (Mann)
SC	:	Scheduled Castes
SDF	:	Sikkim Democratic Front
SHS	:	Shivsena
SP	:	Samajwadi Party
ST	:	Scheduled Tribes
TDP	:	Telugu Desam Party
UDP	:	United Democratic Party
UGDP	:	United Goan Democratic Party
UKD	:	Uttarakhand Kranti Dal

Introduction

Political parties are an indispensable part of modern democratic politics. They occupy a central place in India's democracy. The success of India's democracy, especially its electoral democracy may be attributed, at least in part to the existence and relatively unhindered operation of a large number of political parties. They have played a crucial role in electoral mobilisation, interest aggregation; institutional representation and government formation, thereby contributing to the process of democratisation.

In the last six decades, the world of political parties in India has been in constant flux. The one party dominant system of the 1950s and 1960s has gradually been replaced by multi-party system. Old parties have disintegrated and new ones have emerged. Even those parties that have survived have seen significant transformation. One of the distinctive characteristics of India's party system since the 1990s has been the growing importance of regional political parties. According to the Election Commission of India, the number of state political parties has risen from 11 in 1957 to 34 in 2009. Their vote share in parliamentary elections has increased by 20 percent while that of national parties has declined by 13 percent. The growing importance of regional political parties can be further gauged by the fact that all the governments at the centre from 1989 to 2014 have been formed with the support of several state/regional political parties. Further, regional political parties were in power in 12 states out of the 29 states in 2004.

One of the causes for the emergence and growth of state/ regional parties has been their ability to mobilize the masses on the basis of cleavages of religion, region, caste, language or ethnicity. The failure of the Congress, since 1967 to accommodate diverse regional and local interest, together with the growing centralisation of the party organisation gave political space to many political formations. Yogendra Yadav, an eminent psephologist points out that regional political parties gained prominence due to their ability to give salience to dormant social identities. He describes them as the "third electoral system." A large number of local parties emerged that espoused the cause of certain groups, which in turn became its primary support base. Thus, for instance, the Bahujan Samaj Party (BSP), the Samajwadi Party (SP) in Uttar Pradesh and the Rashtriya Janata Dal (RJD) in Bihar derive support from the backward classes of society, i.e. the Dalits. The SP and RJD have gained prominence with the support of the Yadavs in UP and Bihar respectively (Chandra, 2004; Verma, 2004; Pai, 2002). Similarly, the Shiromani Akali Dal (SAD) gets supports mainly from the Sikhs in Punjab.

The success of the mobilisation strategy of State Parties has had a far-reaching impact on almost all political institutions, including the Parliament, which was the basis of their political influence at the national level. The Parliament has provided the state political parties with a national political space. It has given them an opportunity to influence the political process at the central level and restructure the political discourse. Given the growing numerical strength of State Parties in the national legislature, the manner in which they perform their role determines the nature of parliamentary functioning.

In the light of these, the performance of regional parties within the institutional framework of the Parliament is of particularly interesting. It is ironical that although the Parliament plays a pivotal role in India's democratic polity, and the functioning of State Parties within the Parliament determines not just efficacy of Parliament, but throws a light on the character of political democracy, there has not been much attempt to understand it.

Broadly speaking, the literature on relationship between Parliament and political parties fall into two categories: firstly, literature that is concerned primarily with the Parliament and secondly, literature on regional political parties. There is a serious paucity of work on the Parliament in India. W.H. Morris -Jones's work, *Parliament in India*, published in 1954, is one of the best works in the field till today. Morris- Jones analyzed the nature of representation in the first three Parliament in terms of the socio-economic composition of the Lok Sabha. R.K. Bhardwaj also carried out a similar study covering the period 1951-1974. Several other scholars like A.R. Mukherjea (1983) and T.S. Rajagopala Iyyengar (1972) made a study of the Indian Parliament. However, most of these works are dated. Subhash Kashyap's (1997) *The History of Parliament in India* provides a historical study of evolution of Parliament in India. More recently, B.L. Shankar and Valerian Rodrigues'(2011) work on *Parliament of India* studies the composition and functioning of Parliament in India. However, none of the works on Parliament in India attempts to relate the membership of Parliament with its functioning, i.e. the eternal question of politics : who represents, what, when and how?

Much of the work related to political parties and party system in India have studied the causes for the emergence and increased influence of regional political parties. However, there has been little or no work relating their parliamentary membership with their support base. One of the earliest studies on state politics and state based parties was *State Politics in India* by Myron Weiner (1968). Since then much has been written on the changing dynamics of party system in India and emergence of regional political parties. Ajay Mehra, D.D. Khanna and Gert W. Kueck (2003) *Political Parties and Party System*, Verney and Arora (ed) (1995) *Multiple Identity in a Single State: Indian Federalism in a Comparative Perspective;* Balveer Arora, "Centrists and Regionalist Parties in India's Federal Polity in Atul Kohli (ed) (1988) *India's Democracy*. S. Bhatnagar and Pradeep Kumar (ed) (1988) *Regional Political Parties in India*; G Gopa Kumar's *Regional Political Parties and State*, Suhas Palshikar's (2004) article, Revisiting State Level Parties, The Regional Political Parties and Democracy: Romantic Rendevouz or Localised Legitimation in *Economic and Political Weekly* provide a view of role of regional political parties in India's party system. Similarly, some literature is also available on functioning of specific parties within specific states such as Angela Sutherland Burgers' (1966) *Opposition in a Dominant Party System: A Study of Jan Sangh, The PSP and Socialist Party in UP, India,* Sudha Pai's work, *The BSP in Uttar Pradesh* (*Seminar*, No. 472, 1998), etc.

Scholars like Kanchan Chandra (2004), Suhas Palshikar (2004), have made attempts to study the social base of regional political formations like the BSP and the Shiv Sena. The survey work carried out by the Centre for the Study of Developing Societies, New Delhi, since 1996 also attempts to study the social bases of regional political parties. However, as mentioned earlier none of these work attempt to correlate the support base of a party with their legislative work either at the state or at the national level.

The present book attempts to fill in this gap in literature by conducting an empirical study of the socio-economic background of parliamentary membership of regional political parties and their performance in the national legislative body and correlate it with their social base to answer the main research questions: What do members of regional political parties represent in the parliament? How do they represent? And what is the impact of the representation on the institution itself.

The work attempts to answer these questions within the theoretical and conceptual framework of the idea of representation. Political representation is a multi- dimensional and multifaceted concept that is open to a wide variety of interpretation. However, in the present context of two aspect of representation may be considered:

- Representation of persons or descriptive representation which postulates similarity between the representative and represented.
- Representation of interests or representation of what the representative perceives as the interests of the constituency that he seeks to represent.

Both these interpretation of representation have inbuilt in them the principle of representation of a collective by a party where the electorate mandates a representative from a several competing parties based on their policy promises and performance. The application of this model of representation in the context of legislatures in India is not free from problems. Among the many issues involved is the one that the electorate in India can influence the Parliament of India both indirectly and directly; indirectly through their choice of governments in the states and directly through elections to the Parliament. Further, India has a large number of political parties that are not always distinguishable in terms of either their ideology or in terms of their programme. Their classification as state national and state/ regional/local is also not universally accepted. Parties too do not always accept the nomenclature given to them.

In light of these complicated issues this work attempts to raise and answer the following questions:

- Who are the representatives of State Parties in the Lok Sabha? What is their socio-economic background? What is their educational, occupational and economic background?
- What is the support base of State Parties? Is there a similarity between the MP's of State Parties and their electorate in terms of their socio-economic background such as age, education and occupation? In the descriptive sense, is the membership of State Parties in the legislature conducive to representation of persons?
- What is the nature of 'activity of representation' carried out by the MPs of State Parties within the parliament? What kind of parliamentary business do members of State Parties participate in and why? What are the procedural devices that are favoured by members of State Parties, within the Parliament to perform their

function? Do they take part more frequently in proceedings that allow them to raise constituency concerns?

- Whom do the MP's of State Parties try to represent: persons or interests? Whose interest do they represent: political constituency, State, region, or nation?
- If State Parties, seeks to represent the interests of their constituencies, what is the nature of interest/issues they represent? Are there correlations between the interest that they represent within the legislature, the interest of the constituencies that have elected them and their own socio-economic background?

Scope of the Work

There are large number of schemes of classification of parties and there is little consensus on both the nomenclature of political parties and the basis on which they are classified, this work has adopted Election Commission of India's (ECI) categorisation of parties. The ECI categorizes all registered parties, for the purpose of allocation of election symbols, into two types – recognised and unrecognised. Within the recognised parties there are what is referred to as the National and State Parties. A political party that is a recognised political party in less than four States is included in the ambit of "State party". It is known as a "State party" in the State or States in which it is so recognised. However, the party has to continue to fulfill these conditions for recognition on the results of any subsequent general election to the House of the People or, to the Legislative Assembly of the State. This work is based on ECI's definition of State Parties in 2009 and uses the term accordingly. Other nomenclatures such as regional parties, State based parties are not taken into account

The scope of the work is limited to analysis of social bases and parliamentary performance of MP's of State Parties in the 14th Lok Sabha in the period 2004-2009. The 14th Lok Sabha was constituted in 2004 when the ruling National Democratic Alliance (NDA) lost power in the run up to the Lok Sabha elections and the United Progressive Alliance (UPA) led by the Congress Party came to power. The 14th Lok Sabha had the largest presence of members from the State Parties (173). These parties had varying ideologies, support base and programmes.

They played a significant role in the 14th Lok Sabha both in the government and the opposition. Thus, while the Rashtriya Janata Dal (RJD) was a part of the ruling coalition, the Shiv Sena (SHS) was a part of the opposition NDA. In addition, there were a number of other parties which were not aligned to any particular formation.

The political context of 14th Lok Sabha is also important. The UPA government, among many others in the period 1989-2004 completed its term in office. A bi-polar alliance with the Congress and the BJP leading the two poles was established by 2004 and the political positions of most of the State Parties was also clear. Though the regional parties, were not in a position to form a third front, their importance within the coalition was nonetheless significant. The norms of coalition politics had taken roots and institutional arrangements such as the Common Minimum Programme (CMP) gave a definite say to regional political parties in the process of policy-making process. State Parties and their leadership had also amassed adequate experience of negotiating with national parties both within and outside the institutional framework.

The 14th Lok Sabha had the distinction of passing a series of significant legislation including the Indo-US Nuclear deal, the MNREGA and Right to Information Act. The State Parties were contributors to the enactment of such legislations. Thus, both in terms of institutional framework as well as in terms of experience and policy output the 14th Lok Sabha provided a platform to State Parties to achieve their goals.

Data Sources and Methodology

The study was conducted using three research pathways namely use of in-depth study and analysis of primary data, survey, and interviews

This work is based on detailed examination of the social, educational and economic profile of the members of State Parties. The Lok Sabha secretariat provides disaggregate data on the age, education and occupation of members of Parliament. This data was aggregated in terms of age, education, educational specialisation and occupation of MPs of State Parties and national parties. Further, data relating to income of MPs State Parties from secondary sources was also analyzed

It is widely believed that State Parties get their support from poor, less educated and lower castes. To test this belief primary data from National Election Studies (NES) 2004 and 2009 conducted by the Centre for the Study of Developing Societies, New Delhi, a premiere research organisation was utilised. Since 1996, the CSDS has carried out survey after every Lok Sabha elections. The sample size of the National Election Study- Post Poll Survey in 2004 was 22,000. The voters selected on a random sampling basis from two polling stations in an assembly segment of every parliamentary constituency were interviewed. They were asked 61 questions by interviewers who were specially appointed and trained for the purpose in each state. The entire process was coordinated by state level coordinators. Data so collected were complied and tabulated at the CSDS, New Delhi. This aggregate data made available by the CSDS constitutes the basis of the present research.

The procedures of Parliament provide many opportunities to Members of Parliament (MPs) for daily and periodic interventions on behalf of their electors. It also gives them an opportunity to influence the policies of the government through debates at various stages of the passage of a bill, discussions within the committees, proposals for amendments of bills, etc. Legislation itself is an obvious technique of intervention: new laws can be enacted and old laws can be revised with a view to change in administrative behaviour or policies. The deliberations in course of law making give opportunity to the MPs to exercise supervision through cross-questioning. In addition, Question Hour, Calling Attention, Motion, Adjournment Motion, Short Duration Discussion, Half an Hour Discussions and Discussion under Rule 377 also provide members an opportunity for deliberation. The participation of members of State Parties in all these parliamentary procedures both in quantitative and quantitative sense, such as language of discussion, nature participation, issues raised in select sessions of fourteenth Lok Sabha in course of its life span of five years were analysed to understand the nature of participation of members of State Parties.

Scheme of Work

This work is based on two broad interpretations of representation viz descriptive and procedural representation within the institutional structures; in the context of this work representation within the Parliament. It opens with a discussion on the idea of representation and its theoretical underpinnings. Political representation is an often used term. The multi-faceted and multi-dimensional nature of the term makes it difficult both to interpret it and understand its various dimensions. The chapter outlines the two main dimensions of representation- representation of persons and representation of interest- that is relevant in the context of nature of political representation attempted by political parties in India. It also looks into the role of political parties in a democracy with special reference to representation. The second chapter looks at the origin, typology and development of State Parties in India. This chapter offers a detailed understanding of the various bases on which State Parties have been created or based. It also briefly traces the electoral rise and the growth of State Parties, not just at the regional or state level but also at national level on the basis of electoral data. It attempts explore the causes for the phenomena.

The third chapter, 'Support Base of State Parties' looks into the social profile of voters who elect MPs of State Parties. Herein, the All India Post Poll Survey conducted by CSDS during the 2004 election has been used to identify the support base of State Parties. The chapter analyses both All India data as well as data from those constituencies (in 17 states) in which State party MPs were elected to clearly establish the support base of State Parties. A cursory correlation between the profile of MP's and their support base is also attempted to understand their representative character.

The fourth chapter 'Who are the Representatives of State Parties? Understanding the Socio- economic Profile of Members' examines representation of members of State Parties in the 14th Lok Sabha in descriptive terms. It looks into the socio- economic profile of MPs of State Parties in an attempt to answer two questions: first, who are the members of State Parties and what is their social and economic background and is there a significant difference between the social and economic background of MP's along party line? Here the representative-ness of State Parties is associated with its sociological interpretation, which holds that the legislative assemblies that have cultural 'congruence' with the populace that elects them are in a better position to represent them. For the purpose of the present work important variables namely; age, education, educational specialisation and occupation were considered. This chapter is based on data drawn from the parliamentary records.

The second section of the work attempts to look at representation by State Parties in terms of their parliamentary performance. This section includes two chapters. The fifth chapter 'Relating Performance to Profile: Are State party Members Different' looks into the performance of State party MPs in the Lok Sabha. It looks into statistical data relating to their participation in Debates, Question Hour. It also looks into the attendance record of the State party MPs. The chapter throws a light on the mechanisms of intervention that are used by MPs of State Parties and examines any differences that may exist between the State Parties and national parties. It also co relate the nature of representation with the profile of MPs to determine whether their own background influences their parliamentary performance.

The penultimate chapter 'What to State party MPs Represent and How?' is a qualitative study based on content analysis of Lok Sabha debates and looks into issues and concerns that are represented by State party MPs? It relates the issues raised to two aspects which may play heavily on the nature of representation; the party manifesto, which is the basis on which the MPs of State Parties are elected, and the profile of MPs. The chapter examines, on the basis of opinion polls and survey data, the issues that people consider as important and analyses whether the parliamentarians are guided by it. Interviews of nearly 200 supporters of State Parties have also been used to ascertain what people expect from their MPs. Members of Parliament represent disparate constituencies of territory, occupation, class, community, ethnic groups and the like. The nature of representation depends upon what the MPs seek to represent. This chapter brings forth the challenges that members face in representing and the various roles that State party MPs assume in the process of representation. The chapter shows that the popularity of certain procedures of Parliament is on account of its ability to give rooms to members to represent local concerns.

The concluding chapter attempts to put together the findings of the preceding chapters and attempts to unravel the nature of representation carried by State party MPs. They are, as the work shows, imagining new roles for themselves, constrained by their own interpretation and imagination of 'representation', which has altered the nature of parliamentary functioning. It dispels notions of the underperformance by members belonging to State Parties and underlines their contributions towards a new interpretation of representation in a large and diverse democracy like India.

Chapter - 1

Interpreting Political Representation & Role of Political Parties

Democracy as an idea and as an institution is a human contravention designed to organize public life. Modern Democracies had its origin in the ancient Greek city states of Athens. It emerged in Mesopotamia, simultaneously. Democracy as it existed in classical Greek city states was associated with large gatherings of citizens in assemblies and public places. The small size and limited population of the ancient Greek *polis* meant that citizens could directly participate in public affairs.[1] However, as the focus of democratic government shifted to large-scale units like nations, and the concept of citizenship widened, the problem of participation of the majority in controlling the agenda of the government emerged. This led to the emergence of representative democracy; a system, where rule-abiding, elected officers undertake to represent the interest or the views of the citizens, within the framework of the rule of law (Held, 1999). The classic statement of this view was found in the works of James Madison, Jeremy Benthem and later John Stuart Mill.

Central to the concept of representative democracy, as propounded by these liberal theorists, is the idea that government represents a means of enhancing individual interest. The representative state is a mechanism for aggregating individual interest and protecting individual rights. The sovereign powers of the state therefore, are constantly sought to be justified while at the same time being limited by the people.

By the 19th century, representative democracy came to be regarded as the only viable form of democracy in a large country. As J. S. Mill has observed,

> That the only government which can fully satisfy all the exigencies of the social state is one in which the whole people participate; that any

> participation, even in the smallest public function is useful; that the participation should everywhere be a great as the general degree of improvement of the community will allow; and that nothing less can ultimately be desirable than the admission of all to a share in the sovereign power of the state. But since all cannot, in a community exceeding a single small town, participate personally in any but some minor portions of the public business. It follows that the ideal type of a perfect government must be representative. (Mill, 1858: 217)

In the later 19th century and early twentieth century, a cluster of rules and institutions permitting the broadest participation of the citizens in the choice of representatives, who could make political decisions for the entire community developed and modern representative democracy assumed its contemporary form. Robert Dahl (2001) an American political scientist and an authority on democracy, has attempted to identify the main institutions of a democratic political system in our times. This is summarised below:

1. Elected officials - a deliberative democracy is characterised by the existences of elected officials who have been vested by the constitution to make policy decision. Such elected officials must be chosen through elections, which are conducted in a free and fair manner.
2. Freedom of expression - the success of democracy depends upon the extent to which citizens have the right to express themselves on political matters, including criticism of officials, the government, the socio-economic order and the prevailing ideology without the threat of coercive sanction.
3. Access to alternative sources of information - in a democracy citizens must have access to information other that those provided by the government, through independent channels like newspaper, telecommunications, etc which must be free from governmental control or the control of any other group attempting to influence the attitude of the people.
4. Associational autonomy- Citizens in a democracy must have the right to form relatively independent associations or organisations such as political interest groups etc.
5. Inclusive citizenship - a country can be designated as a democracy only if all adult, permanently residing citizens, subject to the laws of the country are not denied rights like the right to vote, to contest for office, to express freely, to form and participate in independent political organisations, etc

The criterion for democratic governance did not emerge simultaneously in any country. For instance, universal adult suffrage was introduced only in the 20th century even in countries which had a long history of democratic government.[2] In countries where the full set of democratic institutions arrived and has endured, common patterns of emergence of these institutions are discernable. Election to the legislature was the first step towards the establishment of democratic polity.[3] Gradual rights of the citizens to express themselves on political matters and seek information followed the practice of electing law-making officials. Table 1.1 indicates some such devices that have found acceptability in most democratic countries to achieve the ideals of democracy.

Table 1.1- Procedural Devices & Institutions Ensuring Democratic Values

Functions/ Values	*Procedural devices*	*Institutions*
Representation of electorate	Political equality, universal adult suffrage, independent election commission, Open party competition, freedom of speech and expression.	Political Parties, Elections, Legislature, Interest Groups
Representation of issues	Procedural devices like debates in the legislature. These devices ensure the rights and independence of opposition	Political Parties, Legislature, Pressure Groups
Transparency	Legislative proceedings must be open to the media and public alike ensuring transparency of the legislative process	Legislature
Public participation in legislative process or accessibility to legislature	Legislatures power to refer bills to the public	Political Parties, Legislature
Autonomy of decision/ policy making	Parliamentary sovereignty, separation of legislature from judiciary, office of an independent speaker, financial autonomy of the legislature and finally the provision of a separate professional staff for the assistance of the members.	Political Parties, Legislature, Opposition, Judiciary, Free Press, Periodic Elections
Accountability	Time bound electoral process, the election commission which monitored the electoral process and elected members, a code of conduct for the members and a constitutionally sanctioned remuneration for members.	Political Parties, Legislature, Opposition, Judiciary, Free Press, Periodic Elections

Political parties soon emerged, initially as fractions and partisan organisations, but later as full-fledged political parties. The emergence of political parties changed the nature of political participation. With the emergence of political parties, representative democracies became party democracies and political parties' vehicles of representation. The centrality of political parties to democracy is evident from the fact that scholars began to describe political parties "at the heart of political system", as "endemic to democracy"- as an unavoidable part of democracy. Susan Scarow refers to the rise of party based democracy as "one of the transformative inventions of the 19th century (Dalton et all, 2011). Henry George coined the phrase "Party Government" and Walter Bagehot stressed on the importance of cohesive parliamentary parties as the unifying element of representative democracies, indicating the growing importance of political parties in democracies.

Political Parties: Their Role in Representative Democracies

Political parties are multi-faceted and multipurpose organisations that have multiple linkages to both the society and the state. Political parties may not be regarded merely as political organisations, as they arise out of civil society and their continued existence and utility is determined by the civil society. However, they overlap and shape the institutions of state, particularly the legislature and if they acquire the requisite numbers, even the executive. Yet, they are not completely political as they have a social programmatic content, an ideology and a vision that encompasses both the society and the state. They further the interests of both the individuals within the organisation and of groups within the society, as well as their own interest.

There are a plethora of definitions of political parties, though a universally acceptable definition of political parties is yet to be crystallised. Among the many definitions of political parties, a well-known definition comes from the American political scientist Antony Downs, who wrote:

> A political party is a team of men seeking to control the governing apparatus by gaining office in a duly constituted election (Downs 1957)

Giovanni Sartori (2005) a well-known researcher on political parties, defined a party as:

> ...any political group identified by an official label that presents at elections, and is capable of placing through election, candidates for public office.

Both these definition of political parties are different, though accurate indicating the various vantage points from which political parties may be understood. While Downs (1958) emphasizes on seeking power and occupying office, Sartori (2005) places importance on contesting elections.

Broadly however, parties are widely understood as

- Permanent associations of citizens
- Based on free membership and a programme
- Keen to occupy political offices
- Relying on elections as a means of gaining entry into the political process
- Resolve problems through a pre-determined course of action.

The above interpretation of political parties encompasses the characteristics/ features of political parties and their objectives, as well as the means that they seek to achieve these objectives. Broadly however, political parties may be understood as permanent organisations that seek to perform assimilative and integrative function, through acquisition of state power. They are essential links between the unorganised civil society/ masses and organised state structure.

While there may be many organisations that attempt to arbitrate between the people and their agents, the essential difference between a political party and all such organisations is the absence of desire and effort to assume responsibility for 'delivering' through acquisition of power. Organisations other than political parties may seek and sometimes acquire influence, but only parties seek, compete, and acquire power over state apparatus and control over public funds, government, bureaucracy and legislative mechanism. They are, in that sense, a part of the delivery mechanism that is responsible to its clients and accountable for its acts. Political parties have emerged as 'democratic instruments' of democracies.

Table 1.2: Distinction between Party and Non Party Organisations

Type of institution /Purpose	***Party***	***Non Party***
Objective	Gain power, Occupy offices to implement its programme	Influence policy making
Methods	Voting, Assuming office Canvassing, Campaigning, Net working,	Campaigning, Networking, Canvassing
Recruitment	Open	Restricted
Purpose	Political representation	Social/Political/Religious

This is, however, not to say that existence of political parties is limited to democracies alone. Non-democratic, authoritarian and totalitarian regimes too, are characterised by existence of strong political parties.

However, what distinguishes political parties in a democracy from a non-democratic political system is:

- Reliance of parties on people for support and acceptance
- Near complete freedom on the creation of such groups
- Their unrestricted right to seek public support and assumption of office responsibilities on winning such support.

Political Parties in a Democracy

The earliest attempt at classifying the roles and the functions of political parties in a democracy was made by Gabriel Almond. Since then innumerable attempts have been made to address the issue. Political parties perform a range of functions in political organisations, government formation and mass representation. They reduce the complexity of governmental process by aggregating interest and converting them into understandable options that can be exercised by the voters.

Broadly however, the functions of political parties may be classified as that of interest articulation, aggregation and political recruitment, policy formulation and government formation. Of these, the first two functions are performed by the political parties at the level of civil society and the last two at the institutional levels. These functions are often interlinked and interelated to one another in such a way that the strength of the political system and the nature of the political process depends upon the performance of political parties. It may be mentioned here, that all political parties may not perform each of these functions. Nor do they emphasize on each of these functions, and perform them equally well.

Elite Recruitment and Electoral Mobilisation

Larry Diamond and Richard Gunther (1993) characterize elite recruitment and electoral mobilisation as the core function of a political party. Political parties recruit potential leaders, train them for office, socialize them about the norms of democratic governance and in the process ensure continuity and stability. This function is performed both during the phase of candidate nomination, where candidates who are to contest the elections are chosen and electoral mobilisation, where parties, mobilize their supporters to support their candidates. In both these stages, political parties play a crucial role in structuring the choices of individuals.

Interest Aggregation

In representative democracies, political parties are crucial instruments of molding and melding the interest of various social groups into broader and more universalistic goals. In a pluralistic society such as India, this function assumes significant importance. This function may take place either before the elections or after the elections, where a government coalition is formed after aggregating interest of all parties. This function also paves the way for policy stability and policy sustenance over a long period of time.

Government Formation

In the ultimate analysis, political parties compete for power. Political power allows parties to occupy institutions of decision-making and mould the political process in the most conducive manner. Hence, government formation after the success of the party in the election is a key performance function of political parties. In fact, in multi-party parliamentary democracies and coalitional governments considerable energy of the political parties is spent in formation and sustenance of government.

Social Integration

Political parties enable the conversion of people into citizens and assist successful participation in the political process. In societies characterised by diversities of race, religion, region and socio-economic difference, the role of political parties in integrating diverse interest is of considerable importance. These safety valve functions help in smoothly accommodating the interest into the political process and prevent revolutionary outbreaks.

Political Representation

Parties also play a vital role of political representation. This function of representation is central to the existence of parties in a democracy and can be performed by parties during the electioneering stage, where political parties seek the support of their clientele to implement their policies and programmes; within the legislature, where parties represent the interest of their supporters; within the domains of institutions where they influence, draft and enact policies. The function of political representation is of primary importance because it allows political parties to establish roots within the institutional framework of the political system as well as within the civil society.

The important question that arises is; what constitutes representation, what and how do political parties represent? Is there a single universally acceptable definition of political representation? Where and when is the function of representation performed? What is the role of political parties in the process of representation? Do different types of political parties perform representative functions differently? The answer to these questions requires an understanding of "representation" and its varied interpretation.

Decoding the Idea of Representation

The concept of representation is essentially a modern one. The Greeks had no corresponding word for it though they elected officials and sent ambassadors. The Romans had the word '*representare*' from which the word representation is derived, but they used it to bring the literal idea of bringing into presence something which is absent, or embodiment of an abstract in an object. The usage of the term 'representation' to refer to a person acting on behalf of others in a political context emerged in Latin around the 13th and 14th centuries.

Etymologically, representation means representing; making present again. It means making present in some sense, something which is nevertheless not present literally or in 'fact' (Pitkins, 1967:8). In common parlance, it is used to refer to:

> ...a relationship between two persons, the representative and represented or the constituent, with the representative holding the authority to perform various actions that incorporate the agreement of the represented. (Grazia, 1964: 461)

The relationship is not simple, for every action and every type of communication is open to representation. Moreover, representation is a social, psychological as well as a political phenomenon. As a scholar (Singh, 1995) said, Representation is a vague concept and "may sometimes be one thing, sometimes another". When used in the context of political representation "it becomes a multi-faceted and multi-dimensional concept". It has several usages and shades of meaning attached to it. It may broadly be defined as "a range of expectations that people possess in regard to government and hence in regard to public officials and leaders."[4] The scope of political representation is indicated by Robert Von Mohl's unpretentious" definition.

> Representation is a process through which the influence which the entire citizenry, or a part of them have upon governmental action with their expressed approval exercised on their behalf by a smaller number among them, with binding effect on those represented. (Van Mohl cited in Friedrich, 1950: 266)

There are numerous theories of representation, which attempt to interpret and decode the multiple meanings of this complex idea. For the purpose of simplification, it is possible to classify the theories of representation into three broad groups (Pitkins, 1967);

- The Authorisation Theory
- The Accountability Theory, and
- The Descriptive Theory of Representation.

Each of these theories includes several others that are based on different principles of representation. They cannot be called theories in the strict sense of the term, since they represent certain principles or models on which representative government is based. Moreover, a view espoused by a single scholar or practiced in a single nation may be a combination of a number of such "theories" of representation. They also identify the role of the representatives in a democracy.

The Authorisation theory was first put forward by Thomas Hobbes, the 17th century English political philosopher. Thomas Hobbes opined that the representative is a person authorised by the society to act on its behalf for the purpose of preservation of society. The representative is conferred with a right which he did not previously possess. However, he/she has no special role or duties to perform. As a representative, a person is free to do as he pleases with binding consequences. According to Hobbes,

> ...a multitude of men, are made 'one person', when they are by one man, or by one person represented.... For it is the unity of the Representer, that maketh the person.... Unity, cannot be otherwise understood in a multitude... Because each individual composing the multitude is being utterly apart, like a particle of a matter, moving through time and space in search of power after power unto death. (Friedrich, 1950: 262)

Hobbes, however, suggests that there are certain limits on what the representative may do. His/ her failure may deny him/her the responsibility of representation. Critics opine that Hobbes's theory is disproportionately skewed in favour of the representative and is in consonance with his idea of absolute monarchy. It portrays representing as a transaction that takes place at outset, even before the act of representation takes place. The area of rights of the representatives is enlarged while his duties are minimized. Hobbes views were later shared by a number of German scholars.[5]

The Liberal Democratic theory was built on Hobbes idea, but did not reconcile with the idea of unlimited authority. It held that representation occurs whenever one person is authorised to act in place of other; to represent means "to act with binding authority in the name of others." Even an elective body is truly representative only if it "has representative authority" which means "the authority to deliberate and decide for other".[6] The authority is given by voters through elections, to the elected officials. The grant of authority is limited and always circumscribed. Critics point out that the main drawback of this version of Authorisation theory is that it does not limit the time for which authority is given. Accordingly, elections may not be held regularly.

The Authorisation theory in all its versions, fails to explain the concept of representativeness. It provides a formalistic view stressing only the representatives' capacity to bind others to some external standards, or act in accord with special considerations" (Pitkins, 1967:49).

The second main theory is the Accountability theory of representation. It has not been systematically put forward by any scholar, nor has it been developed into a theoretical system (Pitkins, 1967:55)). This theory shows that representation entails responsiveness to the needs and desires of those who are being represented. They define a representative as anyone who has to account for his action. Thus, accountability is the essential prerequisite and the very essence of representation. For accountability theorists, being represented involves special duties and obligations. Elections to them serve as an instrument to hold the representative on-account. It is this characteristic of responsibility, which distinguishes representation in a democracy from other forms of government.

Responsibility, as denoted in the context of this theory, may be of two types:

(a) personal or dependent responsibility where the representative is directly responsible to the constituent, and

(b) functional or technical responsibility, which implies meeting given standards such as capable and efficient conduct or the right course of action. This kind of responsibility is also referred to as independent responsibility where the representative is accountable to none other than his own conscience. The first kind of responsibility is associated with responsiveness, and the second with efficiency.

However, the accountability theorist makes it impossible for the idea of representation to serve as a guide for action. The conduct or the act of the representative remains irrelevant to the process of representation. Moreover, elections may be one of the many means of ensuring accountability. It may also be pointed out that a responsive legislature can also be very irresponsible (Prezworski, 1999). The more responsive it become to a section of the electorate that have elected it, the less it is in a position to behave responsibly, for the interest of the whole and will give way to the interest of a group or a section on account of conflicting interests.

The Descriptive theory of representation likens representation to replicating the existential features of a group or a nation and ensuring accuracy of representation. John Adams, the second American President argued that in the American revolutionary period, the legislature should have been an exact portrait, in a miniature, of the people at large, as it should think, feel reason and act like them.(Adams cited in Pitkins,1967) Other point out that just "as the portrait is in excellent in proportion to its being a good likeness", so "the legislature ought to be most exact transcript of the whole society, the faithful echo voice of the people". Even Edmund Burke (1901) has maintained that, "the virtue, spirit and essence of a representative body lies in its being the express image of the feelings of the nation" Other writers have required the legislature to be a mirror of the nation or of the public opinion. Representative government has been described as an "accurate reflection of the community of the general opinion of the nation or of the variety of interest in the society." (Emden, 1956: 59).

Such interpretations of representation are not based on 'representation being an activity or being held accountable for an act'. Rather, representation depends on the representative's characteristics, or on what he is like. It depends on being something, and not doing something. As J. S. Mill (Mill,1862: 239) observed, a legislative body "is an arena in which each opinion in the nation can produce itself in full light. Others such as Simon Strene (Strene, 1864) speak of the "right of a man to appear by deputy" in the legislature appearing in what matters. Jennings has urged that common people representing other common people can best represent the will of the people. They are the best to tell the people what the government cannot do and what the people will not stand (cited in Pitkins, 1967:89).

The major features of this view were developed by theorists of proportional representation. Proportional representation scholars emphasized on representation precisely because they believed that the composition of the legislature determines its activities. Such scholars often, ascribe a talking function to the legislature in contrast with the acting function that belongs to the executive. The principal function of the legislature, according to this view, is to depict, or present, or reflect popular opinion. And, it is the composition of the Parliament that determines its ability to do so. The legislature cannot govern because it is unfit for political action. Its task is to criticize the actions of the government. As J.S. Mill (1867) observed that instead of the function of governing, for which it is radically unfit, the proper office of a representative assembly is to watch and control the government: to throw light of publicity on its acts. (Mill: 1867:34)

Such theorists further argue that representation when applied in the political context implies a supply of information. The information supplied is likely to be accurate if the representatives reflect the aspirations of the people accurately.[7] There are three different but related ways of bringing this view to bear in the political context.[8] In each, the purpose is action by the representative, but that action by itself is not representation.[9] It is also assumed here that the main function of the legislature is to decide by majority vote, the same way as the nation would vote. The representative in such theories is an inanimate object.

A more subtle version of this theory was put forward by J.S. Mill (1876) who assumed that the role of the representative is of presenting the information. Mill coupled the idea of proportional representation with a view of how a representative body should be composed. In his opinion, a representative body is an arena in which not only the general opinion of every section of the nation must be reproduced.

In this theory, representatives are specialists in transmitting and analyzing information. The legislature provides the institutional infrastructure whose function is to scatter information into the corners of the nation and discover the will of the people. On issues on which people have no will, the representatives have nothing to represent.

Critics charge that perfect accuracy of representation is impossible. Since perfect accuracy cannot be reached, similarity of information too, cannot be ensured. The zeal for accurate reflection in the composition of the legislature has made descriptive theorists blind to the governing functions. Besides representation, the legislature is also concerned with other functions, for instance forming the government or supporting a stable government. Accurate reflection of public opinion in the legislature is not a guarantee of the effective performance of other functions.

Thus, in its nuanced version, the term political representation is associated with three different types of meanings: (1) the idea of authority; (2) the idea of responsibility or accountability; (3) the idea of representativeness.

The three meanings of representation are often inextricably intertwined with one another. It is, however, the third meaning that has assumed greatest importance in the context of political representation. (Grazia, 1964: 461-463).

On the basis of these three theories of representation it is possible to surmise that any substantive attempt to understand the concept of representation within legislative institution in the India involves two main areas of enquiry:

- What constitutes the nature of the activity of representation?
- What or who is a representative?
- What is the role of the representative?

The difference between the two, as Hanna Pitkins (1967:50) observes, may be expressed by contrasting two German words, *vertreten*, to act for another, and *darstellen*, to stand for another. In the first sense, representation is an activity, while in the second, representation means impersonation. These two senses are intertwined. Both are equally important to the ideal of representation. Accordingly, we may attempt to understand the representative character of Lok Sabha in terms of two main themes:

- Representation as an activity of 're-presenting interests'
- Representation as impersonation or 're-presenting persons'.

A water tight compartmentalisation between the two is impossible. There is a large number of interpretations that overlap each other.

Representing Interests

As mentioned earlier, representation implies making present something which is absent. In performing this task of representation, the representative must do what the principal himself might do if he were acting. However, in a large modern democracy like India characterised by social, economic and religious diversities, the representative acts not for a single principal, but an entire group, consisting of community, constituency, state or nation: an unorganised group with motley interests and ideas. The representation of such diverse groups/ interests may not be feasible. Perhaps, this kind of representation within the legislature may be achieved through:

- Voting in the way (manner) that the majority of the principal may vote;
- Ensuring that the interest of the representatives is identical to those of the voters;

- Discussion/ Raising issues that concern the supporters/constituency; and
- Institutional set up such as separation of powers, checks and balances that force the representative to act in the interest of the people.

The important question is, whether the representative must act on his own free will or whether he should act on the basis of a mandate or an instruction of those being represented. The Mandate-Independence theory attempts to tackle this issue in addition to others. Mandate theorists view the representative as an agent of his constituents, and must, to a greater or lesser extent, abide by the instruction of his constituency. They interpret national interests as the sum of constituency interests. There are a variety of positions within the mandate theory.[10]

On the other hand, the independence theorists view the representative as a trustee, as a free agent, an expert who is best left alone to do his work. It points out that a constituency does not have a single, unified, homogenous interest with a readymade will or opinion on every issue. Moreover, political questions are complex and beyond the capacities of common men. Thus, the representative must have the discretion to unravel complicated issues and represent them. As Edmund Burke opined,

> ...what sort of a system, is it in which the determination precedes the discussion; in which one set of men deliberate and another decides; and where those who form the conclusion are perhaps 300 miles distant from those who hear the argument? (Burke, 1901, cited in Pitkins, 1967: 57)

To allow a representative to act only on instructions is to rob him of all his dignity and thus undermine respect for the government (Burke, 1901) .

The emergence of political parties has further complicated the issue. One argument is that representatives are neither bound by the wishes of their constituencies, nor free to act on their own discretion, but that they are bound to act in accordance with the programme of their respective parties. They are thus, the representative of their parties. It has been argued by some theorists that the interest of the party are partial and are not equal to national interest so, the representative must be left free of party obligations to act in the national interest as he sees it (Strene, 1871).

A second view is to regard the political party as a link between local issues and national interest. All political parties have a national programme. The voters express their preference for a particular programme by electing a particular member from the constituency to express their wishes. The legislator is thus bound by the duty to the party on whose programme he has contested, and by the duty to the constituent's wishes because it is in accordance with his views on the national interest. Some compromise positions have also been taken, which argue that the representative has an obligation to both the party and the constituents as well as to the best policy. However, they do not tell us how a reconciliation of the two can be achieved. Some theorists opine that the representative must plead and speak for the constituency, but vote according to national interest; others argue that he is not bound by the whims and fancies of his constituencies but must abide by long range deliberate desires.

Another important issue in the substantive interpretation of the 'activity of representation' involves the important question of interpretation of interests. It may be questioned whether the interpretation of what is in the interest of the constituents should be based on what the representative perceives it to be, or on what constituents perceive it to be. This further complicates the issue, and there are scholars on both sides of the issue. Under normal circumstances, the representative will be forced to act on the basis of what he thinks (possibly) the constituent think, in the absence of a concrete/ permanent referendum. It is assumed that if the representative acts in the interest of the political principal, they too will want what is in their interest and will approve of what is done by the representative (Pikins, 1967).

Canning, an 18th century British statesman expressed this idea succinctly when he said,

> It may happen that your judgment may occasionally come into conflict with my own... In all such cases, I promise you, not indeed wholly, to submit my judgment to yours;..... but I promise you that any difference of opinion between us will always lead me to distrust my own views, carefully to examine, and if erroneous frankly to correct them. (Cannings cited in Pitkins, 1967:164)

The wishes of the political principal must be potentially present and potentially relevant, though the representative need not act in response to the wishes of the political principal. It is possible that the constituents may not have an opinion on every issue, or may not care to formulate a will on every issue or even know about them. On these the representative can act in his constituent's interest, but he must not normally come into conflict with their will when they have an express will.[11] In a modern democracy, the voter may decide on the success of representation by re-electing the representative, though it is not unusual for a representative to be unjustly voted out of office.

Representation of Persons

Scholars such as Alexander Hamilton, John Jay and James Madison in America and James Mill and Bentham in Great Britain focused on the representation of persons. The American scholars opined that representative democracy was a substitute for direct democracy on account of the practical difficulties facing large assemblies. However, these scholars were skeptical of popular democracy and representation allowed for participation in safety. In their ideas, representation assumed the character of representation of persons, though interests are not altogether absent. These scholars recognize the diversity of interests in any society that are personal, shifting, unreliable and antagonistic to national interest. A representative government provided the cure for the ills of factions. The representative in Madison's conception is superior, dispassionate and debates calmly in the light of reason. He refuses to give way to factions. The representative, however, does not know the interests of his constituents better than they themselves do. He is roughly their equal. He, therefore, acts in response to their interest. He is not a trustee, in the Burkesian sense of the term.

English Utilitarianisms interprets interests as personal to each individual. Each man, according to Benthem, is the best judge, if not the only reliable one, of his own interest and no government can act for the best interest of its subjects or at least not as well as they could if left to themselves (Wolin1960: 34). Given this idea of interest, representation becomes impossible, for the representative can act only in his own interest. However, all Utilitarian writers (for instance Benthem) recognize the idea of common good or general interest that is based on the good of the society as a whole. The job of the legislator is to attach rewards to social or

Table 1.2: Representation, Related Activity and Institutional Structures

Representation	*Nature of Activity*	*Institutional Structures*
Representation of Interest	Electioneering, Legislative debates , Policy Making	Political Parties, Legislature, Free Press, Media
Representation of Persons	Political equality, universal adult suffrage, Campaigning, Question Hour, Scrutiny, Legislation, Resolutions and Motions, Discussions independent election commission, open party competition, freedom of speech and expression.	Political Parties, Legislature, Executive,

other regarding actions and punishment to self-regarding action. This is done by means of law. A single legislator may be altruistic and may pursue social interests diligently. However, in an institutionalised legislature altruism is replaced by institutional safeguards such as "the principle of dislocalability.[12] The problem lies in the fact that control of the government by the people involves control by each individual who is guided by his selfish interest. The Utilitarian's simply ignore this problem (Pitkins, 1967: 60).

Institutional designs such as electoral process, term limits, the system of checks and balances, the constitution, have all been designed to ensure representation. In addition, a free media which airs public opinion appears to assist in the process of representation. It is assumed that legislators, chosen through elections would be representative of the parties that they represent, the constituencies that have elected them.

Political Parties and Collective Representation

Broadly however, the idea of representation as commonly understood and practiced in modern democracies is that of 'responsible party government' model. In this model the electorate selects representatives from a number of parties based on their policy promises and performance this understanding of representation however, involves three minimum conditions:

- Existence of disciplined parties that provide an alternative set of programmes on the major issues facing the country;
- Voters who choose parties based on past records of the parties government/opposition, or prospective evaluations of their policy platforms;
- And lastly free and fair elections held at regular intervals to translate votes into parliamentary seats.

Through these means, citizens can hold parties in power collectively accountable for their actions. If these conditions are met, the parties (or parties) are understood to have a democratic mandate to implement their agenda for the duration of their term of office this mechanism provides a link between the preferences of citizens and the actions of governments since it emphasises that parties compete by offering alternative solutions to policy problems, responding to public concerns.

Governments with a parliamentary majority are allowed considerable discretion for effective decision-making, even on difficult and controversial issues. Parties in power remain accountable on a day-to-day basis to Parliament and at regular intervals to the electorate, who retain ultimate control. Voters can evaluate at regular intervals and can vote them out if dissatisfied with their promises or performance.

However, the application of this model is not free from problems. Political parties can carry forth the process of representation at different level and through different mediums. They can represent within the institutions such as the legislature, government at both the national and state level. They can also represent in the public domain through the media, social networking, electioneering and the like. Likewise the electorate can influence the legislature through two channels: *indirectly* through their choice of governments in the states, and *directly* through elections to the parliament. They can also influence the nature of representation through their choice of political parties, party manifestoes and candidates. The application of this model depends on certain pre-condition:

- Recognised political parties
- Clearly distinguishable policy programmes at least on major issues
- Continuous presence of parties allowing evaluation of their policies over time
- Presence in parliament

However, political parties are not always distinguishable from other groups or from one another in terms of either their ideology or in terms of their programmes. Most parties in India, for example, claim to be secular, socialist and centrist in terms of their ideology. Their party manifestoes are also a general statement of their belief. They do not clearly specify their programmatic content. An understanding of India's parties and the basis on which they are classified is a precursor to, analyzing their parliamentary role. The subsequent chapter attempts to understand type of political parties and the basis of their classification

References

1. Held, David (1999). *Prospects of Democracy-East West, North South*, Stanford, Stanford University Press.
2. John Stuart Mill, (1876). *Considerations on Representative Government*, Liberal Arts Press, New York.
3. Benthem. J, An Introduction to the Theory of Morals and Principles, in J.S. Burns, H.L. A Hart (Eds) (1996). *Collected Works of Jeremy Benthem*, Delhi, Oxford University Press.

4. A. Dahl, Robert. (2001) *On Democracy*, East- New Delhi, West Press Private Limited, p. 65-68.
5. J. Dalton, Russell, M. Farrell, David and McAllister Ian, (2011). *Political Parties and Democratic Linkage: How Parties Organize Democracy*, Oxford, OUP.
6. Downs, Anthony (957) *An Economic Theory of Democracy*, New York, Harper Collins.
7. Sartori, Giovanni (2005) *Parties and Party System: A Framework for Analysis*, Colchester, Cambridge University Press.
8. Diamond Larry and Gunther, Richard (1993). *Political Parties and Democracy*, London, John Hopkins University, pp. 3-9.
9. Russell J. Dalton, David M. Farrell, and Ian McAllister, *Political Parties and Democratic Linkage: How Parties Organize Democracy*, Oxford, OUP.
10. Pitkin, Hanna (1967*) Theories of Representation*, Berkley, University of California Press, p. 2.
11. Grazia, Antonio (2004) *Encyclopaedia of Political Ideas*, Blackwell Publication, London, p. 461.
12. Friedrich, Carl. J. (1950*) Constitutional Government and Democracy in Theory and Practice*, Boston: Ginn & Co., Boston.
13. Leisersson, Avery (1949).*Problems of Political Representation in Government and Private Groups*, Journal of Politics, Vol. 11, August.
14. Barker, Ernest (1964) *Greek Political Theory*, New York, Methuen, p. 35.
15. Prezworski, Adam, Stokes, Susan, Manin, Bernard (1999), *Democracy, Accountability and Representation, Cambridge*, Cambridge University Press, pp. 10-12.
16. Edmund Burke, (1901), *Speech to the Electors of Bristol*, Vol. 2 Boston, Little Brown and Company.
17. J. Ford, Henry. (1924) *Representative Government*, New York, Henry Holt & Co.
18. Sterne, Simon (1871), *Representative Government*, Philadelphia, J.B. Lippincott, p. 51-61.
19. Howard. Lee Mac Baum, (1948) *The Living Constitution*, New York, Macmillan.
20. Jeremy Benthem, (1835) "Constitutional Code", in Samuel Bailey, *The Rationale of Political Representation,* London, R. Hunter and Co.
21. Wolin Sheldon (1960), *Politics and Vision*, Boston, Little Brown and Co.
22. Yadav Yogendra & Palshikar, Suhas (2008) Ten Theses on State Politics, *Seminar*, Vol. 591 November.
23. Ranney, Austin and Kendell, W. (1956). *Democracy and American Party System*, New York, Harcourt Brace and Company.
24. Kendell, W. (1956). *Democracy and American Party System*, Harcourt Brace and Company, New York.
25. Lee Mac Baum, Howard. (1948) *The Living Constitution*, New York, Macmillan.
26. Downs, Anthony (1952). *An Economic Theory of Democracy*, New York, Harper.

Notes

1. For extensive discussion of democracy in Greece one can refer to Hansen Mogens, Herman *The Athenian Democracy in the Age of Demosthenes: Structures, Principles and Ideology,* translated by J.A. Cook, (1991) Oxford, Blackwell.
2. Belgium, France, Switzerland, introduced Universal Adult Suffrage only after the Second World War.
3. Britain started the practice of electing members to the legislature as early as 13th century, U.S.A, in the 18th century.
4. Interview with D.L Sheth, Professor, Centre for the Study of Developing Societies, New Delhi, on 11 March 2005 in New Delhi.
5. The best known writers who developed such views were, Gierke and Jellinek, Max Weber and Hans Wolff. Gierke and Jellinek argue that the representative is an official, a specialised organ of the group authorised for the performance of certain activities. Weber opined that representation is a state of affairs in which the actions of certain members of the group is ascribed to the rest. It exists only when some members have the authority to act on behalf of others and others do not have. Wolff defined representation as a person whose behaviour rights and duties accrue to the group. His activities are ascribed to the group.
6. A detailed discussion on this is provided by Avery Leisersson (1949) "Problems of Political Representation in Government and Private Groups", *Journal of Politics*, Vol. 11, p. 566; Ernest Barker (1964) *Greek Political Theory,* Methuen, New York, p. 35.
7. Anthony Downs approaches the problem of representation from an economic theory perspective has formulated similar views. He suggests that representatives, as agents of political party are concerned with transmitting information to the party, as to what people want and sometimes vice versa.
8. The first view may suggest that the legislature is like a map or a mirror, essentially a passive object, so put together that the spectator can gather information about the people. That is to say, that it reflects or resembles the nation by its composition. Secondly, it may suggest that the legislature is like a painter or a maker of representation to someone else, represents by its activity, the interest of the people of nation. Thirdly, there may be a suggestion that the representative legislature is a sufficiently accurate copy, a perfect replica, then it may safely be allowed to substitute for the whole people.
9. This theory is linked to radical democratic ideology that believes that direct democracy is the best form of government and representation the second best option.
10. A restricted mandate theorist may maintain that representation occurs only when the representative acts on the basis of explicit instruction of his constituents. A more moderate position may allow the representative some discretion. However, it too insists that the representative must consult his constituency before taking any controversial decision. A third, more liberal position opines that the representation may act in the best interest of the constituents, until he is instructed by them and when instructed must obey.

11. Some scholars like Gosnell argue that the constituents have a latent or unconscious or unexpressed will on everything which the representative must anticipate. This however is not always possible or desirable. See...

    Foote Gosnell, Harold. (1948) *Democracy, The Threshold of Freedom*, New York, Ronald Press, p. 134-135.

12. The principle of dislocalbility implies that the legislator wishes to get re–elected and will hence do what the voters want him to do. Elections enable the voters to further their interest.

Chapter - 2

State Parties in India: Typology, History and Development

India's political scenario is characterised by the existence of a large number of parties. Each of these parties has a huge membership and sometimes a large support base. At the same time, the turnover of the parties in India is also large. A number of parties have a very short life span and may either merge an existing parties or became a part of a new political formation. In terms of ideology too, India has diverse parties with substantial overlap among them. The existence of a large number of organised political parties makes any attempt at classification of the parties highly difficult, if not impossible. Parties in India may be classified on the basis of their geographical spread, ideology and objectives, social base, organisation and functioning, etc. It is possible to identify different types of parties based on each of these characteristics. A combination of these characteristics would give us a more complex typology of parties.

The Election Commission of India (ECI) categorizes all registered parties, for the purpose of allocation of election symbols, in to two types – recognised and unrecognised.

A political party is treated as a recognised political party, if it satisfies any one of the following two conditions:

- It has been engaged in political activity for a continuous period of five years and has, at the last general election in that State to the Lok Sabha or to the Legislative Assembly of the State, returned at least one member to the House of the People for every twenty-five members of that House or any fraction of that number from that State;
- The total number of valid votes polled by all the contesting candidates set up by such party at the last general election in the

State to the Lok Sabha or to the Legislative Assembly of the State, is not less than six percent of the total number of valid votes polled by all the contesting candidates at such general election in the State.

Within the recognised parties there are National and State Parties. A recognised political party in four or more States is known as a 'National Party' throughout India. It continues to be recognised as a National Party so long as it continues to fulfill the conditions for recognition in four or more States on the basis of results of any subsequent general election either to the House of the People or to the Legislative Assembly of any State. A political party is treated as a recognised State party if it has presence in less than four in the State or States in which it is so recognised, but only so long as the party continues to fulfill the conditions for recognition on the basis of results of any subsequent general election to the House of the People orto the Legislative Assembly of the State, in the said State or States.

Accordingly, in the 14th Lok Sabha, the Election Commission of India recognised six parties as National parties and 56 parties as State Parties. Among these State Parties there were parties that were recognised as State Parties in one State (such as the TDP, BJD, AGP etc.) and parties that were recognised as State Parties in more than one State (JDU, SP, RJD, ADMK,AITC etc.).

This classification of parties into National and State Parties may not be satisfactory. This is because a National party under the present definition of the ECI need not have reasonable national or all India presence. In fact, apart from the Congress and the BJP none of the political parties can rightfully claim to be national parties. Even the BJP had limited presence in southern states such as Tamil Nadu and Kerala and North eastern parts of the country. The presence of National parties in the 14th Lok Sabha can be seen in Table 2.1.

Table 2.1: Presence of National Parties

Parties	*Seats*	*No of states in which candidates were put up*	*No. of states/UT in which Party won seats*	*Vote share*
BJP	138	31	18	22.1
BSP	1	25	1	5.33
CPI	10	15	5	1.41
CPM	43	19	5	5.66
INC	26	33	31	26.53
NCP	1	11	1	1.80

Source: Election Commission of India: Statistical Report of the 14th General Election, 2004.

As may be seen from the above table, four of the six national parties' listed by the ECI do not have significant presence in most of the States. Nor did they get six per cent votes in the elections to the Lok Sabha; (CPM got 5.66%, BSP 5.33%, NCP 1.80%, and the CPI 1.41%). They are treated as national parties by applying the other criterion. In 2000 CPM lost national status temporarily; CPI was in the danger of losing it after 2004 elections; for all practical purposes, NCP is limited to Maharashtra and BSP is confined mainly to Uttar Pradesh.

Table 2.2: Presence of State Parties

State parties	*Seats Contested*	*Seat Won*	*Total Candidate Contested*	*No. of states*	*States in which contested*	*% Vote*
Arunachal Congress	1	0	1	1	Arunachal Pradesh	0.02%
All India Anna Dravida Munnetra Kazhagam	33	0	33	1	Tamil Nadu, Pondicherry	2.19%
Asom Gana Parishad	12	2	12	1	Assam	0.53%
All India Forward Bloc	10	3	10	5	West Bengal	0.35%
All India Trinamool Congress	33	2	33	5	Meghalaya, West Bengal	2.07%
Biju Janata Dal	12	11	12	1	Orissa	1.30%
CPI (ML)	65	0	65	18		0.33%
Dravida Munnetra Kazhagam	16	16	16	1	Tamil Nadu	1.81%
FPM	1	0	1	1	Manipur	0.02%
Indian National Lok Dal	20	0	20	4		0.50%
Janata Dal (Secular)	43	3	43	12	Karnataka, Kerala	1.47%
Janata Dal (United)	73	8	73	16	Bihar, Uttar Pradesh, Lakshadweep	2.35%
Jammu & Kashmir National Conference	6	2	6	1	Jammu and Kashmir	0.13%
Jammu & Kashmir National Panthers Party	7	0	7	3	Jammu and Kashmir	0.02%
Jammu & Kashmir Peoples Democratic Party	3	1	3	1	Jammu and Kashmir	0.07%
Jharkhand Mukti Morcha	9	5	9	4	Orissa, Jharkhand	0.47%
Kerala Congress	1	1	1	1	Kerala	0.09%
Kerala Congress (M)	1	0	1	1	Kerala	0.05%
Lok Jan Shakti Party	40	4	40		Bihar	0.71%
Maharashtrawadi Gomantak Party	2	0	2	1	Tamil Nadu	0.00%
Marumalarchi Dravida Munnetra Kazhagam	4	4	4	1	Tamil Nadu Pondicherry	0.43%
Mizo National Front	1	1	1	1	Mizoram	0.05%
Manipur Peoples Party	1	0	1	1	Manipur	0.02%
Muslim League Kerala State Committee	10	1	10	6	Kerela	0.20%
Nagaland Peoples Front	3	1	3	2	Nagaland	0.18%
Pattali Makkal Katchi	6	6	6	2	Tamil Nadu, Pondicherry	0.56%

(Contd...)

RJD	42	24	42	6	Bihar, Jharkhand	2.41%
RLD	32	3	32	11	Uttar Pradesh	0.63%
Revolutionary Socialist Party	6	3	6	3	West Bengal	0.43%
Shiromani Akali Dal	10	8	10	1	Punjab	0.90%
SAD (M)	6	0	6	1	Punjab	0.10%
Sikkim Democratic Front	1	1	1	1	Sikkim	0.04%
Shivsena	56	12	56	14	Maharashtra	1.81%
Samajwadi Party	237	36	237	23	Uttar Pradesh, Uttarakhand	4.32%
Telugu Desam	33	5	33	**1**	Andhra Pradesh	**3.04%**
United Democratic Party	1	0	1	1	Goa	0
UGDP	1	0	1	1	Goa	0%
Uttarakhand Kranti Dal	4	0	4	1	Uttaranchal	0.01%

Election Commission of India: Statistical Report of the 14th General Election, 2004.

Some of the parties that are classified as State Parties by the ECI do not consider themselves as State or regional parties. They perceive themselves as national parties both in terms of their ideology and their programme. Thus, for instance, parties such as the SP, RJD, RLD, JD(S), JD (U), etc. have fielded candidates in many States. In terms of votes and seat share too, the SP and the RJD are ahead of three national parties, namely, the BSP, NCP and CPI. DMK and SHS too were ahead of two other national parties in this respect. CPM, CPI, BSP and the NCP could be called multi-State Parties, as their presence and representation in the Lok Sabha is limited to a few States.

Typology of State Parties in India

For purposes of better understanding according to K.C. Suri (2010) it is possible to identify several factors or issues that have contributed to the emergence of large number of recognized State Parties in India. These factors may also be regarded as the basis of classifying State Parties.

Table 2.3: Classificatory Scheme of State Parties in India

Classificatory Types	*Parties*			
Presence	***One state***	***More than one states***	***Region***	***All India***
	National Conference, Telegu Desam Party, Shiromani Akali Dal, Shiv Sena, NCP, MGP, JD(S). DMK.	Trinamool Congress, CPI(M), Rashtriya Janata Dal(United)	Samajwadi Party BSP, CPI, CPM	Congress, BJP

(*Contd...*)

Party Organization and leadership	Individual AIDMK, TMC, TDP (Lakshmi Parvati, PRP	Family DMK	Collective	
Ideology	Caste- ethnic identities Rashtriya Janata Dal, Samajwadi Party, Assam Gana Parishad, Shiv Sena	Religion: Shiromani Akali Dal, National Conference, Muslim League	Leftist /Socialist SP, BSP, CPI, CPM	linguistic/ regional nationalism Telegu Desam, DMK, AIADMK, Trinamool Congress
Origin	Social Movement the SAD, JKNC, DMK, AGP, JMM, and Shiv Sena	Break Away NCP, AITC, ADMK, MDMK, KEC, BJD, SP, RJD, JD(U), LJSP, RLD,	Revolutionary MUL, RSP, FB	
Objective/ Purpose	Ethnic/ Community concerns: SP, BSP, RJD, SHS, DMK, AIADMK,	Secessionist SAD, JKNC, JKPDP, NPF	Autonomy AGP, AUDF, DMK, AIADMK	Power Sharing TDP,BSP

Presence/Support Base

State Parties may be classified on the basis of their presence. Nearly 95% of parties are small parties' referred to as minor parties or letter head parties(Suri, 2010)[1]. While some parties have presence in only one state, others may be broad-based. Their support base and organisational presence may extend to two or more states and may well cover an entire region. They may also have reasonable hope of coming to power at the state level, or share power at the Central level. Though none of the State Parties would like to concede to the contrary, all recognised parties come under this category, although the magnitude of such parties vary greatly. Parties such as the DMK and the AIADMK may have much greater say at the national level than parties such as the Arunachal Congress or Sikkim Democratic Front, which are limited to one state. Only 12 of the State Parties in India have contested elections in more than one state.

Organisation/Leadership

A second basis of classification of political parties may be based on their leadership styles. In their styles of functioning too, most parties are leader-centered and personality driven. This is true of both parties that have presence in a number of states such as the SP, RJD, Shiv Sena or State-based parties such as the TDP, BJD, TRS, SAD and the National Conference.

In most cases State Parties are created and led by a charismatic leader. The leader's charisma may be drawn from either the fact that he may have led a social movement, such as; BSP led by Kanshi Ram and Mayawati, who worked for the upliftment and political mobilisation of the Dalits; or because the leader may be popular/glamorous due to his association with popular media such as cinema, M.G. Ramachandran, founder of the AIADMK, N.T. Rama Rao, founder of TDP and Chiranjeevi, founder of Praja Rajyam Party fall under this category. In all such parties, the leader exercises absolute control over the rank and file of the party and the party is often co-terminus with the personality. Often many of such parties fail to survive after the death of the leader.

A "charismatic party", as described by Panebianco (1988), does not require strong party organisation. The supreme leader does not allow any institutionalisation of party machinery or the committees, as he tends to see them as impediments to the exercise of his personal power. The TDP, DMK, AIADMK, Shiv Sena, SAD, Trinamool Congress, BJD, National Conference, INLD are parties led by strong leaders with weak organisation.

Very often in such parties, the mantle of leadership passes on to the heir of the party leader, making the party organisation family-driven. Samajwadi party, the RJD, the DMK, and SHS are examples of parties which were founded by a charismatic leader, but which have eventually evolved as family run organisations.

Ideology

A third basis of classification of State Parties is the Ideology. Formally all parties in India are secular, socialist and democratic, as it is mandatory for the parties to declare true faith in these principles while they register with the EC. Even parties that appeal to people on the basis of caste and religious identities and are founded to promote the interests of particular communities, regard themselves as secular and socialist, of course imparting them with their own meanings (Suri, 2010).

In the immediate post-independence period, the nationalist movement and the different perceptions for the attainment of independence provided the broad framework for the ideologies of political parties in the country. Nationalism, socialism, secularism and democracy were the basic ideological foundation stones of Congress party (Suri, 2010). The most serious opposition to the Congress ideology was from the Communist Party. In the immediate post-independence period, the Communists waged armed struggle in some parts of the country to overthrow the Indian state, although they soon gave up that course and participated in the first general election. They differed significantly from the Congress in terms of their perception of the character of the Indian state, the path to revolution in India. However, their participation in elections brought them within the fold of parliamentary democracy in India. Despite this they constitute the second major ideological stream in Indian Politics.

The rise of the BJP in the late 1980's and the strategies it adopted to increase its electoral support base provided the third axis of the ideological framework of Indian parties. The BJP attempted to unite the Hindus by awakening a sense of vulnerability among them through militant Hindu nationalism. Yogendra Yadav and Palshikar point out that in the economic sphere the BJP attempted redefine the nation and articulate the cultural and material aspirations of the new middle class in India through its ideology (Yadav, 1999; Palshikar, 2004).

In the working of state political parties in India, caste, religion, language and region also have acquired ideological overtones. Religion has been an active element in party domain before and after. The origins of such parties can be traced to the pre-Independence period. During the freedom struggle the Muslim League mobilised Indian Muslims on religious identity. In Punjab, the Shiromani Akali Dal (SAD) had its roots in religion and there are Christian parties in Kerala. However, despite the existence of parties claiming to represent people of specific religious beliefs, the followers of those religions did not support such parties en masse.

Language and region also acquired the nature of ideology in India. Most of the regions of India are based on linguistic nationalities. The linguistic reorganisation of the states in 1956 has meant that most states have a single language. Independent linguistic identify has provided fertile soil for the emergence of parties in India. The Dravidian parties, Shiv Sena, TDP, AGP and BJD are all based on linguistic pride.

In most cases, as a language is confined to a region, the region has assumed the form of an ideology.[9] Such parties are based on a broad range of regionalist sentiments and are based on the invocation of regional pride and identity. They have often demanded preservation and even predominance of regional culture, history and language. Demands for state formation and inclusion of certain territories into a state have become potential instruments for mobilisation for such parties. Thus, for instance, the AIADMK, TDP, Shiv Sena strengthened their power base through regional identity policy. Such regional pride is also accompanied in some cases with sentiments of deprivation by the 'sons of the soil'. Both the Shiv Sena and AGP emerged as anti-migrant movements, which was the basis of their regional pride.

However, the regional and linguistic ideologies have often acted as a counterpoise to other ideologies such as religion and caste.

Origin

Yet another basis of the typology of State Parties in India could be linked to their origin or the way in which parties have come into existence. Under this category we may identify parties that have been the products of long and sustained social movements and are the result of breakaway from the parent organisation.

The basis of such movements may be varied and may range from the feeling of deprivation to regional prides or religious identity. Thus, for instance, parties like the SAD, JKNC, DMK, AGP and Shiv Sena fall into this category. The DMK, the strongest of all regional parties was an outburst against the social oppression suffered by non-Brahmins at the hands of Brahmins and Aryan invaders of the north.

The demands for formation of a separate state or the inclusion of certain territories within the state become potent weapons for political mobilisation and creation of new party organisations. The Akali Dal which was formed in 1920, as an offshoot of the Sikh Gurudwara Reform Movement of the 1920s, engaged in issues of sectarian representation and self-determination of Sikhs. The SAD successfully carried out a campaign for a Punjabi Suba (separate State for Sikhs) that excluded the Hindi-speaking areas, where the Hindus were in preponderant numbers, and included areas where the Sikhs were in a majority. In the 70s and 80s it carried out a militant struggle for Khalistan, a separate state for the Sikhs which resulted in a split in the party. However, in Punjab, the policies of the party gave rise to civil strife and have often been taken to question the secular nature of party leadership. (Palshikar, 2004)

Similarly, the National Conference, one of the oldest regional parties in India which was formed in 1939, emerged as a party claiming regional political autonomy within the state and has been struggling for the rights of Kashmiri Muslim identity.

Among the many State Parties in India, there are some State Parties which were founded as a result of split in a parent party. The AIADMK, DMK, MDMK, KEC, BJD, SP, RJD, JD(U), LJSP, RLD, etc. are parties which emerged out of a split. A large majority of these parties have also emerged as a result of a split within the Congress. Examples include NCP and AITC etc. However, some of the parties like the AIADMK have emerged as a result of a split within the State Parties.

Another category of parties function to launch struggles to bring about major social and political changes, such as the CPI, CPM and CPI (M-L) The ideology and the objective of such parties are, therefore, very "revolutionary' in nature. Within this category, it is possible to make distinction on temporal grounds, for example those which emerged in pre-independence period, both left-ideology parties such as RSP, SUCI, FB etc. and those which emerged during the Janata period in 1967-77, were implosion of the Janata Party (Arora et all, 2013)

Finally there are parties that were formed with an exclusive objective of entering electoral politics and forming government: such as the BSP, TDP, etc. However, it may be mentioned as a word of caution that parties emerge due to multiple factors or motivations. For example, the formation of SP or RJD is due to split in the parent party, as its leaders formed the party to capture power through electoral politics, although they may claim that they were striving in the cause of social justice and secularism.

Purpose/Goals

Finally, one could distinguish between State Parties based on their goal or purpose. Accordingly, it is possible to identify parties that have aims to uplift certain sections of the society or community to the exclusion of other. Kanchan Chandra (2004) identifies them as ethnic parties; parties that are secessionist, that demand greater degree of autonomy. K.C. Suri (2010) points out that in a multi-cultural society like India, political parties draw their support mainly from social groups who belong to one religion, caste or tribal population. Although leaders of most parties claim that they draw support from all sections of the society, some parties draw more support from specific social groups, such as the SAD from Sikhs in Punjab, NC in J&K and MUL in Kerala from the Muslims of these States; BSP from the Dalits; SP and RJD from the Yadavs in UP and Bihar respectively. Kanchan Chandra points out that the distinguishing feature of such parties is not inclusion but exclusion of certain groups. Such parties have often couched their ethnic identities in left of the centre and socialist ideologies.

Though all political parties claim allegiance to the Indian constitution and even abide by it, there have been parties which have demanded secession from the Indian state, though this may not be the stated goal of the party.

Thus, for instance the SAD during the 1970's and 80's demanded an independent state of Khalistan, the JKNC for Independent Kashmir, etc.

Almost all State Parties and leaders in India have demanded greater autonomy for the states and greater federalisation of Indian polity. They demand more powers to the States within the federal framework (cooperative federalism or true federalism); the regionalist ideology taking the form of demands for states development. Such parties deal with issues of backwardness, industrial progress and investment. The first manifestations of such parties were found in the period after 1967 when the Congress's strength in the Lok Sabha was substantially reduced and 8 out of the 16 states had non-Congress governments. The relations between the centre and the states not only became tension-ridden but an important arena for the expression of party rivalry as well. Agitations by such parties is also the clearest expression of regional diversity in India (Morris Jones, 1957). Such parties are as nationalistic as the national parties are. The founder of the TDP, N.T. Rama Rao, described his party as a regional party with national perspective.

Finally, like the Liberal party, or Greenbacks in the USA, India also has parties that are issue-based. Though these parties are small/minor parties, their support base is small, their presence in the classificatory scheme is important. The Save United Goan Democratic Party could be cited as an example.

Origin of State Parties in India

The Indian National Congress emerged as a political group that aimed at inculcating a sense of solidarity and nationalist consciousness against British colonialism in the 1880's. From a modest beginning as a group of nationalist Indians demanding concessions from the British Government, it became a mass movement that demanded complete independence from the British. It retained its historical legacy in the post-independence period and emerged as a political organisation. The INC succeeded in giving the movement against British colonialism an institutional form retaining the affection of the nation, which regarded it as the architect of India's freedom. The conversion of a movement into an organisation was a significant development, unparalleled in the history of political organisations in India or even the world. As a result, the Congress enjoyed not just a vast support base but also a varied social base (Chandhoke, 2009). This constituted the basis of Congress's electoral success between 1950 and 1962.

In the later years, however, the Congress party began to show lack of an idealistic vision many a time, as leaders became more interested in nurturing their own ambitions. Slowly, conflicts originated and gradually it got aggravated between the legislative and organisational wings of the Congress due to personal rivalries and differing interests. Gradually, the Congress went through various splits (1969, 1980, 1994 and 1999). During the tenure of Indira Gandhi and Rajiv Gandhi, the Congress displayed authoritarian and monopolistic tendencies, as evidenced by the emergency imposed in 1977 by Mrs. Gandhi. The governance became centralised and personalised resulting in the decline and decay of the Party. From 1980s onwards, it became increasingly difficult for the Congress to sustain its mass support. It gradually became incapable of providing the leadership accommodating varied interests (Chandhoke, 2009).

Even though the Congress remained dominant for a very long time, it would be wrong to conclude that it had always held 'monopoly over power'. Even before 1967, this was not true. There was always a multiplicity of parties opposing the Congress. In terms of votes the combined strength of non-Congress parties has always been much more and even in terms of seats the Congress never commanded absolute majority, apart from two spells from 1952- 53 and 1963- 64. It becomes imperative to recognize continuing significance of regional political parties because of several reasons: first, it suggests that the 1967 elections did not represent a sharp break; second, it recognizes the political reality of Congress belonging to the center of politics; third, the view of continuity and change brings out the true role of Congress as a socializing agency and norm setter; fourth, it explains why dissidence within Congress is as important as that outside it; and lastly, it explains the significance of changes of elections of 1967- 69 elections (Kothari,1970).

Since the elaborate group structure within Congress reflected all shades of opinion,opposition parties were able to influence dominant-dissident relations within the Congress. The 'other' parties are said to have an important role to play vis-a-vis the Congress. Operating as parties of pressure on a party of consensus (Kothari,1970:176) and providing refuge to dissident elements within the Congress, some opposition parties focused on new hitherto neglected issues while others are formed by an amalgamation of defectors from the Congress.

With the decline of Congress hegemony and subsequent rise of the BJP in the era of coalition politics, the nature of political participation since the 1990s has witnessed remarkable changes. There has been a clear shift from a one-party dominant system to a multi-party system and minority governments in Indian politics. "The rise of regionalism has led to a growing demand for greater autonomy by the States in the 1980s, culminating in the mushrooming of regional political parties" (Chandhoke, 2009: 267). The regional parties thus assumed prominent national roles (in forming coalition governments at the Central and State levels bringing new castes and classes into their fold and deepening the process of democracy in India.

The Congress had led a successful national movement and, as a result, enjoyed considerable popularity and legitimacy. Congress leaders utilised the inherited political capital wisely in accommodating rival elites within the political umbrella of the Party. This strategy enabled the Congress to succeed for a while and long enough for practices of democracy to take root. A further factor that contributed to Indian democracy was the nature of political mobilisation of the Indian society, which was at its minimum. Political conflict mainly took the form of claims and counter-claims by rival elites, especially regional elites, claiming greater share in power and resources at the level of the Central government. However, due to the heterogeneous nature of India's polity, these conflicts rarely spread from one region to the other (Kohli: 2009). 'The Indira period witnessed the emergence of regional–based parties as an alternative to the national catch-all parties. The centralization of Congress party paved the way for the consolidation of regional parties.

Some believe that the decline in Congress hegemony was facilitated by two factors: the rise of the BJP in the Hindi heartland, the growing significance of regional political parties in South India and peripheral states like West Bengal (Kohli, 2009: 8). Regional nationalism had a greater appeal to the peripheral states than Hindu nationalism, as a result of which regional political parties gained significance in these states. They derived their power base from the backward castes; a social strata which the Congress had so long ignored. The agenda of these parties was focused on their respective regions and they also exhibited a distinct lack of ideology, ready to tilt towards either the Right or the Left, depending on the chances of gaining maximum political currency. The recent rise of a party whose support base is rooted in the lower castes, such as the Bahujan Samaj Party (BSP) led by Mayawati, is an example of this phenomenon (Kohli, 2009:8).

A theoretical explanation of the development of regional parties would require us to negate the prevailing theoretical idea that there is a direct relation between a country's party system and electoral system. Myron Weiner states that even though according to Duverger's hypothesis the is not the case. In fact, India's electoral system is such that it definitely acts to discourage emergence of minor parties. However, the very fact that it has not led Weiner to justify the emergence of minor parties in the light of only the electoral system, in the following ways: first, opposition would have been more splintered in case of a single – majority system, while India's proportional representation encourages dissident groups to break away from the Congress. Second, in spite of an electoral system that discourages smaller parties, these parties might not have felt the need to consolidate because the Congress was so far ahead of them in terms of power. However, this does not mean the power is beyond the reach of the opposition. Though the combined strength of these parties would still be less than the Congress, they would still be in a better position to win seats and further popular support. Though combined opposition vote was unlikely, what it indicates is the size of discontent with the Congress (Weiner, 1957).

Another factor that has been said to facilitate the rise of state-based parties in India is the political economy of globalisation. It is often argued that as globalisation propels the importance of 'localities' as sites of political agency and domination become more pronounced. Economic liberalisation enhances the power and bargaining leverage of the states. Moreover, economic liberalisation has affected competitive ability of states to attract investments, which increases the clout of rich states and the gap between rich and poor states. However, economic disparity is a non-factor to describe the strength of regional parties, since economically strong states like Haryana and Punjab have regional formations that are as strong as those in economically backward states like Bihar or the North East (Palshikar: 2004).

State Parties in National Politics

State parties are not new to Indian politics. They are however, new entrants to national politics. The Akali Dal (SAD) and DMK were partners in the first coalition government of Janata Party government, although it had a clear majority (295 seats) on its own. 51 members belonging to various regional parties were part of the Janata Party government in 1977. This was the first time in India's political history that regional parties were part of the government at the national level. When Congress came back to power in 1980 after the collapse of Janata Party government at the centre, the total tally of regional parties including the smaller left parties of West Bengal was reduced to 35 in the seventh Lok Sabha. The elections to the eighth Lok Sabha were held in the backdrop of the assassination of Indira Gandhi and there was a sympathy wave for Congress Party. The Rajiv Gandhi led

Congress, won a massive majority. Despite the wave of support for the Congress Party, regional parties increased their seat share in the Lok Sabha. 76 members belonging to different regional parties were a part of the eighth Lok Sabha. The rise of Telugu Desam Party (TDP) in Andhra Pradesh and Asom Gana Parishad (AGP) in Assam added to the strength of the regional parties. However, the role of regional parties was insignificant in national politics as the Congress dominated the Lok Sabha with 415 seats.

Since 1989, State parties have come to occupy important role in national politics. The rise of State parties has been both consistent and of consequence to democratic politics. This has often been at the cost of national parties, particularly the Congrss, as can be seen from the improving tally of the State parties, compared to that of national parties (see Table 2.4). Thus, the number of seats that the State parties contested and won has increased from 27 in the 1989 Lok Sabha to 146 in the 2009. Their vote share has also increased by 20 percent; from 9.28 per cent in 1989 to 28.4 per cent in 2009, while that of the national parties has declined by 13 per cent from 79.3 per cent to 63.6 per cent in the period between 1989 and 2004 in the national legislature.

Table 2.4: Performance of State and National Parties; 1989-2009

Year	*State parties*		*National Parties*	
	Seats	*Vote Share*	*Seats*	*Vote Share*
1989	27	9.28	471	79.34
1991	51	13.08	478	80.58
1996	129	22.43	403	69.08
1998	101	18.97	387	67.98
1999	158	26.93	369	67.11
2004	159	28.90	364	62.89
2009	146	28.4	376	63.58

Source: Election Commission of India, *Statistical Report on the General Elections to the Lok Sabha*, First to the Fifteenth Lok Sabha, 1952-2009 (1990, 1991, 1996, 1998,1999, 2004, 2009, New Delhi)

In the period 1996-2014, regional parties were indispensable in the formation of government at the national level. They have been important partners in the coalition governments that came to power; from the United Front government in 1996 to the National Democratic Alliance in 1999 and the successive United Progressive Alliance (UPA) in 2004 and 2009. It was however, the United Front (UF) government that brought forth the centrality of regional parties in national politics. In the 1996 Lok Sabha,

129 MPs belonged to State Parties. Being the third largest group in the Lok Sabha after the BJP and Congress, the Janata Dal led UF got a chance to form a government after the BJP failed to muster a majority in the hung Parliament. 95 of the MPs belonging to regional parties were part of the UF coalition that was supported by the Congress Party. This gave rise to the impression that regional parties were occupying the 'third' space-outside of Congress and BJP (Palshikar, 2010).

The voter preference for regional parties also increased, since 1996. At least one fourth of India's electorate voted for State Parties in 1996. While, the BJP and Congress together polled a little over fifty per cent share of the total votes. The Communist parties, BSP and Janata Dal together, had about 20 per cent votes. In 1999, the State parties increased their vote share to nearly 27 percent votes. The BJP polled 23.5 per cent votes, while its regional allies of BJP secured 18 per cent votes. The regional allies of Congress too, polled 5 per cent votes. Other regional parties polled 15 per cent votes. Thus, in terms of vote share forty percent of the votes were polled by State Parties and 60 percent by national parties.

The rise in the vote share of regional and state level parties was accompanied by the broad alliances that they forged with national parties like the BJP, since 1998. In 1999 general elections (Twelfth Lok Sabha) the BJP allied with 19 regional parties. This was unlike the situation in 1996 (Frankel et al, 2000: 181) when the BJP despite being the single largest party in the Lok Sabha was not supported by the regional parties to form the government. In the thirteenth Lok Sabha, the NDA-led coalition consisted of 25 parties and in the fourteenth the UPA-led coalition had the support of 16 regional parties/allies.

The growing strength of State parties in the Parliament, was however, not accompanied by a trust in their abilities to provide a stable government. Both the National Front in 1989 and United Front governments in 1996 that were short lived, were led by State parties. The success of Vajpayee led NDA government and Manmohan Singh led UPA coalition government in completing their terms (in the period 1999 to 2014) restored popular confidence in the stability of coalition governments. However, they were both led by national parties, though state parties had an important role to play in both the government.

The political developments of 1990s underscore the centrality of State parties to government formation at the national level. The decline of the Congress Party gave an opportunity to the smaller parties to become assertive. In addition to this, the State parties also built on their own core support base, which was reflected in their increasing vote share. Both in terms of vote share and seat share, the State parties moved from strength to strength. As the events unfolded, it seemed that the national parties were supporting entities to regional parties (Frankel et al, 2000:2) or dependent entities relying on the support of State Parties. This however did not mean that the role of national parties in providing a government, or an alternative government had declined (Jaitley, 2013). It only indicated that despite the changing fortunes of parties, the State parties continued to play an important role not just in the state level politics, but at the national level too.

It can therefore be concluded that the character of representative democracy, as reflected in its national legislative institution, namely the Parliament is determined not just by the ideas, ideology and profile of the members of the national parties. The State parties too emerged as important actors and played a critical role in shaping of the Parliament as a representative and deliberative institution.

References

Suri, K.C. (2010) Parties under Pressure; *Working paper Series*, CSDS-Lokniti, New Delhi.

Palishkar, Suhas. (2004) 'Regional Parties and Democracy: Romantic Rendezvous or Localised Legitimation?' Democracy- Asia. Org, pp. 92-93.

Arora, Balveer and K.K. Kailash (2013) 'The New Party System; Federalised and Binodal' in Mehra, Ajay K. (ed.) *Party Sytem in India; emerging Trajectories* (Atlanta: Lancer Publishers.

Morris Jones, W.H. (1957) *Parliament in India London*: Longmans, Green and Co., pp. 16-21.

Chandhoke, Neera. (2009) *Contemporary India: Economy, Society and Politics,* New Delhi: Pearson, pp. 264-268.

Kothari, Rajni. (1970) *Politics in India* Delhi: Little Brown and Company, pp. 176.

Kohli, Atul. (2009) *Democracy and Development in India: from Socialism to Pro-Business* (New Delhi: OUP, pp. 5-Roy, Ramashray and Paul Wallace Paul (ed.), (1999) *Indian Politics and the 1998 election* New Delhi: Sage Publications, pp. 52.

Kohli, Atul. (2009) *Democracy and Development in India: from Socialism to Pro-Business,* New Delhi: OUP, p. 8.

Myron, Weiner. (1957) *Party Politics in India: the Development of a Multi-Party System,* London: OUP, pp. 224-228.

Frankel, R. Francine. et al, (2000) *Transfroming India: Social and Political Dynamics of Democracy,* New Delhi: OUP, 2000, p. 181.

Jaitley, Arun. (2013) *Third Front: My Opinion* (Available atwww.arunjaitley.com, http://www.arunjaitley.com/en/my-opinion-inside.php?id=77&mode=Read &icatId=16 (Accessed on September 3, 2013).

Chapter - 3

Support Base of State Parties

In any representative democracy, the members of the democratic community give the power to the representatives to act in a specific way and for a certain period of time. This does not mean that the community is deprived of its ultimate control. The body of representatives, or the parliament, derives its authority from the community. The relationship between the representative body and the community, therefore is of prime significance. As James Madison, a founding father of American Constitution, opined,

> The effect (of delegation of government) is.... to refine and enlarge public views, by passing them through the medium of chosen body of citizens, whose wisdom may best discern the true interest of their country, and whose patriotism and love of justice will be least likely to sacrifice it to temporary partial considerations. Under such a regulation, it may well happen than the public voice, pronounced by the representatives of the people, will be more in consonant to the public good than if pronounced by people themselves, convened for the purpose (Madison, 1787)

The success of a democratic polity depends to a large extent on the essential representativeness of the system. According to V.B. Singh (1984), an eminent political scientist, "how representative a system is, in fact an indicator of the democratic-ness of the polity." The representativeness of the system would depend on two main factors, among others:

(a) Who are the representatives and what is their relationship with the community; and

(b) How do they represent the community in the institutional forums?

The answer to the first question would relate to the socio-economic characteristics of the representatives, namely, age, education, occupation, income, etc. It would also be related to the socio-economic profile of the electorate that has voted the representatives. Congruence between the two would indicate some representativeness. The answer to the second question would relate to the manner in which representative's carry out their functions, namely, what they represent, how do they represent and where do they represent.

The present chapter attempts to answer the first question in order to determine the nature of representation carried out by State Parties. It seeks answers to three specific questions: who are the voters for State Parties? Is there a core support base of State Parties, especially in constituencies where the State Parties have won seats and elected members to the Lok Sabha? What is the socio-economic profile of the voters of State Parties? Are the supporters of State Parties and national parties different? If so, what is the difference between the two?

The answer to these questions may be found by looking at data relating to voters of State Parties. The Election Commission of India provides aggregate data relating to vote share of different parties. It also provides state-wise and constituency-wise vote share of various parties. However, it does not provide data of voters of State Parties on the basis of caste, education and income. The National Election Study (NES 2004) provides data relating to these.

The NES 2004 provides disaggregate data on the socio-economic profile of the voters based on age, education, occupation, income, caste, etc. The present chapter mainly analyses the responses to one question from the survey questionnaire of the National Election Study 2004, "Which party did you vote for?" along with some of the background variables of the respondents, namely, caste, education and income. We look into two sets of data in this respect; first, data relating to support base of state and national parties across the country on the basis of education, income and caste and secondly, support for State Parties in constituencies where their contestant won elections.

This data, together with the data provided by ECI may be helpful in identifying the supporters of state party MPs, and analysing their socio-economic characteristics.

All India Support Bases of State Parties

Data shows that 5141 out of the total of 27189 respondents, constituting nearly 19 percent of the respondents, preferred state party representatives at national level. This data together with the Election Commission of India data on vote share of State Parties in the 14th Lok Sabha elections (Table 3.2) indicates the importance of State Parties in the 14th Lok Sabha.

Table 3.1: Distribution of Vote by National and State Party Groups

	Number	*Percent*	*Valid Percent*
National Parties	15863	58.3	70.8
State Parties	5141	18.9	22.9
Small parties and independents	1416	5.2	6.3
Total	***22420***	***82.5***	***100.0***

Source: NES 2004, n=27189.

Table 3.2: Distribution of Vote for State Parties

Sl. No.	*Party*	*Number*	*Percent*
1.	03: JD(United)	344	1.3
2.	11: RJD (Laloo)	224	.8
3.	12: LNJP(Paswan)	120	.4
4.	13: KEC(M)	22	.1
5.	16: DMK	172	.6
6.	17: PMK	78	.3
7.	18: JMM	127	.5
8.	22: Shiv Sena	294	1.1
9.	23: BJD	289	1.1
10.	24: Akali Dal	203	.7
11.	25: AIADMK	245	.9
12.	26: Trinamool Congress	313	1.2
13.	27: TDP	412	1.5
14.	30: SP	435	1.6
15.	31: JD(S)	168	.6
16.	32: RLD (Ajit Singh)	80	.3
17.	33: INLD (Chautala)	145	.5
18.	40: CPI (ML)	44	.2
19.	42: RSP	84	.3
20.	53: AGP	276	1.0
21.	56: UGDP	3	.0
22.	60: JKNC	55	.2
23.	61: JKPP	5	.0
24.	62: JKDP	35	.1
25.	73: FPM	33	.1
26.	75: MPP	16	.1
27.	76: UDP	1	.0

(Contd...)

28.	79: MNF	211	.8
29.	82: NPF	280	1.0
30.	86: Akali Dal (Mann)	12	.0
31.	88: SDF	351	1.3
32.	89: MDMK	61	.2
33.	93: UKD	3	.0

Source: NES 2004, n=27189.

State Parties polled nearly 19 percent of the votes. Out of all the State Parties mentioned above, AITC and BJD in the East, SP and JD (U) in the North, SHS in the West, TDP in the South and NPF, MNF, AGP in the North East were the major State Parties that had the support of more than one percent of the total number of respondents. The RJD, the MNF and AIADMK also had the support of nearly one percent of the respondents. State Parties were thus important in every region of the country; the North East had a large number of regional parties and each of them enjoyed considerable support compared to national parties. Similarly, the East and the North of the country too had a large number of State Parties that enjoyed considerable support. The West had the least number of State Parties.

Though most of the respondents supported national parties, the support of nearly one-fifth of the respondents to State Parties in an election to the national legislature is of significance.

The data indicates that the smaller State Parties and independents did not offer any serious competition to either the national or State Parties, or much choice to the electorate.[1] The competition was between the national parties which were aligned either to the Congress-led United Progressive Alliance or the BJP-led National Democratic Alliance. There were also some State Parties which offered issue based support/opposition to UPA/NDA.

Table 3.3: Caste-wise Support for Parties

Sl. No	*Caste*	*National Parties*	*State Parties*	*Small parties and independents*	*Total*
1.	**SC**	77.9	17.8	4.3%	100.0
		17.7	12.5	10.8%	16.0
2.	**ST**	56.9	27.0	16.1%	100.0
		13.0	19.0	41.3%	16.2
3.	**OBC**	68.9	26.3	4.8%	100.0
		33.1	39.0	25.6%	34.0
4.	**Others**	75.8	20.0	4.2%	100.0
		36.2	29.5	22.2%	33.8
	Total	70.8	22.9	6.3%	100.0
		100.0	100.0	100.0%	100.0

Source: NES, 2004, n=27189.

It would be important in the present context to disaggregate the data in terms of caste, education and income to ascertain the support base of State Parties.

Caste-wise disaggregation of data shows that of those who supported State Parties, a majority belonged to the OBC (39.5%) followed by the others (29%), ST and SC. The national parties received greater support from the category "others" (36.2%) followed by the OBC and the SC and it received least support from the ST. Interestingly, nearly 5 to 6 percent more respondents from the marginalised groups including the OBC, SC and ST supported the State Parties than the national parties. In the case of the "others" nearly 10 percent more respondents supported the national parties.

This shows that the marginalised sections, particularly the OBC and the SC preferred the State Parties to the national parties, irrespective of the nature or level of political institution (viz. national or state). The ST preferred the smaller unregistered parties and the general category of respondents favoured the National parties.

Table 3.4: Income-wise Support for Parties

Income	*National Parties*	*State Parties*	*Small parties and independents*	*Total*
Very low	70.2	23.9	5.9	100.0
	66.6	69.5	69.0	67.4
Low	72.2	22.3	5.5	100.0
	16.9	15.9	15.9	16.6
Medium	73.4	21.3	5.3	100.0
	15.0	13.3	13.6	14.6
High	73.5	20.4	6.1	100.0
	1.5	1.3	1.5	1.4
Total	71.0	23.2	5.7	100.0
	100.0	100.0	100.0	100.0

Source: NES, 2004, n=27189.

The income-wise data indicates an interesting trend. As we move from the lower to higher income level, the support for State Parties declines. In other words, State Parties are most preferred by the respondents of very low and low income groups. (69.5 and 15.5%) Together, nearly two-thirds (85%) of the respondents who voted for State Parties belonged to the weakest economic category and only 15% were from the middle or higher income groups. This figure was 83 and 17 percent for national parties. The smaller parties and independents too enjoyed a support base similar to that of State Parties.

Thus, two conclusions may be drawn from the above data. Firstly, the lower income groups preferred the State Parties to that of the national parties. Secondly, as we move from the lower to the higher income category, the support for State Parties declines and for the national parties increases. This indicates that the supporters of the State Parties come mostly from lower income groups and lower the income levels the more likely is the support for State Parties.

Table 3.5: Education-wise Support for Parties

Education	*National Parties*	*State Parties*	*Small parties and independents*	*Total*
Non Literates	72.0	22.6	5.4	100.0
	31.1	30.0	26.3	30.5
Primary	69.2	24.4	6.4	100.0
	35.0	37.9	36.1	35.7
Matriculate	70.2	24.3	5.5	100.0
	12.7	13.5	11.2	12.8
Intermediate	72.0	22.2	5.9	100.0
	10.1	9.6	9.2	9.9
Graduate	69.9	19.1	10.9	100.0
	8.4	7.1	14.8	8.5
Post Graduates	76.1	18.1	5.8	100.0
	2.7	2.0	2.3	2.5
Total	70.7	23.0	6.3	100.0
	100.0	100.0	100.0	100.0

Source: NES, 2004, n=27189

Similarly, support for State Parties comes more from those with lower level of educational qualification. But for the lowest level of education i.e. non-literates, the support for State Parties declines as there is an upward movement along the educational ladder. Thus, nearly 37.9 percent of those with primary level of education, 13.5 percent of Matriculates and 9.6 percent of Intermediate level of education supported State Parties, compared to the support of 35, 12.7 and 10 percent respectively of respondents from the same categories to national parties. The data shows similar pattern in the case of income as well as education, that the support for State Parties increases as we move down the education ladder. In other words, those with lower level of education are more likely to support State Parties than those with higher level of education. In contrast, national parties gain support largely from two categories i.e. those with the lowest level of education and those with medium and higher level of education.

The above data amply illustrates that State Parties get greater support from lower castes, lower income groups and those with lower levels of educational qualifications. Despite the indicative nature of the above data, the large support for State Parties highlights the importance of State Parties at the national level. It also shows that the State Parties are more popular in states of North East and East India compared to that of North and Western India. This is evidenced by the large number of significant State Parties as well as the overall support that they seem to enjoy.

Support Base of State Parties in Seats Won by State Parties

All India data may not provide a nuanced understanding of supporters of State Parties, as it includes data from those constituencies where State Parties may not have had much support. The above conclusion therefore may be indicative rather than conclusive. Further, since most states in India have moved towards a two party model, the support base of each party may vary from state to state. In view of this, a state-wise analysis, where the candidates of State Parties have won (and where survey has been carried out) may help in accurately capturing the support base of the State Parties in terms of the points of reference mentioned at the outset, namely

- Caste
- Education
- Income

For the above purpose, the All India data has been further been segregated into five different zones.

- **North Zone** – Jammu and Kashmir, Punjab, Uttarakhand, Uttar Pradesh
- **West Zone** –Maharashtra
- **East Zone** – Bihar, Odisha, Jharkhand, and West Bengal
- **South Zone** –Andhra Pradesh, Karnataka, Kerala, Tamil Nadu, Puducherry
- **North-East Zone** - Assam, Sikkim, Nagaland, Meghalaya, Mizoram

Data of each state in the zone is analysed to understand the nature of representation from each unit and make suitable comparison.

Following is the list of important State Parties in each of the states mentioned above:

Table 3.6: List of Important State Parties in States

Sl.No.	*State*	*Important State Parties*
1.	Jammu and Kashmir	J&KNC, J&KPDP
2.	Punjab	Akali Dal
3.	Uttarakhand	SP
4.	Uttar Pradesh	SP, BSP
5.	Maharashtra	SHS, MNS
6.	Bihar	JD(U), RJD
7.	Odisha	BJD
8.	West Bengal	TMC
9.	Andhra Pradesh	TDP,TRS
10.	Karnataka	JD(S)
11.	Kerala	KEC(M)
12.	Tamil Nadu	DMK, AIADMK, PMK, MDMK
13.	Puducherry	DMK, AIADMK, PMK, MDMK
14.	Assam	AGP
15.	Sikkim	SDF
16.	Nagaland	NPF
17.	Meghalaya	MPP, RPA
18.	Mizoram	MNF

North Zone

The North Zone includes the state of Jammu and Kashmir, Punjab, Haryana, Uttarakhand and Uttar Pradesh. Post poll survey carried out in each of these states reveal a definite caste pattern in the supporters of State Parties.

Table 3.7: Caste-wise Support for State Parties in North Zone

	Caste			
	SC	*ST*	*OBC*	*Others*
		Jammu & Kashmir		
BJP	0	0	0	100
J&KNC	25	12.5	0	62.5
J&KPDP	7.1	0	14.3	68.6
Congress				
		Punjab		
Cong	30.7	0.8	10.4	58.1
BJP	12.2	2	9.2	76.5
BSP	72	0	8	20
SAD	17.3	1.5	11.4	69.8

(*Contd*...)

Uttar Pradesh				
Cong	15.8	2.7	46.4	35
BJP	8.3	1.1	36.4	54.2
BSP	68.8	0.3	22.4	8.5
SP	11.5	1.1	57	30.5
RLD	3.8	0	58.8	37.5
Uttarakhand				
Cong	20.4	2.1	17.3	60.2
BJP	7.2	0	11	81.8
SP	40	6.7	13.3	40

Source: NES, 2004, n=27189.

In Jammu and Kashmir, the J&KNC received majority of its votes (62.5%) from the caste group "Others" which includes all groups other than SC, ST, OBC and Muslims. In other words, this category includes upper caste Hindus and Brahmins. 25% of respondents belonging to SC and 12.5% of ST category supported J&KNC. It was found no favour amongst the OBCs. In the case of J&KPDP, the other important state party in the state, it received 14.5% votes from OBC voters and only 7.1% from SCs, and the rest from "others".

This reveals that the State Parties of Jammu and Kashmir had greater support amongst the upper and intermediary castes. Amongst the marginalised, SC and ST favoured the National Conference, while the OBC favoured the PDP to the J&KNC.

In Punjab, the upper caste voters mostly preferred the BJP (75%), followed by the SAD (69.8%) and Congress (58.1%). The SC supported the BSP more than the Congress. The ST and OBC supported the Congress and SAD more than other parties.

The SAD received highest vote share from "Others" followed by the SC and OBC votes. For BSP, 72% of the vote share came from SC voters and 8% from the ST. On the other hand, Congress received highest vote share from "Others" followed by SC (30%), very few ST votes and only 10% of the OBC votes. Thus, theCongress was more popular amongst the ST and OBC.

In Uttarakhand, SC, ST and OBC constituted 60% of votes of SP. This was 37% for Congress, and 18.2% for the BJP. For BJP the majority of support came from "Others" category. Clearly the marginalised sections of the voters constituted the core of the supporters of State Parties in Uttarakhand.

Interestingly, in UP 57% of total votes received by SP were from OBC and only 11% from the SC, whereas in the case of BSP, 69% of vote was from the SC voters and only 22% from the OBC voters. Thus, while the BSP had most supporters from the SC, the SP had bulk of its support from the SC. The Congress supporters consisted mainly of the OBC and the Upper and intermediary castes. In the case of RLD, their highest vote share came from OBC voters. The BJPs support base consisted largely of the category "others", while BSP received the least share of votes from "Others" category. The data indicates the two main State Parties namely, the SP and BSP had maximum support of the two main marginalised groups namely, the SC and OBC. Among the national parties, the Congress had a greater support of OBC and ST while the BJP voters were mainly from the upper castes.

Two broad conclusions emerge from the above data. In the first place, there is a significant difference in the support base of parties in the North and North West region of Jammu and Kashmir and Punjab and that of Hindi Heartland states of Uttar Pradesh and Uttarakhand. While the supporters of State Parties in the North West region are largely from upper castes, the regional parties of North India gets most support from marginalised sections of the society.

West Zone

The main regional party in Maharashtra is Shiv Sena (SHS). The NCP though having largely a regional base is categorised as a national party.

Table 3.8 : Caste-wise Support for State Parties in West Zone

Caste				
Maharashtra				
	SC	**ST**	**OBC**	**Others**
Cong	23.8	18.5	25.5	32.2
BJP	6.7	8.8	39.6	45
SS	5.5	4.1	40.9	49.5
NCP	15.4	9.6	23.4	51.6

Source: NES, 2004, n=27189.

The data in Table 3.8 illustrates that the Shiv Sena received a majority of its votes from the upper castes categorised as "Others" (50%). The Party was equally popular amongst the OBC (41%). Together the SC, ST and OBC constituted 51% of the support base of the SHS. The NCP's vote share was spread out between the different caste categories. NCP received highest votes from upper caste category, 23% from OBC and 15.4% from SC voters and 10% from ST. It was Congress that received the highest share of votes from the ST category. The Congress and the BJP had better support amongst the marginalised (55% and 68 %) than either the SHS or the NCP (51% and 48% respectively) sections.

The data indicates that regional parties of the West zone have almost equal support amongst the marginalised and the upper castes. while the national parties have greater supporters from the marginalised. The SHS the main regional party of this region is most representative of the backward castes.

East Zone

As mentioned earlier,the East zone for this study comprises Bihar, Jharkhand West Bengal and Odisha. The main regional parties in these states are JD(U), RJD and LNJP in Bihar, JMM, JDU, JDS and RJD in Jharkhand and AITC in West Bengal and BJD, Congress and in Odisha. Let us analyse the caste wise data of different regional parties in these three states of East Zone.

Table 3.9: Caste-wise Support for State Parties in East Zone

	Caste			
	SC	*ST*	*OBC*	*Others*
		Bihar		
Cong	10	0	55	35
BJP	15.7	2.9	43.1	38.2
JDU	13	0.9	50.5	35.6
RJD	24.2	2.7	50	23.1
LNJP	10.9	0	68.5	20.7
		Jharkhand		
Cong	5.8	30.8	46.8	16.7
BJP	11.6	21.3	32.9	34.2
JDU	4.3	17.4	52.2	26.1
JMM	11.8	47.9	23.5	16.8
RJD	25.9	3.7	63	7.4
JDS	9.1	4.5	77.3	9.1
		West Bengal		
Cong	13	19.3	8.7	59
CPM	28.2	7	11.7	53.2
CPI	17.1	11.4	14.3	57.1
AITC	35.7	7	9.6	47.8
BJP	22.7	19.7	10.6	47

(Contd...)

Odisha				
Cong	23.2	20.2	31.5	25.2
BJP	13.3	18.1	45.7	22.9
BJD	15.0	6.6	45.3	33.1

Source: NES, 2004, n=27189.

The data in Table 3.9 shows that in Bihar, of the two main regional parties, the JD(U) received its highest share of votes from OBC voters i.e., 50.5% and 13% from SC voters. For RJD, 50% of vote share came from OBC and 25% from SC. After RJD, the party that had the highest share of votes from SC voters is BJP which received 15.7% votes. All the major political parties of Bihar received their majority of votes from OBC category but LNJP got maximum support, almost 69%, from OBC category. The two parties which got maximum support from OBC and SC (74% and 79% respectively) were RJD and LNJP. The data reveals that the support base of regional parties varies, though they may have similar ideologies. Thus, while the RJD, the LNJP and JD (U) are all important regional parties of the state and profess to espouse the cause of the marginalised, the support base of the RJD and LNJP is more representative of them. The Congress and JD (U) are almost similar in terms of their support base.

In case of Jharkhand, the JMM received highest share of votes from ST (47.9%) and the least share from SC. For other regional parties the majority of vote share came from OBC voters. After OBC, it was SC that voted mainly for RJD. JD (U) received the least votes from SC amongst all caste categories and JDS received the least share from ST. So, for JMM the most important caste category was ST, for JDU it was OBC and ST, for RJD it was OBC and SC that were important.

In case of West Bengal, the data in the Table 3.9 reveals that the Congress received maximum support from the upper castes (50%), followed by the CPI. Amongst the regional parties, the AITC had maximum vote share from the SC voters (35.7%), followed by the CPM which received the highest SC votes (28.2%) and CPI (17.1%). SC and ST constitute 42% of the voters of AITC. CPI also received the highest share of votes from ST category amongst the parties (11.4%). Although AITC and BJP had almost similar support from the SC, ST and OBC categories put together, the BJP had larger vote share from the ST and AITC having greater vote share and was less preferred compared to the national parties from SC, the Congress and the left parties were more representative of the non-marginalised groups.

In case of Odisha BJD got support from SC and ST (15% and 6.6 respectively). It got maximum support from OBC (45.3%) and 33.1 percent from Others.

The above data indicates that the support base of regional parties varies from state to state. While the JD (U) has greater support from the upper castes in Bihar, it has greater support amongst the OBC in Jharkhand. Similarly, while the Congress support base in Bihar is largely from the marginalised, in the case of West Bengal it draws maximum support from the upper castes. Secondly, some State Parties like RJD have similar support groups across the states. Thirdly, left parties such as CPI and CPM have less support from the marginalised groups than the regional parties. Fourthly, some State Parties that cater to specific groups such as the JMM has greatest supporters from the group.

South Zone

South Zone for this study comprises Andhra Pradesh, Kerala, Tamil Nadu, Puducherry and Karnataka. The main regional parties in these states are: TDP in Andhra Pradesh, KEC and KEC(J) in Kerala, DMK, PMK, AIADMK and MDMK in Tamil Nadu, PMK in Puducherry and JD(S) in Karnataka. The table below shows the various caste categories and their representation in various states.

Table 3.10: Caste-wise Support for State Parties in South Zone

	Caste			
	SC	ST	OBC	Others
		Andhra Pradesh		
Cong	24.2	3	42.4	30.3
BJP	20	0	53.3	26.7
TDP	7	4.4	64	24.6
		Kerala		
Cong	4.9	1.4	49.9	43.9
CPM	17.7	2.8	60.9	18.6
KEC	11.8	0	64.7	23.4
KEC(J)	30	0	15	55
		Tamil Nadu		
Cong	9.7	1.4	88.2	0.7
BJP	12.1	0	84.8	3
DMK	16.4	1.2	72.5	9.9
PMK	18.2	1.5	75.8	4.5
AIADMK	22.6	1.2	69.5	6.6
MDMK	23.3	0	73.3	3.3
		Puducherry		
BJP	10.7	NA	71.4	17.9
PMK	0	NA	83.3	16.7
		Karnataka		
Cong	35.8	22.6	37.7	3.8
BJP	33.3	7.4	48.1	11.1
JD(S)	9.1	4.5	77.3	9.1

Source: NES, 2004, n=27189

The data in the above table reveals that in Andhra Pradesh, TDP received highest share of votes from the OBC. Nearly three quarters of the supporters of TDP were SC, STs and OBC, with OBC constituting about 64% of its supporters which was higher than the Congress and the BJP. The BJP too has a similar support base. However, SC vote share to Congress and BJP was much higher than that for TDP. Among the category 'Others', the TDP was the least popular. It appears therefore that TDP was popular amongst all marginalised groups, though it was slightly less popular amongst the SC.

In case of Kerala, the KEC received the highest OBC votes at 64.7%. This was nearly four percent more than the CPM and 15 percent more than the Congress. Together the SC and OBC constitute more than three quarters of the supporters of State Parties. Only 23 percent of the voters of KEC are from the upper castes and 'Others' category. However, amongst SC and ST the Communist Party was more popular. The Congress and KEC(J) have more supporters from them. Interestingly, the supporters of KEC and CPI (M) are almost similar in terms of Caste background with only a marginal difference

In Tamil Nadu, all the major political parties drew maximum support from the OBC voters. The Congress was most popular amongst the OBC. All the State Parties had lesser though similar support from the OBC. However, their support amongst the SC and ST was higher than that of Congress or BJP. The AIADMK received 22.6% of SC votes and 1.2% of ST votes while MDMK received the highest SC votes (23.3%) but no ST vote. PMK and DMK's voting pattern based upon caste categories was almost the same with around 17% votes from SC and 75% from OBC. The DMK was most popular amongst 'Others' category.

It appears therefore that in Tamil Nadu, though the national parties, particularly the Congress had greater support amongst the OBC and lesser support amongst the SC and 'Others', in the case of regional parties it was the other way round.

In the case of Karnataka, the JD (S) the most popular of the State Parties had largest support from the OBC (77.3%). Its support amongst the OBC was nearly double of that of the Congress (37.7%) and the BJP (48.1%). The Congress had larger support amongst the ST (22.6%), while similar percentage of supporters from the ST voted for the BJP and the JD(S). The upper castes and 'Others' preferred the BJP to the Congress or the JD(S). It appears therefore that in Karnataka, the bulk of the support for the JD(S) came from the OBC followed by the SC and Others category. Though the OBC preferred the JD(S) overwhelmingly, the SC and ST supported the Congress.

In Puducherry, the BJP received 10% SC votes and 71% OBC votes. PMK received 83.3% OBC Votes and 16.7% of Others category vote.

When voters for political parties of the south are categorised on the basis of caste, it is clear that the support base for the State Parties comes largely from the OBC. In almost all the southern states, the OBC constituted the bulk of the supporters of the State Parties that have contested the elections from the state. The support of the SC and ST was divided between the national and regional parties. In most cases the SC support was either for the Congress or for the State Parties except in Kerala where it was for the Communist party.

North-East Zone

Table 3.11: Caste-wise Support for State Parties in North East Zone

	Caste			
	SC	*ST*	*OBC*	*Others*
		Assam		
Cong	4.5	6.8	20.5	68.2
BJP	8.6	22.9	25.7	42.9
AGP	3	6.1	47	43.9
		Meghalaya		
Cong	1.1	93.1	0	5.9
BJP	8.1	40.5	8.1	43.2
RPA	0	98.1	1.9	0
		Mizoram		
Cong	100	0	0	0
MNF	98.1	0.9	0.9	100
		Nagaland		
Cong	1.4	94.4	0.7	3.5
BJP	0	100	0	0
NPF	0.4	94.6	2.1	2.9
		Sikkim		
Cong	9.2	25.5	35.7	29.6
SDF	7.1	24.6	44.3	24

Source: NES, 2004, n=27189

In Assam, the AGP, the most important state party with three seats in the Lok Sabha, got 47% of its support from OBC voters, and 6.1% from ST indicating large support from the OBC. The OBC supporters of AGP were nearly two times more than that of the national parties. Together, the marginalised constitute nearly three quarters of the supporters of AGP. Among the national parties, the BJP had 22.9% votes from ST and 8.6% from SC voters and 25% from OBC. The Congress which has a substantial presence in the region and is the largest national party, had the highest vote share from the category "Others" followed by from OBC.

In Meghalaya, the regional party RPA, which was a federation of all the regional parties in the state, received 98.1% of votes from ST and rest from OBC. Clearly, the national parties came nowhere close to the State Parties in terms of either support or support of the ST and OBC. The BJP received 40.5% votes from ST and 43.2% from "Others" category.

In Mizoram, the MNF, the major regional party of the state,the supporters were predominantly from SC (98.1%), while in Nagaland, NPF's vote base was predominantly from the ST voters (94.6%) and 2.1% from OBC. In Sikkim, SDF vote base was such that 44.3% votes came from OBC, 24.6 from ST and 7.1% from SC. Congress received highest vote share from OBC followed by Others, ST and SC.

All the North Eastern states except Assam, showed similarity in terms of their support base for the parties. In the whole of North East, the regional parties were the main claimants of the support of the ST, SC and the OBC. The OBC and SC population in the states of North East except Assam was small. Under the circumstances, the popularity of the State Parties amongst the ST indicates the predominance and popularity of the State Parties at large and among the marginalised in particular. The upper castes and other religious groups had greater preference for the Congress. The BJP though included in the study had a minor presence in these states.

Support Base of State Parties: Zone-Wise Analysis for Education Categories

Table 3.12: Education-wise Support for State Parties in North Zone

	Education						
	Non Literates	*Primary*	*Secondary*	*Inter-mediate*	*Graduate*	*PG*	*Total*
	Jammu & Kashmir						
BJP	5	0	0	0	0	0	0.2
J&K NC	4.3	5.5	1.5	0	3.3	0	4.1
J&KPDP	3.9	8.2	7.7	3.0	10.0	0	6.2

(*Contd...*)

Punjab							
Cong	30.7	31.2	30.2	29.1	27.0	17.2	29.5
BJP	6.8	10.9	16.5	9.4	17.4	20.7	11.9
BSP	7.3	9.9	5.0	6.0	.9	0	6.1
SAD	27.8	18.2	25.9	34.2	21.7	20.7	25.0
Uttar Pradesh							
Cong	9.1	12.6	9.5	10.5	10.6	9.1	10.4
BJP	15.1	18.8	17.6	31.5	36.5	36.4	19.6
BSP	25.7	16.4	13.1	10.5	8.2	9.1	18.7
SP	22.5	20.2	24.9	16.7	20.0	15.9	21.3
RLD	2.9	6.4	6.3	5.6	3.5	2.3	4.6
Uttarakhand							
Cong	35.5	44.8	32.9	35.4	51.4	41.7	39.2
BJP	28.3	30.8	50.0	49.4	37.8	50.0	37.0
SP	6.5	1.4	1.4	2.5	0	8.3	3.1

Source: NES, 2004, n=27189.

North Zone: In Jammu and Kashmir, educated voters voted mainly for PDP and only those that were not literate voted mainly for J&KNC, indicating that the J&KNC was far more popular among the less educated voters, who formed its major support base.

In Punjab, Akali Dal, the main regional party of the state, received highest share of votes from those who had studied up to college but did not have a degree (34.2%) followed by the non-literates (27.8%). The Congress had maximum support from those with education up to primary level.

In Uttar Pradesh, amongst the non-literates, BSP had the highest vote share – 25.7%, followed by SP – 22.5%. For the low and middle education category, it was SP that received the highest share of votes (20.2%) and so is true for the next category of Matric pass as well. However, for all higher education categories following Matric it was the BJP followed by SP that had highest share indicating the popularity of SP. It may be mentioned that though the BSP is categorised as a national party, the party is largely confined to Uttar Pradesh. The SP and BSP together gained maximum support from the non-literate and least educated category of voters (i.e. below matric level category), while the BJP and SP were more popular amongst the less educated category of voters.

In Uttarakhand, where the main contest was between the two major national parties viz., Congress and BJP, amongst non-literates and primary school education categorizes, Congress received higher vote share than BJP. But amongst Matriculates, intermediates and Professional degrees categories, BJP took the lead. The SP which was the most important state party in Uttarakhand received maximum vote amongst the non-literate category (6.5%). It was also very popular amongst the highly educated (Post graduates and above) 8.5% of whose voters supported the SP.

The State Parties across the northern states received more votes from the non-literate, below matric category of voters. This was true not just in those states where the contest was essentially amongst the State Parties, such as UP but also in those states where the contest was between the national parties in states like Uttarakhand. While the SP and BSP derived support largely from those with lower level of education, the other State Parties of the region such as the SAD and SP were also popular amongst those with higher level of education. On the other hand, the State Parties of Jammu and Kashmir had support across educational categories. Further among the national parties, the Congress had a variegated support base and was popular both with educated elite and masses.

West Zone

Table 3.13: Education-wise Support for State Parties in West Zone

	Education						
	Non Literates	*Primary*	*Matriculate*	*Inter-mediate*	*Graduate*	*PG*	*Total*
	Maharashtra						
Cong	20.1	20.4	18.8	13.5	15.4	25.0	19.4
BJP	13.2	13.1	17.6	27.1	29.7	20.8	15.8
SS	9.9	20.1	19.9	22.9	14.3	12.5	19.7
NCP	22.5	21.4	18.8	17.7	14.3	12.5	20.6

Source: NES, 2004, n=27189.

In Maharashtra, there appears to be no clear pattern based on educational level of the voters. The highest share of votes from non-literates and those from lower education category (primary) went to NCP followed by Congress, both of which are national parties, though NCP is confined to the state and since 2009 has been categorised as state party. Those who had studied up to matriculation gave larger vote share to Shiv Sena. In contrast, those with higher education (category of College and Graduates), the votes went mainly to BJP. Amongst the most educated (those with a Post Graduate degree), the vote share went largely to Congress.

In Maharashtra too, the main state party i.e. Shiv Sena's support base is mostly from those with the low education status while the BJP supporters belong to the better educated category. Interestingly, the NCP is supported mostly from the lower educational category.

East Zone

Table 3.14: Education-wise Support for State Parties in East Zone

	Education						
	Non Literates	*Primary*	*Secondary*	*Inter-mediate*	*Graduate*	*PG*	*Total*
Bihar							
Cong	2.9	2.2	2.9	.0	.0	.0	2.2
BJP	8.0	12.5	13.8	7.0	9.7	23.8	10.6
JDU	16.3	22.7	31.9	38.0	29.2	19.0	23.2
RJD	23.1	19.4	15.9	15.5	15.3	28.6	19.9
LNJP	9.4	10.3	7.2	8.5	16.7	14.3	9.9
Jharkhand							
Cong	14.7	20.8	17.6	18.5	19.4	10.0	17.4
BJP	25.5	32.7	43.2	46.7	37.1	50.0	33.7
JDU	2.3.	3.5	3.4	2.2	0	.0	2.6
JMM	16.1	14.2	12.2	5.4	12.9	10.0	13.5
RJD	4.7	3.5	1.4	1.1	.0	.0	3.1
Odisha							
Cong	37.5	35.1	28.3	22.9	22.8	16.7	32.9
BJP	21.1	19.4	20.4	25.7	14.0	33.3	20.4
BJD	23.1	32.4	38.9	34.3	36.8	27.8	31.0
West Bengal							
Cong	17.4	15.9	11.1	9.4	16.7	25.0	15.8
BJP	6.8	5.5	7.8	7.5	10.6	.0	6.5
CPI	5.8	2.8	1.1	1.9	1.5	.0	3.4
CPM	28.9	34.1	32.2	28.3	25.8	25.0	31.3
TMC	10.0	15.5	16.7	28.3	19.7	25.0	14.9
FBI	2.6	1.3	1.1	.0	1.5	8.3	1.7
RSP	10.3	8.1	8.9	5.7	1.5	.0	8.2

Source: NES, 2004, n=27189.

In Bihar, in terms of educational attainment, 23.1% of people who fell into the Non-literate classification voted for RJD, and 16.3% of non-literates voted for JD(U). As we move to the next category of voter with a primary education, we find that it was JD (U) that had the highest share of votes at 22.7% followed by RJD and BJP at 19.4% and 12.5% of vote share respectively. Further, once we move to the categories 'Matric', 'College but no degree' and 'Graduate'; it is again JD(U) that gets the largest share of votes at 31.9%, 38.0% and 29.2% respectively. However, 28.6% of respondents that were Post graduates voted for RJD. Thus, among the two main State Parties in Bihar, the main vote share for JD (U) came from the voters that were primary school educated and the support continues amongst all education categories till Graduate level. It was the RJD that got more votes of non-literates and below primary level educated voters.

In Jharkhand the main contestants were the BJP, the Congress and the JMM. The highest vote share for JMM came from non-literates and for Congress it comes from the primary level educated voters. The BJP got the highest vote share amongst all education categories. It got 25.5% support of the non-literates, 32.7% of primary level educated, 43.2% matriculate, 46.7% college educated but without degree, and 37.1% graduates voted for BJP. BJP's support from the more educated voters was more than that of those with less education. The opposite was true of Congress, the JDU and even the JMM.

In Odisha, amongst higher education categories, matric and above, BJD had the higher vote share. However, amongst non-literates and Primary level educated, Congress got higher share of votes. For West Bengal, amongst all the education categories, higher vote share was received by CPI (M). Among the State Parties, the TMC got greater support from the more educated than among less educated. However, the RSP and FBI, were more popular among the less educated compared to the CPM and the TMC.

The eastern region is characterised by the presence of large number of State Parties. While the congress and the BJP are the main national parties in all the states, except West Bengal where the CPM is the main national party, the State Parties include, JD (U) and RJD in Bihar, the JMM in Jharkhand, the BJD in Odisha and the TMC and FBI in West Bengal.

The contest in all these states is usually between a national party and a state party, as is it in the rest of India. And the support for the vote share of the national party is less than that of state party, except in West Bengal.

On the basis of educational attainment, in all the states except West Bengal, the State Parties drew support mostly from those who are less educated, particularly those who are non-literates, and those with school level education. Among the national parties, the support of the educated voters was more than that of the less educated. The Congress and the CPM where they were strong were popular among non-literate and those with lower educational attainment.

Since the support of those with lower level of educational attainment is crucial to the success of a political party, the party that had greater support among this category was also successful in the formation of the government in the state. In this context there was tough competition between the Congress and the State Parties.

South Zone

Table 3.15: Education-wise Support for State Parties in South Zone

	Education						
	Non Literates	*Primary*	*Secondary*	*Inter-mediate*	*Graduate*	*PG*	*Total*
Andhra Pradesh							
Cong	28.3	37	28.6	27.8	72.7	0	32.3
BJP	4.2	7.4	0	5.6	9.1	0	5.2
TDP	40.4	30.9	57.1	44.4	9.1	100.0	37.8
Karnataka							
Cong	40.0	32.6	18.8	20.0	0	0	32.5
BJP	8.8	30.4	18.8	13.3	16.7	0	16.6
JDU	3.8	13	18.8	6.7	16.7	0	8.6
Kerala							
Cong	20.0	30.8	32.1	44.9	35.6	36.0	32.9
BJP	6.0	6.8	12.7	3.7	9.2	8.0	7.8
CPI	14.0	6.6	7.1	5.1	3.4	4.0	6.5
CPM	34.0	31.6	28.3	25.7	27.6	24.0	29.7
KEC	2.0	1.3	1.4	2.9	1.1	4.0	1.6
Puducherry							
Cong	0	.0	7.7	0	..0	.0	2.4
BJP	100	53.8	61.5	80.0	60	80	64.3
PMK	.0	30.8	30.8	20.0	40.0	20.0	28.6
Tamil Nadu							
Cong	12.7	17.8	16.2	25.6	23.3	.0	17.1
BJP	6.1	3.0	5.1	2.6	2.3	0	4
DMK	14.6	20.8	25.3	20.5	27.9	33.3	20.2
PMK	12.3	7.4	5.1	3.8	7.0	.0	7.9
AIADMK	34.0	29.2	25.3	23.1	20.9	33.3	29.0
MDMK	3.8	8.6	9.1	6.4	4.7	.0	6.9

Source: NES, 2004, n=27189.

In Andhra Pradesh nearly 40.4% of people that fell into the category of non-literate, supported the TDP. Only 28.3% of non-literates voted for Congress. This pattern reverses for those who belonged to the Primary level education category with share of votes to Congress at 37% and to TDP at 30.9%. Once we move to the categories 'Matric' and 'College but no degree', it is TDP again that gets the largest share of votes at 57.1% and 44.4%, and share of Congress is around 28%. The BJP got highest votes from the category of 'Graduates'. Thus, the main vote share of TDP came from the voters that fell in the categories of 'non-literate', 'Matric' and 'College but no degree', whereas the support for the Congress came from the categories: 'Primary' and 'graduate'.

In Karnataka, Congress dominated the vote share especially amongst the non-literate and below primary categories. But voters with higher education and graduates largely supported the BJP and the JDU got maximum support from the category 3. It was also supported by those with the highest level of education (16.7%).

In Kerala, the non-literates and those with primary level of education voted mostly for CPI (M) while those with higher educational qualifications, supported the Congress. As we move up the educational ladder the support for the Communist party increases. The Kerala Congress appears to be a more popular among those with higher educational qualifications than those with less.

In Tamil Nadu, when classification of support is done on the basis of educational qualification of the voters, the data shows that the AIADMK had higher share of votes amongst all categories except from Graduate and professional degree holders. The voting share of DMK and Congress varied across the education categories. However, the DMK had greater support from those with higher educational qualifications compared to the AIADMK which has greater support from amongst those with lower educational qualifications.

In Puducherry voters of all education categories gave a higher share of their votes to BJP. However, among the supporters of PMK, a third of the respondents were those with primary and middle level of education, while 40%, 33% and 28% belong to the category 4, 5, and 6.

It is difficult to identify a single broad trend about the support base of State Parties in the Southern Zone. However, certain broad trends are identifiable. There appear to be two categories of State Parties in the Southern zone based on the classification of support based on the educational status of the voters; firstly in the states of Andhra Pradesh and Tamil Nadu, the State Parties (TDP and AIADMK) clearly have greater support from voters with lesser educational qualifications. Other smaller parties in the state such as PMK and MDMK also seem to have similar support base. Second, there are parties such as JD (U) in Karnataka and KEC in Kerala which have greater support from those with higher and intermediate level of education qualification. The DMK too seems to have a large following amongst the educated elite. In the absence of strong independent regional parties and coalitional nature national parties, the Communist party has greater support from the subalterns.

North-East Zone

Table 3.16: Education-wise Support for State Parties in North East Zone

	Education						
	Non Literates	*Primary*	*Secondary*	*Inter-mediate*	*Graduate*	*PG*	*Total*
			Assam				
Cong	27.4	27.8	3.2	17.2	14.8	14.3	20.5
BJP	37.1	31.5	29.0	37.9	29.6	28.6	33.3
AGP	24.2	25.9	45.2	31.0	40.7	14.3	30.5
RPI	0.	1.9	.0	0	0.	0	0.5
			Meghalaya				
Cong	44.4	40.4	28.2	47.4	21.4	0	40.0
BJP	5.1	5.7	10.3	15.8	50.0	0	7.7
RPA	14.5	8.9	12.8	10.5	21.4	0	11.1
MPP	0	.0	.4.	0	.0	0	.2
			Mizoram				
Cong	.0	1.3	2.9	4.3	11.4	0	2.6
MNF	38.9	42.8	50	31.9	34.1	50	41.8
Indpt	38.9	40.8	39.7	48.9	40.9	33.3	41.2
			Nagaland				
Cong	27.5	27.7	32.0	23.9	24.7	33.3	27.7
BJP	2.5	.5	.0	3.0	1.4	.0	1.2
NPF	45.0	55.0	48.5	61.2	60.3	66.7	53.8
			Sikkim				
Cong	13.3	20.1	21.7	25.8	17.9	.0	19.1
SDF	70.0	69.6	63.8	56.5	67.9	100.0	67.5

Source: NES, 2004, n=27189.

In Assam, the AGP has been enjoying larger support base from voters with intermediate and higher level of education. Thus, while only 24.2% of non-literates voted for AGP, twice the number of matriculates (45.2%) voted for it. This was also the category from which AGP got the highest share of votes. Similarly, 31% of the voters who were 'College educated but without degrees' had voted for the AGP. AGP also got a large share (40%) of votes from Graduates.

Among the national parties, 37.1% of the voters who belonged to the Non-literate classification (lower) voted for BJP, and 27.4% of non-literates voted for Congress. The BJP also got significant support from those with higher level of education. For voters that fell in the category 'College but no degree' 37.9% voted for BJP while 29.6% of respondents that had a college degree (graduates) voted for BJP.

In Meghalaya, Congress got the highest share of votes from all educated categories of voters, except Graduates. The Congress support was greater from the non-literate voters and those with primary level of education (44% and 40%) than those with higher level of education (21% and 0). The support for RPA was spread across educational groups.

In the case of Mizoram, voters who had studied up to Matriculation level gave a higher vote share (50%) to MNF. The MNF also had a sizeable support amongst those with higher educational qualifications. Among the post-graduate respondents 50% reported to have voted for MNF. The pattern reverses for education categories after that. College/no degree holders and Graduate voted mainly for Independent candidates. Though the Congress has a marginal presence in the state, the party received its support more from those with higher level of education.

In Nagaland, NPF was the favoured party for all education categories. However, it secured greater support from those with higher educational qualifications (average of 63%) than those with intermediate (54%) and lower levels of education (55%) or non-literates

In the cases of Sikkim, the highest share of votes went to SDF. All the post-graduates from among the respondents and an average of 71% of the voters from all other educational categories supported the SDF. The largest share of votes for the Congress came from those with intermediate level of education (College educated but no degree education category).

The State Parties in the North East seem to have some similarity when their support base is examine on the basis of educational status of the voters. All the State Parties in the North East have greater support from those with higher level of education than from those with lower level of education. In this context it is important to bear in mind that the North Eastern states have a high level of literacy and this may have some bearing on the nature of support base of different parties.[2] The national parties such as the Congress and the BJP do not have significant support in the states of North East India. However, their support is more from those with intermediate and lower levels of education than the regional parties.

Zone-wise Support Base of State Parties Based on Income

North Zone

Table 3.17: Income-wise Support for State Parties in North Zone

	Income				
State	***Very low***	***Low***	***Middle***	***High***	***Total***
		Jammu & Kashmir			
BJP	1.9	.0	.0	.0	.2
NC	0	4.5	4.2	10.7	4.2
PDP	3.7	7.5	6.0	3.6	6.2
		Punjab			
Cong	38.8	27.8	27.8	31.7	29.9
BJP	15.3	7.1	13.3	14.8	12.3
BSP	9.4	13.1	4.3	0.5	6.2
SAD	17.6	31.3	23.8	23.0	24.8
		Uttar Pradesh			
Cong	10.3	8.9	13.6	12.7	10.4
BJP	15.3	19.4	29.0	25.5	19.9
BSP	27.6	16.5	7.1	10.9	18.7
SP	20.6	23.3	18.5	18.2	21.2
RLD	3.8	4.3	6.2	7.3	4.6
		Uttarakhand			
Cong	46.9	37.0	35.8	23.5	39.1
BJP	26.5	38.8	43.4	52.9	37.1
BSP	2.0	4.2	5.0	11.8	4.1
SP	2.0.	6.1	1.3	0	3.1

Source: NES 2004, n=27189.

In Jammu and Kashmir, the PDP received the highest vote share followed by J&KNC and BJP. PDP's vote share was higher than the other parties amongst all income categories except in the high income group in which the J&KNC had a substantially higher vote share (10.7% to NC and 3.6% to PDP). PDP's highest share of votes came from low income voters (7.5%). BJP could manage to get 1.9% of votes from the very-low income category voters.

In Punjab, the respondents gave a higher percentage of votes to Congress (29.9%) followed by Akali Dal (24.8%) and BJP (12.3%). Congress received the highest share of votes from all income categories except from the 'low income' category. For Congress itself, the highest share of votes came from the 'very low income' category voters (38.8%), whereas, for Akali Dal it was from 'Low income category (31.3%). For

BJP, highest share of votes came from very low income category and the lowest share of votes came from low income category.

In Uttar Pradesh, SP got the highest share of votes (21.2%), followed by BJP (19.9%) and BSP (18.7%). Although SP had the overall lead, from among the various income categories, it had received the highest share of votes only from the Low income category voters (23.3%). For other categories of income the division of vote share is such that the highest share of very low income category votes went to BSP (27.6%) followed by SP (20.6%); the highest share of votes from both Middle income and High income category went to BJP (29% and 25.5% respectively) followed by SP (18.5% and 18.2%) signifying the influence of BJP over middle and high income group of voters.

In Uttarakhand, Congress may have taken the highest share of votes (39%) followed closely by BJP with 37.1% of vote share; but it was BJP that had a higher share of votes amongst all income categories except the Very low income group. This indicates the importance of voters coming from "very low income" category and their support for Congress party. The lead that BJP had over Congress amongst income categories other than the very low income categories only increased as we move up the income levels with 52.9% of high income voters voting for BJP and just 23.5% voting for Congress.

The State Parties across the northern states received more votes from the non-literate and below matric category of voters. This was true not just in those states where the contest was essentially amongst the State Parties, such as UP but also in those states where the contest was between the national parties like Uttarakhand. While the SP and BSP derived support largely from those with lower level of education, the other State Parties of the region such as the SAD and SP were also popular amongst those with higher level of education. The State Parties of Jammu and Kashmir on the other had support across educational categories. Further among the national parties, the Congress had a variegated support base and was popular both with educated elite and masses.

West Zone

In Maharashtra, the NCP took the lead with 21% vote share followed by Shiv Sena with 19.5%, Congress with 19.3% and BJP with 15.8%. An interesting pattern can be seen in Maharashtra in that the very low and low income category voters gave higher share of votes to NCP followed by Shiv Sena, which are regional parties. However, it was Congress that received the highest share of votes from the middle income voters (23.1%) followed by BJP (19.2%). In the high income group, it was BJP that received the highest vote share (27.4%) followed by Congress (21%). NCP, in fact received the least share of votes from middle income and high income category voters.

Table 3.18: Income-wise Support for State Parties in West Zone

		Income			
State	***Very low***	***Low***	***Middle***	***High***	***Total***
		Maharashtra			
Cong	17.3	18.5	23.123.1 21.0	21.019.3	19.3
BJP	13.4	14.6	19.2	27.4	15.8
SHS	20.8	19.4	18.4	14.5	19.5
NCP	26.5	20.8	14.8	11.3	21.0

Source: NES, 2004, n=27189.

East Zone

In Bihar, of the total number of people surveyed, the division of votes was such that the JD(U) got the highest percentage (23.2%) of votes followed by RJD with 19.9%, BJP 10.9%, LNJP 9.9%, and Congress receiving only 2.1% vote share.

Table 3.19: Income-wise Support for State Parties in East Zone

		Income			
State	***Very low***	***Low***	***Middle***	***High***	***Total***
		Bihar			
Cong	3.5	1.3	1.6	0	2.1
BJP	7.4	12.9	10.8	28.6	10.9
JD(U)	16.5	26.3	30.3	14.3	23.2
RJD	21.2	21.1	16.2	14.3	19.9
LNJP	9.7	8.7	11.4	17.9	9.9
		Jharkhand			
Cong	16.3	21.8	12.3	20.0	17.7
BJP	28.0	30.5	42.0	53.3	33.8
JDU	0.8	3.7	3.2	2.2	2.6
JMM	17.8	11.9	12.3	6.7	13.5
RJD	6.1	2.3	1.4 .	0	3.1
		Odisha			
Cong	41.7	29.6	23.2	31.6	32.9
BJP	18.1	20.9	25.4	10.5	20.5
BJD	26.1	36.4	32.6	26.3	31.0

(Contd...)

West Bengal					
Cong	17.5	16.0	13.6	11.1	15.9
BJP	5.2	6.8	7.6	5.6	6.3
CPM	27.0	33.0	35.2	25.0	30.8
CPI	4.0	4.6	1.7	.0	3.5
AITC	11.2	16.0	16.1	36.1	14.9
FB	2.5	1.2	1.7	.0	1.8
RSP	11.5	8.3	4.7	.0	8.4

Source: NES, 2004, n=27189.

The JD (U) received the greatest support from the "Low and Middle" income voters (26.3% and 30.3%). On the other hand, the RJD got the largest share of support from very low income category votes (21.2%) followed by JD(U). Thus, maximum support from both very low and low income groups went to the two main State Parties.Among the high income category, the BJP received the highest share of votes at 28.6%. Interestingly, the LNJP, a newly emergent state party had greater support from the middle and high income group.

Both the Congress and the BJP were marginal players in the state and had allied with regional parties. The BJP had greater support from the middle and high Income groups, while the Congress had greater support from the low and the middle income groups.

In the state of Jharkhand, the highest vote share went to BJP (33.8%) followed by Congress with 17.7% and JMM with 13.5%. The JMM was supported mostly by the very low and low income groups. The RJD, like the JMM, was supported largely by the very low and low income groups, while the JD(U) had the support of low and middle income groups. Across the spectrum of income categories, it was BJP that received the highest support from the middle and high income category of voters (42% and 53.3% respectively).

In Odisha, the Congress had the highest vote share of 32.9%, closely followed by BJD with 31% of votes. The BJP had the third largest vote share of 20.5%. Among all income categories, the very low income category vote share went mainly to Congress (41.7%). However, the largest share of high income votes also went to Congress (31.6%), implying that in Odisha, the vote base of Congress came mainly from very low income or high income category voters. The highest share of low income category support and middle income category vote share was received by BJD (36.4% and 32.6% respectively). Together they comprised over 60% of the support for it. Thus, it appears from the data that both the Congress and the BJP had similar support base with Congress having more "very low" income category votes and BJD having greater "low income category support.

In West Bengal, the CPI (M) had the largest overall share of votes (30.8%) followed by Congress (15.9%) and Trinamool Congress (14.9 %). The CPI (M) received the highest vote share from all income categories except the high income category. From the high income category the largest vote share was received by Trinamool Congress. Interestingly, the other smaller State Parties too had greater support from the lower income groups. In all it appears that lower the income level greater is the support for left parties.

When voters are categorised on the basis of income in the eastern region, certain trends seem to emerge. In the first place, the states of Bihar and Jharkhand have similar characteristics with maximum support to the State Parties from the low and very low income group, while BJP has greater support among the high income group. In Odisha, both the Congress and the BJP have similar support base of low and middle income, while in West Bengal it is ideology that seems to be the basis of support for parties. The left parties, whether national or regional have greater support from very low and low income groups, while AITC and Congress have more support from the middle and high income group.

By and large, it appears is that the low and very low income groups support the State Parties and parties with a left of the centre ideology.

South Zone

Table 3.20: Income-wise Support for State Parties in South Zone

	Income				
State	**Very low**	**Low**	**Middle**	**High**	**Total**
		Andhra Pradesh			
Cong	27.1	41.8	46.3	25.0	33.0
BJP	6.4	1.5	4.9	0	5.0
TDP	36.7	37.3	41.5	50.0	37.7
		Karnataka			
Cong	37.4	15.9	57.1	25.0	32.1
BJP	8.4	36.4	14.3	25.0	16.7
JDU	9.3	6.8	0	25.0	8.6
JDS	12.1	15.9	14.3	25.0	13.6

(Contd...)

Kerala					
Cong	28.2	32.9	42.8	41.2	33.2
BJP	10.4	7.0	5.9	11.8	8.3
CPI	9.5	5.5	3.2	0	6.5
CPM	29.7	30.5	26.1	17.6	28.9
KEC	1.3	1.6	.5	5.9	1.4
Tamil Nadu					
Cong	14.4.	19.9	19.4	0	17.1
BJP	4.6	2.9	3.7	10.0	3.9
DMK	15.2	23.2	27.6	30.0	20.3
PMK	10.3.	6.1	5.2	0	7.8
AIADMK	32.5	26.4	24.6	20.0	28.8
MDMK	7.7	6.8	6.0	10.0	7.1
Puducherry					
Cong	0.	7.1	.0	0	2.3
BJP	33.3	57.1	72.0		65.1
PMK	66.7	21.4	28.0	.0	27.9

Source: NES, 2004, n=27189.

In Andhra Pradesh, the TDP received its largest vote share from two distinct categories of supporters- the high income category (50%) and the very low income (36.7%) category, whereas the Congress got the larger share of votes from the Low and Middle income categories of voters. This indicates that the support for TDP and the ideas espoused by the party cuts across income divides. While the Congress and the BJP have fixed support base amongst the middle classes.

In Karnataka, 32.1% of those covered by the survey supported the Congress, 16.7% the BJP and BSP; and 13.6% the JD (S) and 8.6% JDU. The low income category voters in Karnataka voted mainly for BJP with 36.4% of vote share. The very low and middle income category vote share went largely to Congress (37.4% and 57.1% respectively). Interestingly, the high income voters were equally divided amongst the four main parties equally (25%). The JD(S) was the preferred party of nearly 15 % of low and middle income groups. Obviously, the low income group preferred the Congress to the regional parties in Karnataka.

In Kerala, Congress took the lead with 33.2% vote share and CPI (M) was a close second with 28.9% votes. The Congress received the largest vote share from all income categories except from the very low income category voters, where it was CPI (M) that received the largest vote share from the low and very low income categories. The regional parties appeared to be marginal players in Kerala having greater support of the middle and high income groups.

In Tamil Nadu, among the different income categories, AIADMK received the highest share from the very lower income category, followed by the DMK. Both the parties seem to draw support from similar income categories, with one exception; the AIADMK got greater support from Very Low Income category while the DMK got greater support from High Income group. The difference in terms of percentages is almost equal. The MDMK and PMK are smaller regional parties with the former getting more votes from very poor and the latter from the high income groups. Among the national parties, the support for Congress is equally spread out, with more among the Low and Middle income groups supporting it. However, the High income category vote share went largely to TMC with 36.1% vote share.

In Puducherry, the BJP received the highest share of votes (65.1%), and PMK received the second highest share of votes (27.9%). The poorest income category voters gave higher share of their votes to PMK (66.7%). However the BJP received the highest share of votes from all other income categories. It appears therefore the poorer voters preferred the PMK to any other party including national parties and they constitute the core of the support base of the party.

It is difficult to generalize about the support base of regional political parties in the south. This is due to two factors. First, the number and nature of parties that exist in each of the states is different and secondly, their support base also appears to be different. While some State Parties like TDP and JD(S) have appeal across income boundaries, others such as AIADMK have definite support base. A second interesting observation relates to Congress, which though of limited significance in the states of the region, has almost similar support base across the states of the south, i.e. from the low and middle income group.

In some states like Tamil Nadu, multiple regional parties have almost similar support base when categorised on the basis of income. While the older State Parties are more popular and have polled a greater percentage of votes, the newer State Parties have limited appeal, though the nature of support that they receive from different income groups is almost similar.

Kerala appears to be an interesting study, largely on account of the coalitional nature of the parties in the state. Hence the support is largely divided between the two major formations and the regional parties have limited elbow room.

North-East Zone

Table 3.21: Income-wise Support for State Parties in North East Zone

			Income		
State	***Very low***	***Low***	***Middle***	***High***	***Total***
			Assam		
Cong	31.2	30.6	14.0	9.1	20.7
BJP	44.8	25.8	35.0	27.3	32.9
AGP	24.1	30.6		32.0	36.431.0
			Meghalaya		
Cong	38.5	44.1	33.8	23.1	40.3
BJP	2.0	8.4	17.6	15.4	7.9
RPA	9.5	13.4	7.4	7,7	11.1
TMC	39.2	21.8	29.4	38.5	28.9
			Mizoram		
Cong	0	.0	5.6	5.4	2.6
MNF	45.2	43.4	37.7	41.9	41.8
			Nagaland		
Cong	26.3	30.3	25.2	30.2	27.4
BJP	2.1.	2.0	.5	0	1.2
NPF	47.4	50.0	58.3	56.6	53.7
			Sikkim		
Cong	20.3	15.4	20.2	36.4	19.0
SDF	67.1	71.6	65.3	54.5	67.7

Source: NES, 2004, n=27189.

The division of votes in Assam has been such that the percentage of votes to BJP was the highest at 32.9 %, followed by AGP, a regional party, receiving 31% vote share and Congress receiving 20.7%. BJP received the largest share of votes from the Very low income category and the Middle income category voters (44.8% and 35%, respectively). The AGP received the largest vote share from the low income and high income categories.

In Meghalaya, Congress had the highest vote share 40.3%, followed by Trinamool Congress 28.9% with 11.1% by the Regional Party Alliance. The largest Low income and Middle income category vote share in Meghalaya was received by the Congress. However, the Very low income and the High income vote share went largely to TMC.

From those surveyed in Mizoram, 41.8% voted for MNF and 41.2% voted for Independent candidates and only 2.6% voted for the Congress.

From all income categories, the MNF received the highest share of votes. Its support was uniform across income groups with the highest share emanating from the very low income group (45%).

In Nagaland, the regional party NPF had the highest share of votes followed by Congress at 27.6%. NPF dominates over all income categories and especially among the higher income categories. The support for NPF is slightly more from among the high income group than the low income group.

In Sikkim, SDF received highest share of votes (67.8%) followed by Congress (19%). Unanimously, the largest share of votes was received by SDF. The Congress received the highest share of votes from the High Income Category. However, unlike in the case of NPF the SDF has greater support from the very low and low income groups.

In the North East, the main contest is between the regional parties and the Congress with limited penetration of the BJP in all of the states except in Assam. An interesting feature of the politics of north-east is the sizeable support for independents. As in the case of rest of India, in the North East too the support for the State Parties comes more from among those with low and very low income. While for the national parties, though the Congress does get some support from the low income group, its support base is more from the middle and high income groups.

Highlights

- The support base of a party in depends on certain factors:
  - ***The number of parties in the state***: The number of State Parties determines the nature of support base of the party. In some states there exist only one state party (Assam) while in other States there exist more than one state party (Bihar and Tamil Nadu). In some of the states the support base of all the regional parties is similar like in the case of DMK and AIADMK and in others the support base of State Parties is different (RJD and JDU).
  - ***Nature of party Competition in the state***: In states such as Kerala and Meghalaya, the parties are coalitional in nature. The nature of support base for such parties varies in such states from states which have straight contests.
  - ***Socio-economic Composition of the State Population***: The support base of State Parties is also dependent on the socio-

economic and demographic profile of the states. The support base of political parties is reflective of the population of the state, its level of economic development and level of educational attainment.

- ***Ideology of parties***: In some states like Bengal and Kerala, ideology is an important determinant of the support base. The parties that have left to the center ideology have a large following and widespread support.
- ***Experience of the Party***: Older and established parties have greater support across groups than younger State Parties.

Notwithstanding these differences, certain broad trends about the support base of State Parties may be inferred from the above analysis:

Firstly, each party has a different support base, making generalisation a difficult enterprise. State-wise and region-wise difference in the support base makes each state party unique in terms of its support. However, it is possible to arrive at certain broad understanding. Firstly, State Parties usually get greater support from lower castes, lower income groups and those with lower level of education. This is particularly true of parties particularly of the North Zone except, Jammu and Kashmir. Educational qualifications and economic status of voters are indicative in this respect. Across regions, support for State Parties declines as we move up the social educational and economic ladder.

Secondly, State Parties of Jammu and Kashmir, the North East (Meghalaya, Mizoram and Nagaland) Kerala and West Bengal are different in terms of their support base from State Parties in the rest of the country. In Jammu and Kashmir State Parties get support from the 'upwardly mobile' i.e. more educated and prosperous voters, with some support from others also, while national parties get more support from the non-literates and moderately educated and those with lesser income levels.

In the North Eastern states, the State Parties are stronger than the national parties. They have support from the Tribal population and economically marginalised voters. In Kerala and West Bengal, ideological divide determines the nature of support. The left parties, irrespective of the national or state presence have greater support of lower castes, and those with poorer education and income.

Thirdly, among national parties, the Congress has a support base similar to that of the State Parties, while the BJP seems to be having greater support from upper caste Hindus and economically and educationally endowed voters.

On the basis of the above analysis it is possible to identify certain group of parties, which share similar support base:

Group I: AGP, SP, DMK, AIADMK, PMK, MDMK, JD (U), RJD, KEC, TMC

- Mostly Splinter groups of the Congress
- Centrist ideology
- Support base similar to that of the Congress.

Group II: JD(S), BJD, TDP

- Centrist ideology
- More middle class support
- Has support across groups.

Group III: J&KPDP, J&KNC, MNF, NPF

- These parties are products of the political circumstances in the states
- They are unique in terms of ideology
- Focus more on local issues
- Have varies support base.

Relating Support Base of State Parties to Support for Parties

An important question that arises is why do people support State Parties? Why are State Parties preferred to national parties? A series of interviews of the supporters of major State Parties in almost all states of India have come up with some of the reasons for the support. The responses have also indicated as to what the supporters expect of their MPs at the local and national level.

Question 3a: When you go to vote, what is it that you look for?

	Number	*Percent*
Party	68	81.0
Candidate	55	65.5
Caste of the Candidate	20	23.8
Approachability of the Candidate	22	26.2
Past Record of the Candidate	29	34.5

Source: Author Survey.

In voting for State Parties at national level, people are guided mainly by their perception of the party and its programmes. On probing further, the respondents said that they "looked into the image of the party". This "image" was based on the newspaper and media reports as well as contact with local party workers. The credentials of the candidate are also taken into account by voters while voting. Though caste and the familiarity with the candidate do play a role in voting, their role is next only to that of the party and the candidate.

Question 3b Why did you choose a local/ state party over the bigger national parties?

	Number	*Percent*
History of the Party	14	16.7
Reach of the People	45	53.6
Others (their work, third party to form the government, can develop the region better)	53	63.1

Source: Author Survey.

When asked why they chose State Parties over national parties, majority of the respondents felt that the ability of the state party candidate to reach out to the people, to aggregate and articulate their interest determined their choice of the party. They felt that State Parties were able to perform these functions better than national parties, which were conceived as "distant" and "far removed" from local issues and problems, though their candidates were local. In this context, the choice of the candidates by party leadership is of singular importance. National parties are perceived as choosing candidates on the advice of central leadership, while state party leadership located within the region itself is perceived to be closer.

Question 3c : Do you think State Parties are better than national parties?

	Number	*Percent*
Yes	65	77.4
No	8	9.5

Source: Author Survey.

The approachability of the state party candidates, their understanding of the local issues and problems had a bearing upon the choice of the candidates. Accordingly irrespective of the level for which the voters voted, the nature of political institutions and the limitations of the institutional framework, it was the desire for "representation" that determined the choice of both the candidate and problems.

Question 3d: What makes State Parties better?

	Number	Percent
Commitment to Local Issues	37	44.0
Connect with the Local People	25	29.8

Source: Author Survey.

Voters Perception of Role of State Party MPs

Question 3e: What should be the most important role of the MP

	Number	Percent
Development	33	39.3
Employment	7	8.3
Others (Coordination with state government, Ensuring proper utilisation of funds, Approachability, Empowerment)	55	65.5
Concern with Local Problems	39	46.4

Source: Author Survey.

Most people interviewed had some idea about the role of an MP, though the distinction between the role of an MP and Member of State Legislative Assembly was not always so apparent. Majority of the people interviewed considered the MLA a more familiar a figure. Nearly one third d of the respondents felt local development and concern with local problems should be the primary concern of the Lok Sabha MP. Development herein was interpreted as construction of "basic infrastructure such as roads, railways etc. and provision of basic amenities such has clean drinking water, electricity, schools, etc." When reminded that Lok Sabha MPs were representatives at the national level, the respondents said they knew about it; yet, they felt that the representative should find time and means of ensuring connect with the local people and local problems.

Question 3f: What would be your description of ideal MP?

	Number	*Percent*
Listening to the grievances of the constituents	67	79.8
Work for their area	43	51.2
Approachable	51	60.7
Fulfil all their promises	39	46.4
Getting funds for the constituency	57	67.9

Source: Author Survey.

They observed that they would prefer to vote for candidates who "would listen to them". Herein representation was interpreted as an "act". The act was to be followed up with response in concrete and discernible terms such as speaking on behalf of the constituents, gaining concessions for the constituency, local liaison work. This view shaped their perception of the role of the Lok Sabha representative as well as the functions he is entrusted with.

Question 3g: What should be the most important function of an MP?

	Number	*Percent*
Representing the constituency in the parliament	55	65.5
Solving Local Problems	58	69.0
Discussing the larger national issues	32	38.1
Participated in making laws	32	38.1

Source: Author Survey.

Thus, participation in national debates and law making often appeared far removed in their conceptualisation of the functions of the MPs. The role of the MP, irrespective of the party to which he/she belonged was conceptualised as an individual involved in articulation of interest. Representation through articulation, it was presumed would ensure greater material benefits for the constituents in particular and constituency as a whole. Representation in that sense was closely associated with responsiveness. The information on the "act of representation" was often based on media reports and communication with local party functionaries. Most respondents were satisfied with the manner in which the state party MPs performed this function.

Conclusion

The above discussion clearly indicates that the marginalised voters belonging to lower castes, education and income preferred State Parties to national parties. It is the support of these groups that has contributed to the electoral success and consolidation of State Parties, notwithstanding the regional variations. The reasons for the support varied from State to State and party to party. However here too, the trend seems clear. Supporters across groups preferred State Parties to national parties on account of its proximity to the people; the approachability of their candidates and their connect with the people because of personal contact and understanding of local issues and problems. Further, supporters expected State party MPs to represent their problems and seek redress. As mentioned earlier, irrespective of institutional structures, voters expected State party MPs to represent them and representation was interpreted as an "activity" that ensures concrete measurable gains both in terms of 'presence' and recognition as well as policy outcomes and material gains.

Reference & Notes

1. Madison, James. (1787). The Federalist, vol. 10, cited in Roger Davidson, "Wielding the Broom", in Thurber, James and Davidson, Roger (eds), (1995) *Remaking Congress, Change and Stability in 1990s*, Washington: Congressional Quarterly Inc.
2. Singh, V.B., (1984). Profiles of Political Elites in India, New Delhi, Ritu Publishers p. 5.
3. Suri, K.C. (2010). Parties under Pressure. *Working Paper Series*. New Delhi, CSDS.

Chapter - 4

Who are the Representatives of State Parties? Understanding the Socio-economic Profile of Members

The socio-economic background of the members of the State Parties in the Lok Sabha is an important determinant of representation. Representation may be sociological / descriptive, wherein the representatives share the origin, background or place of residence; or economic similarity, measured in terms of income, assets and occupation; cultural similarity of origin, language, religion, caste etc. with the electorate. There can be little doubt that such similarity helps the representatives in understanding the expectations and issues faced by the representative in the context in which they take place.

As seen in the previous chapter, the support for State Parties often comes from the margins of the society; those with lower levels of income, education and caste. One of the major reasons for the growing support for state level parties has been the perception that they are better able to understand local issues and problems on account of their proximity to the people. The important question however relates to the social and economic background of MPs of the State Parties. Is their background similar to that of the 'people' and the constituency they claim to represent? Is it different from national parties? and how does it assist/desist better representation?

Socio-economic Background of MPs of State Parties

The socio-economic background of MPs of State Parties, which in the present context includes age, educational status, specialisation and occupation provides a good basis for assessing the nature of descriptive representation of MPs of State Parties. Each of these parameters would help in understanding whether the MPs of State Parties are better representatives of their political principals, particularly when compared to their counterparts at the national level and whether their personal background enables them to establish a natural link with the electorate.

Age of MPs of State Parties

In view of the fact that most State Parties have relatively new history and their rise in the national politics is of recent origin, the age profile of MPs of State Parties provides a good basis of understanding the parties. While theoretically age alone may not have a bearing on the nature of representation, it provides a basis of understanding the nature of state party membership in the Lok Sabha.

Table 4.1: Age of MP's of State Parties in the Fourteenth Lok Sabha

Age	*Number*	*Percent*
25-35	10	5.74
36-45	36	20.68
46-55	64	36.78
56-65	41	23.56
66 and above	19	10.91
NA	4	2.2
Total	**174**	**100**

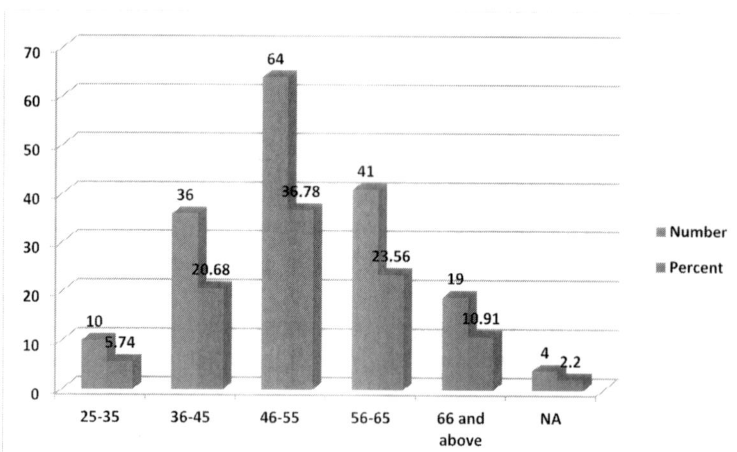

A study of the membership of State Parties in the 14th Lok Sabha indicates that majority of the MPs of State Parties belonged to the middle age group of 46-65 years with maximum members in the age group of 46-55 years. Nearly 57% MP's of the State Parties are in this age group.

This is similar to the all India picture, where nearly 55% MP's belong to the age group of 36-55 years. A comparison between national and State Parties reveals that two-thirds of the MPs belonging to the State Parties and nearly half of the members of national parties were in the age group of 36 to 55 years. However, while the maximum concentration of members in national parties was in the age group of 46-55 years, the State Parties had a greater concentration of members in the 36-45 years age bracket.

If one considers the age below 35 years as the 'youth' category, then the number of MPs representing the 'youth' category is only 5.74% (negligible) when compared to the rest.

Age of MP's that have more than 10 members in Lok Sabha

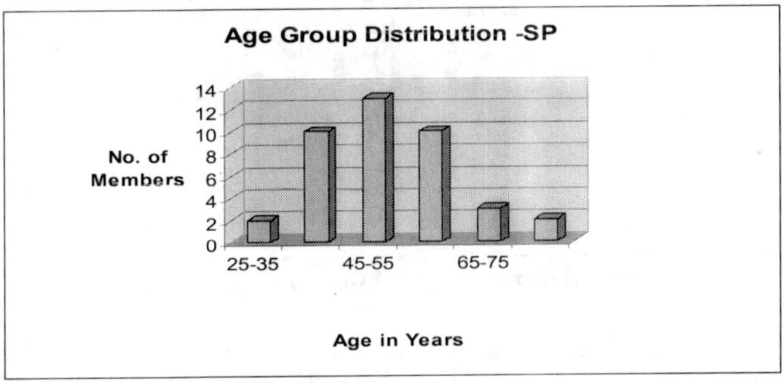

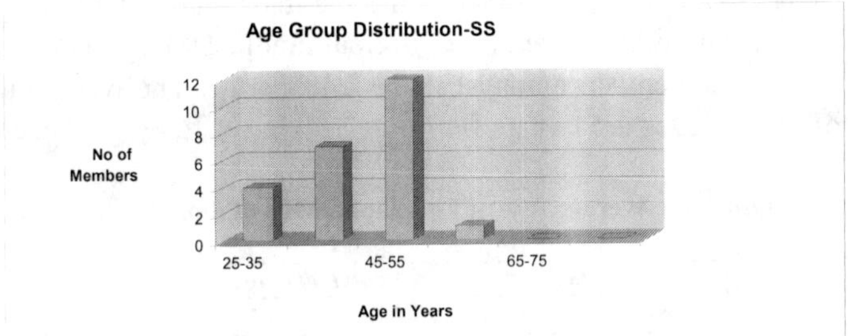

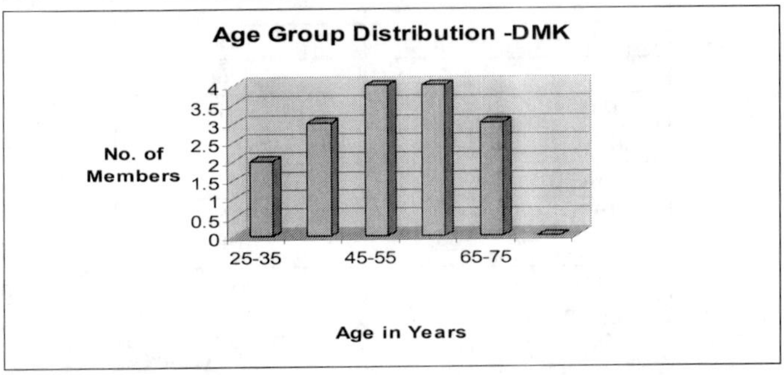

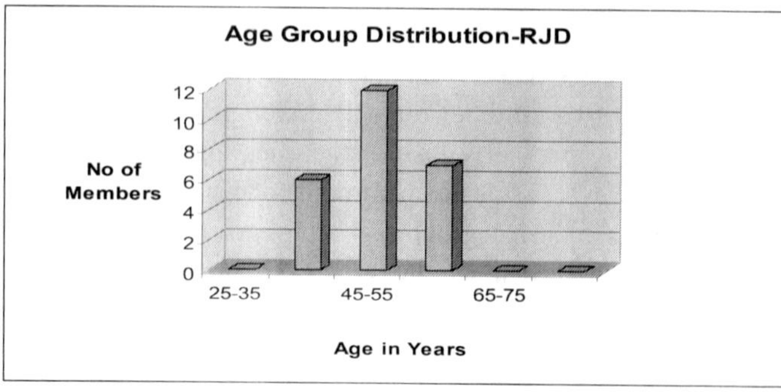

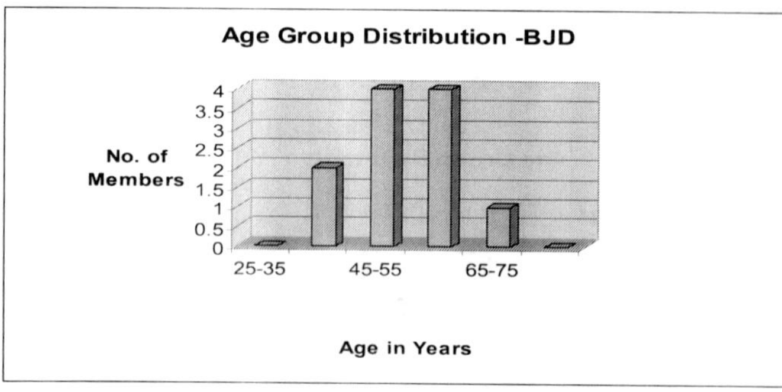

MPs in Different Age Groups in State Parties

The maximum number of younger (25-35 years) members belong to Shiv Sena (16%) and RJD (13%), while the maximum number of older members belongs to the State Parties of South India. DMK had the largest number of older members amongst all the State Parties. The average age of MPs of State Parties is 51 years.

Table 4.2: Average Age of Lok Sabha MPs of State Parties

Party	*Average Age (years)*
AGP	45
AIFB	58.7
AITC	47
BJD	52.6
DMK	51.7
JKNC	57.5
J&KPDP	56
JD(S)	66.6
JD(U)	53.5
JMM	49
KEC	51.5

(Contd...)

LJSP	47.6
MDMK	60.5
MNF	49
NPF	40
PMK	52.83
RJD	49.6
RLD	55
RSP	49.6
SAD	56.6
SDF	44
SP	53.32
SHS	42.3
TDP	60.8

Source: Lok Sabha Secretariat, Computation by Author.

Region-wise data reveals that the majority of the state party MPs belong to the age group of 56-65 years. In the North-East, however, the majority of the MPs belong to the 46-55 years category. The Western and the Southern parties also have the largest number of young MPs in the age group of 25-35 and 36 to 45 years.

Education levels of State Party MPs

Majority of the members of the State Parties (80%) were highly qualified, i.e. graduates and above. While only 10% were matriculates or below.

Table 4.4: Educational qualification of MPs of State Parties in the Fourteenth Lok Sabha

Education	*Number*	*Percent*
Doctorate	12	6.8
Graduate	81	46.5
Post Graduates	47	27
Under Graduates	15	8.6
Matriculate	9	5.1
Under Matric	4	2.8
NA	6	3.4
Total	**174**	**100**

Source: official Webpage of Parliament of India, http://loksabhaph.nic.in/Members/lokaralpha.aspx?lsno=14&tab=2 Lok

The members of State Parties were more qualified than members of national parties. Thus, 71% of national party members and 75% of State Parties were similarly educated. All the the members of AITC, 90% of

BJD members, 85% of SAD members, 85% of SP and 84% of RJD members were similarly educated. Among the larger State Parties that had less qualified members were DMK, TDP and Shiv Sena. Only 62% of the Members of DMK, 66% of TDP were graduates or post-graduates and 58.3% members of Shiv Sena were graduates and post-graduates. This was higher than that of some of the national parties such as the left front (59 percent).

Equally significant is the fact that the 14th Lok Sabha consisted of nearly 20% members who were under-graduates. The State Parties had 16% members in this group. DMK, SHS and JMM were amongst the significant parties that had under-graduates. Incidentally, these parties were the largest amongst the State Parties in the Lok Sabha.

Table 4.5: Zone-wise representation of Educational Qualification of MP's belonging to State Parties

	Zone									
Education	***North East***		***East***		***West***		***North***		***South***	
	No	%	No	%	No	%	No	%	No	%
Doctorate	1	20	6	9.6	0	0	3	5.5	2	5.1
Graduate	3	60	24	38.7	6	42.8	27	50.0	20	51.2
Post Graduates	1	20	18	29.0	3	21.4	16	29.6	9	23.1
Under Graduates	0	0	7	11.3	2	14.8	1	1.8	5	12.82
Matriculate	0	0	2	3.2	1	7.1	5	9.2	1	2.5
Under Matric	0	0	2	3.2	0	0	1	1.8	1	2.5
NA	0	0	3	3.2	2	14.8	1	1.8	1	2.5
Total	5	100	62	100	14	100	54	100	39	100

Source: Tabulated from official Webpage of Parliament of India, http://loksabhaph.nic.in/Members/lokaralpha.aspx?lsno=14&tab=2 Lok Computation by Author

Region-wise analysis of data reveals that maximum proportion of highly educated MPs belong to State Parties of the East and North East, while the maximum number of MPs with intermediate level of education comes from the West and South. On the basis of the above discussion it is possible to arrive at three conclusions:

Firstly, there has been a significant increase in educational qualification of MPs of Lok Sabha and State Parties have contributed to this trend. Interestingly, the State Parties of East, Northeast and Northern region have contributed to the presence of large number of MPs with higher level of education. It can be concluded that State Parties of North India and Hindi heartland provide the 'newly emergent elite' i.e., those belonging to backward castes, with moderate to high level of education and incomes, a vehicle of political recruitment.

The State Parties of West and South have contributed to the presence of members with intermediate level of education. This is indicative of the nature of recruitment in State Parties. Notwithstanding the small number of MPs who are elected from the North Eastern region, the MPs of North East are more qualified than MPs of other regions. This may be attributed to the high level of literacy of the North East region in general.

The membership of State Parties in the Lok Sabha indicates the presence of educated and even erudite members, though most of these parties, as seen from the previous chapter enjoy the support of underprivileged castes. The political leadership of these parties however belongs to the educationally elite.

As D.L. Sheth (1999), an eminent political scientist, explains this phenomenon. He points out that despite tardy implementation, the policies of affirmative action has brought up a significant section of individuals in almost every lower caste group, to acquire modern education and enter bureaucracy and other non-traditional occupations. A new leadership has emerged in different regions and among different groups. They constituted themselves into their own separate political parties. By the 1970s, the Congress party that was presided only by upper caste, English-educated elite was dislodged and replaced by newer State Parties with new leadership. This group competed intensely for political power and found representation either as members of ruling or opposition parties and bargained independently as distinct interest groups. However, the leadership of these parties was not significantly different from that of national parties. The political leadership of State Parties consisted of educated elite of the politically conscious and numerically preponderant and organised, underprivileged communities. Thus, those who entered politics were equipped with higher education, irrespective of their economic status or social background.

The presence of moderately educated members indicates a desire on the part of the lesser educated to participate not merely in the voting process but, also in contesting for office. However, the increased presence of such members was not the singular contribution of State Parties. In fact, a large number of such members found representation through national parties.

Together, the increase in the participation and representation of the marginalised sections of the society (The participation of SCs, STs was almost equivalent to the general population)[4] particularly in the northern states and the Hindi heartland, and the increase in representation of matriculates, indicates a widening of the democratic process. It is also indicative of a strong democratic upsurge that mobilised the hitherto under privileged and provided them with institutional access. To that extent, the marginal improvement in the representation of the less educated, particularly within the State Parties, is symbolic of larger changes that the Indian polity was witnessing, lack of stable majorities and an increased demand for reservation of seats in employment and education, etc.

The education of representatives also indicates the economic character of the State Parties in the context of India's expenditure on education which is lesser than that of many developing countries and a disproportionate share of the education budget devoted to higher education. This at a time when the country's elite sent their children to private schools and virtually tuition-free colleges and universities, while primary public schools were given few resources, schooling was not made compulsory, and dropout rates were so high that half the children in state-funded schools failed to complete fifth standards.(Weiner, 1967)

Social Indices of Assessment of Educational Specialisation

The educational specialisation of the opposition MPs indicates the preponderance of generalists.

Table 4.6: Educational Specialisation of MP's of State Parties in the Fourteenth Lok Sabha

Specialisation	*Number*	*Percent*
Arts	53	31.78
Commerce	9	5.17
Engineering	10	5.74
Finance	1	0.5
Law	40	23
Medicine	5	0.28
Science	13	7.47
No Specialisation	25	14.36
NA	9	5.17
Doctorate	8	5.1

Sourece: Lok Sabha Secretariat, New Delhi

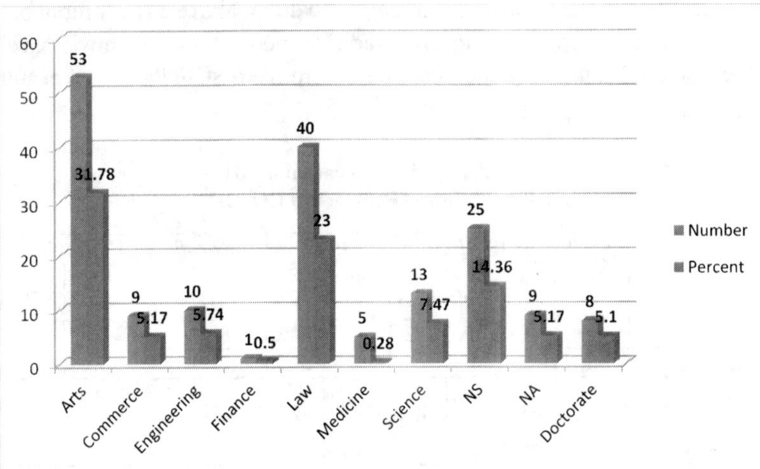

Computaion by Author

Educational Specialisation of MP's of State Parties in the Fourteenth Lok Sabha

Majority of the MPs of the State Parties specialised in Humanities, liberal arts and social sciences, giving a generalist character to the 14th Lok Sabha. The presence of generalist was not unique to State Parties alone; national parties too had a large presence of generalists. Apart from Humanities graduates, lawyers were present in large numbers (23%) in the State Parties. This was in accordance with the general trend of the Lok Sabha. In fact, the percentage of lawyers in the 14th Lok Sabha was significantly higher than the previous Lok Sabha, where the presence of lawyers was on the decline.[5] It is also interesting to note that the maximum percentage of Lawyer MPs were from the State Parties of the North (29%) and East (20%). Nearly 5 % MPs of the State Parties were doctors, engineers or from finance background.

One may find a direct causal link between the educational specialisations with political inclination. The fact that majority of the MPs of State Parties in particular and Lok Sabha in general, come from generalist or law background may lead one to interpret that people engaged in other kinds of profession have less inclination towards politics and institutional participation.

Interestingly none of the MPs of the State Parties belonged to non-traditional specialisations such as architecture, film production and the like. Broadly they belonged to four streams: Humanities, Sciences, Engineering and Law.

The State Parties also had members who did not have any professional specialisation. It also had MPs who had intermediate level or lower level of education. Majority of such members were from State Parties of South and West.

Table 4.7: Zone-wise Education of MP's of State Parties in the Fourteenth Lok Sabha

	North East		*East*		*West*		*North*		*South*	
	No	%	No	%	No	%	No	%	No	%
Arts	3	60	23	37.0	2	14.3	16	29.6	10	25.6
Commerce	0	0	2	3.2	2	14.3	4	7.4	1	2.56
Engineering	0	0	3	4.8	2	14.3	3	5.5	2	5.1
Finance	0	0	0	0	1	7.1	0	0	0	0
Law	1	20	12	19.4	2	14.3	15	29.5	10	11.1
Medicine	0	0	1	1.6	0	0	1	1.8	3	7.6
Science	1	20	5	8.0	0	0	4	7.4	3	7.6
NS	0	0	9	14.5	3	21.4	6	11.1	7	17.9
NA	0	0	5	8.0	2	14.3	2	3,7	1	2.5
Doctorate	0	0	2	3.2	0	0	3	5.5	2	5.1
Total	5	100	62	100	14	100	54	100	39	100

Source: Tabulated from official Webpage of Parliament of India, http://loksabhaph.nic.in/Members/lokaralpha.aspx?lsno=14&tab=2 Lok

Economic Indices of Assessment

Assets

Table 4.8: Assets of MPs of State Parties in the Fourteenth Lok Sabha

Party	*Total assets per Members*	*Less than 10 lakhs*	*10-50 lakhs*	*50 lakhs-1crore*	*Above 1 crore*	*Total Number of members*
SP	153.78	3	13	8	12	36
DMK	105.06	0	5	5	5	15
RJD	56.19	1	11	10	1	23
BJD	53.51	3	4	1	3	11
SHS	151.29	0	6	3	3	12
Total	-	7	39	27	34	97

Source: Paul, Samuel,Vivekananda, M.(2 004). *Economic And Political Weekly* vol. 39(45): 4927-4934.

The data relating to assets of the MPs of State Parties indicates that nearly 40% of the members were millionaires. Majority of the members with large asset base came from the larger and more established regional political parties (see Table). Half of the members of RJD and one-third of the members of SP, SHS and DMK had asset base of over Rs one crore(100 million). However, the difference between the important State Parties of North and South was that while the State party MPs of the North derived their income from agriculture or agri businesses, those of the South were mostly business persons and industrialists.

Economic Indices of Assessment: Occupation

Table 4.9: Occupation of MPs of State Parties in the Fourteenth Lok Sabha

Occupation	*Number*	*Percent*
Advocate	10	5.7
Agriculture	65	37.4
Business	15	8.6
Social & Political Worker	25	14.4
Teachers	9	5.2
Doctors	3	1.7
Engineers	2	0.2
Trade Unionist	1	0.2

Source: Tabulated from official Webpage of Parliament of India, http://loksabhaph.nic.in/Members/lokaralpha.aspx?lsno=14&tab=2 Lok

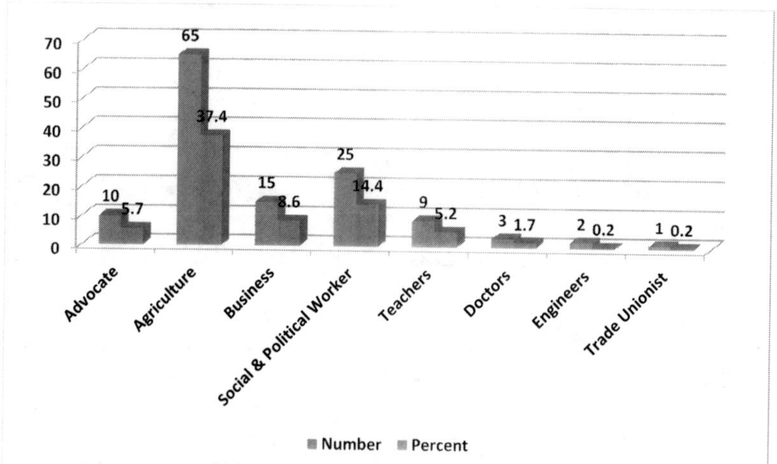

Occupation of MP's of State Parties in the Fourteenth Lok Sabha

The occupational profile of the MPs of State Parties in the Lok Sabha indicates that agriculturists constituted the largest group within the Lok Sabha. The percentage of agriculturists in State Parties (65%) is equal to that of the membership of all parties (65%). Majority of these agriculturists were highly educated and had significant asset base. Most of the agriculturists belonged to the State Parties of the Hindi heartland namely RJD, SP, JMM and SAD. Among the parties of the South, a substantial percentage of members of TDP and all the members of KEC were agriculturists.

Interestingly, industrialists, businessmen and traders constituted a significant group of the State party representatives. Nearly 14 percent of the MPs of regional parties of the opposition were industrialists compared to 8.6 percent of the BJP or Congress. Thus, there appears to be a sizeable presence of business class both within the regional and national parties. Most of the MPs of this category were highly educated (graduates and above). The DMK had the largest number of businessmen among the State Parties.

Table 4.10: Party-Wise Occupation of MPs of State Parties in the Fourteenth Lok Sabha

	Advocate	*Agri*	*Business*	*Social and Political worker*	*Teacher*
AGP	0	0	0	1	1
AIFB	0	1	0	0	2
BJD	2	2	0	1	0
DMK	3	4	5	1	0
J&KNC	1	0	0	0	0
J&K PDP	0	0	0	1	0
JDS	0	2	1	0	0
JDU	0	3	0	3	0
JMM	0	4	0	1	0
LJSP	0	0	0	3	0
KEC	0	2	0	0	0
MDMK	0	1	0	2	0
MNF	0	0	0	0	1
PMK	0	1	1	0	1
RJD	1	14	0	5	0
RSP	0	1	0	1	1
RLD	0	0	1	0	1
SAD	1	4	1	0	0
SP	2	21	5	5	2
SS	0	2	1	1	0
TDP	0	3	0	0	0

Source: Lok Sabha Secretariat, New Delhi,Computaion by Author.

Region-wise disaggregation of the data reveals that State Parties of North India had a greater presence of agriculturists, and social and political workers, while State Parties of South had a larger number of Businessmen, lawyers and medical practitioners.

The interest of the business class in legislative politics since 1989 is indicative of their desire to directly influence the political processes. Their presence, in terms of numbers, is not a reflection of their influence. They have tried to influence the political processes indirectly through interest groups, lobbying, etc., rather than through direct participation in electoral politics.

A large section of MPs are categorised as "Social and Political Workers". It refers to those members who are engaged in full time political activity. A section of members who categorize themselves as full time Social and Political Workers, have no other source of income and are fully dependent on political activity for their existence, while others may have other sources of income such as family business, agriculture, etc. They may also be retired service holders. However, given the rigors of legislative work and the accompanying political activity, most members have to devote almost their entire time to political activity. In that sense, all members of the Lok Sabha may be categorised as full time political activists. Social and political workers constitute a significant occupational group among the state party MPs in the Lok Sabha. 68% of the social and political workers were graduates and above. The largest number of social and political workers also belonged to the State Parties of Hindi heartland.

Conclusion

It appears that a majority of the MPs were middle aged and possessed high academic qualifications with specialisations. By 2004, nearly three quarters of the MPs were either graduates or postgraduates. This kind of high educational standards may be indicative of the continuing desire of the educated elite to influence the political process, directly.

A significant presence of educated, middle aged, upper economic group members, of the State Parties indicates that there has been no significant difference between the national and State Parties in the profile of the political elite. Moreover, if educational qualification and specialisations are indicative, (even partially) of the economic status of members, then it would appear that the members of State Parties belong to economically prosperous sections of the society; both educationally and economically. The beginning of this trend was visible in the Second Lok Sabha itself and accentuated over a period of time.

The members of State Parties like BJD and TDP are not only as qualified as members of the Congress or the BJP, but are often more so. This may be indicative of the desire of the 'new political elite' to influence the political process through state politics and regional political parties. State politics has become the epicenter of political contests in India. The performance of the elite at the state level determines their future at the national level. This indicates the establishment of a truly federal polity, notwithstanding the centralised federation that the constitution establishes. Further, this development may also be indicative of the fact that regional political parties provide greater opportunities for political recruitment for the emerging elite. Whether this is due to the domination of the established parties by the traditional elite or due to their organisational or mobilisation inabilities requires further research.

The asset base of MPs of the State Parties is as large as that of the MPs of the national parties. While some of the MPs of State Parties derived their wealth from agriculture, other have acquired riches through business or professions.

Within the larger picture, there appear sub-trends, which, though not pronounced, may still be noteworthy and tell the story behind the nature of State Parties. There appears to be a significant difference between the nature of State Parties in the North, South and East of India including the North East. This also indicates the nature of political elite in different parts of the country and the way in which politics has evolved in different parts of the country.

First there are State Parties of northern India and Hindi heartland including the states of Punjab (SAD), Uttar Pradesh (SP), Bihar (RJD, LJSP) and Jharkhand (JMM). Though some of these parties like the RJD and JMM technically belong to the eastern part of the country, in terms of the characteristics they share, they are similar to the parties of the North. Hence, logically they may be clubbed under State Parties of North. All these parties (and even BSP, which is technically a national party) consist of members who are middle-aged, highly educated (79%) with specialisation in humanities (47%). Professionally majority of them are Lawyers and derive their income from Agriculture (46%) and related occupations. The number of social and political workers from these parties is also large. The MPs of such parties have large asset base and belong to what may be referred to as the upper middle class.

These parties also consist of a large number of members (12%) who have intermediary levels of education. Although these parties are products of democratic upsurge and assertion of the backward castes in politics, their social and economic profile measured in terms of education was similar to that of the established elite. A large number of members of these parties belong to what may be referred to as other backward classes.

The State Parties of the south consist of members who are older and have greater experience. Though the average level of their education is high (80%), it is lower than that of the parties of East. Their MPs have varied educational specialisation. While 10/37 members are law graduates, 8 have specialised in engineering, medicine, science and commerce and 8 in humanities. These parties also have a large number of MPs with intermediate level of education (16%). They belong to the business class, traders and industrialists. Nearly a fifth of them are businessmen and traders with and another one-fifth of them are lawyers, teachers, and engineers. One-third of them are agriculturists.

There are fewer numbers of State party representatives from the East and North East in the Lok Sabha (BJD, AITC, AIFB, SDF, MNF and AGP). The BJD is the largest State party from the east with a considerable legislative presence. But for the BJD, AIFB and AGP, almost all the parties of this region have only one member in the Lok Sabha. Hence, it is difficult to generalize about them. However, a few features of the State Parties of East and Northeast are amply evident. These parties have older members and more experienced members. They are also more educated (17/20 members) and have almost negligible presence of members with lower levels of education. They have greater presence of Middle class professionals, social workers and almost no presence of businessmen. A large number of them are teachers.

There is only one party in Western India, namely, the Shiv Sena, which has a significant presence in the Lok Sabha. In terms of the socio-economic profile of the members, the Shiv Sena shares similarity with the parties of the South, with some variations. The members of this party are younger than their southern counterparts and less educated. In all other respects, (educational specialisation, occupation and assets), they are similar to the members of the southern State Parties.

What does the socio-economic assessment of MPs of State Parties indicate? It would not be incorrect to state that the State Parties have made no significant change in the character/composition of the representation. The membership of State Parties is similar to that of national parties. It is as elite as that of national parties, if not more. The pattern of political recruitment channeled through political parties is such that only the elite find entry into the political process. A large number factors including organisational structure of political parties, organisation of communities, resources required to electoral politics, criminalisation have contributed to this factor. In all there appears to be a glass ceiling for entry into institutional politics, particularly, legislature.

The entry of middle class intermediary caste into institutional politics may be interpreted as organised assertion by economically affluent, educationally qualified members of such social groups. Such an assertion took place both through the national parties such as the BJP, BSP, NCP and the State Parties. State Parties seem to have given a fillip to the process. As a result, a larger number of under privileged members succeeded in entering the institutional structure.

However, the membership of State Parties indicates a regional pattern in the evolution of political process. It appears from the data that the process of democratisation (entry of intermediary caste members with intermediate levels of education) is a little different in the south from that of the north of India. If the representation of State Parties in the legislature is any indication of the party structure, the State Parties of north are predominantly led by intermediate caste, agricultural community, which may be categorised as middle class with high level of education and asset base. In particular, lawyers of north have particular inclination towards politics.

The parties of south and west on the other hand have evolved into institutions that provide institutional support to intermediary caste members of business community with median levels of education. The educated and social elite of middle classes have abjured from participation in the political process, given their numerical inferiority. They have however, tried to influence the political process from other institutions such as the bureaucracy.

Notes & References

1. Sheth, D.L. (1990) Caste and Class Social Reality and Political Representation in Shah (ed), In V.A. Pai Panandiker and Nandy, Ashish (eds.), *Contemporary India,* New Delhi: Tata-McGraw Hill, p. 220.
2. Pai, Sudha. (2002) *Dalit Assertion and Unfinished Revolution: The BSP in Uttar Pradesh*, New Delhi: Sage.
3. Ombvet, Gail. *(1994) Dalits and Democratic Revolution,* New Delhi: Sage Publications.

   Weiner, Myron. (2001). "The Struggle for Equality, Caste in Indian Politics", in Kohli Atul (ed), *The Success of India's Democracy*, Delhi: Cambridge University Press.

4. Yadav, Yogendra. (2000) Understanding the Second Democratic Upsurge: Trends of Bahujan participation in Electoral Politics in 1990s, in Frankel, Francine., Hasan, Zoya., Rajeev Balveer Arora (eds), (2001). *Transforming India: Social and Political Dynamics of Democracy,* New Delhi: Oxford University Press.
5. Electoral turnout in different types of Constituencies, 1977-1991.

Year	All India	General	SC	ST
1971	55.3	57	51.4	43.4
1977	60.4	61.5	59.5	48.6
1980	57.2	58.2	55.6	48.2
1984	64.1	65.2	62.6	54.1
1989	61.9	62.7	61.8	53.2
1991	55.9	56.6	55.4	48.8

Source: Yogendra Yadav, '"Understanding the Second Democratic Upsurge: Trends of Bahujan participation in Electoral Politics in 1990s", in Francine Frankel, Zoya Hasan, Rajeev Bhargav, Balveer Arora (eds), *Transforming India: Social and Political Dynamics of Democracy*, (Oxford University Press, New Delhi, 2001), p. 129.

Chapter - 5

Relating Performance to Profile: Are State Party Members Different?

Within the ambit of legislative institutions, political parties, irrespective of their nature, size and support base, are concerned with three significant functions. These are also the most important functions of the legislative body, and include[1]: Law making,[2] controlling the executive[3] and representation.[4] In effect, these functions are interrelated. For instance, a discussion on a particular legislation may become an occasion to criticize government's failure to initiate legislation on the matter for a long time. It is also possible that the MPs of the House may use the deliberations on a legislative proposal to spell out the problems associated with a particular issue, thereby performing their representative functions. Similarly, the questions directed towards an individual minister may assume the form of a suggestion for a legislative proposal. A watertight compartmentalisation is therefore not possible. In addition to this, political parties coordinate with similar groups, build consensus, negotiate and bargain and develop legislative strategies. However, these are informal functions, which may be outside the purview of legislative activity. These are also not open to public scrutiny and vary depending on time, issue, political situation and leadership.

For the purpose of understanding the performance of State Parties in the legislature we may distinguish the three main formal functions with which MPs are associated:

- Law making,
- Control of the executive,
- Representation

Law making

According to West Bogdoner (cited in Sill, 1968: 23), the legislature is a corporate entity consisting of popularly elected representatives. It provides political space for active contestation of ideas. It exemplifies the liberal ideal that conflicts between ideas in the political sphere results in best possible decisions. It possesses the ability to perform this function better than other organs of government on account of its corporate character. However, what constitutes law making and the extent of involvement of the Lok Sabha in the lawmaking process needs to be analyzed.

Law making, being a technical process, involves several stages. In the first place, a policy decision has to be taken to make a law. Usually, as in all modern democracies, in India too, the initiative to make a law comes from several sources. The legislative initiative may come from the legislators themselves, the cabinet, or the committees, which have spent considerable time and energy in discussing the need for a particular law. Laws may also originate from the activities of various interest groups or concerned parties, which have conveyed the need for a law on a particular matter either to the executive, or to one or more legislators. In India, as elsewhere in the world, executive initiative in the law making process is significant[5]. The initiative is then drafted and shaped as a bill before it is presented to the House. In the drafting process, the role of the bureaucracy becomes important. The career civil servant, trained and technically better equipped, drafts the bill under the supervision of the minister in charge of the subject. The bill, so drafted, is put up before the House for consideration. The role of the House is therefore limited to:-

- Giving suggestions relating to introduction of a bill,
- Discussion on the bill to remove discrepancies that may have crept in the draft bill,
- To improve on the bill,
- To make suitable amendments to the bill, and
- Ratification of the bill.

Significant in the entire process, is the role of the Members of Parliament (MPs) as debaters. MPs in this capacity perform three significant functions. Firstly, they discuss an issue threadbare brining to focus all the debates around the issue. Secondly, the debates allow the MPs to represent their respective constituencies, both territorial and functional. Thirdly, in the process of deliberations, the MPs of the Lok Sabha prevent executive excesses and ensure governmental accountability.

The central function of the Lok Sabha is to debate vital issues that would ensure open contestation and continuous accountability. Such contestation must be free, fair and transparent. Considerable time must be spent on the performance of this function. The availability of adequate devises to ensure participation is also an important pre-requisite for the successful operationalisation of this function.

Much of this contestation takes place during Legislative debates, Budget sessions, debates on matters of urgent public importance under rules of the Lok Sabha, Question Hour, Calling Attention Motion, amongst others; The performance of these function would depend upon three important factors amongst others. First, the interest of the members in participating in legislative business; second, the importance that the party attaches to these functions; and thirdly, the efficacy of these procedures in enabling the legislators to perform the functions of their representation.

The first two factors are in many ways interlinked. The interest of the members in parliamentary business would depend not only on his/her interest but, also on the reward that such participation would bring. Rewards may be in the form of re-nomination of the member from the constituency by the party and his/her consequent re-election. Both these would in turn depend on the level of satisfaction of the party leadership and the electorate. Studies shows that supporters of State Parties expect MPs to aggregate local issues and represent them at the institutional level. They also expect the MPs to intervene in the decision making process and ensure developmental funds for the constituency. The five most important functions of MPs according to supporters of State Parties according to our survey were as follows:

1. Listening to the grievances of the constituents
2. Getting funds for the constituency
3. Representing the constituency in the parliament
4. Discussing the larger national issues
5. Participated in making laws

Interestingly, supporters of the State Parties did not consider the participation of their MPs in law making or discussions on larger national issues as the most important function of the representatives. For, them the service functions were more important. There is however, the recognition that MPs must also ensure that funds become available and development projects are initiated in the constituency. This makes liaison and not necessarily deliberation with the government necessary.

In the light of such expectations, it is interesting to examine:

1. How do MPs of State Parties participate in legislative business and what is the extent of their participation in the parliamentary business?

2. What are the parliamentary procedures that are favoured by MPs of State Parties?
3. Is it possible to identify linkages between the extent of participation and the socio-economic profile of MPs? Does age, education, occupation or caste of the MPs determine his/her extent of participation or choice of parliamentary procedure?

MPs' Participation in Legislative Business

During last two decades there has been a gradual decline in the efficiency of Parliament both in terms of the sittings as well as the fruitful time spent by the Lok Sabha.

Table 5.1: Sittings and Sessions of the 14th Lok Sabha

Lok Sabha	*Sittings (Hours)*	*Time spent (Days)*	*Average Time Spent (Annually)*[7]
First	3784	677	926
Second	3652	567	894
Third	3733	578	914
Fourth	3029	467	932
Fifth	4072	613	698
Sixth	1753	267	725
Seventh	3324	464	688
Eighth	3224	485	667
Ninth	754	109	603
Tenth	2528	423	514
Eleventh	814	125	528
Twelfth	575	88	531
Thirteenth	1946	356	445
Fourteenth	1737	332	353
Fifteenth	1344	357	269
Sixteenth	1642	331	328

Source: Statistical Handbook of the Lok Sabha, Ministry of Parliamentary Affairs, New Delhi, 2019.

Table 5.2: Time Spent in Different Types of Business

Type of Business	*Time Spent Hrs. Mins.*	*% of total time*
Legislative matters	375 :40	21.63
Budget	352: 52	20.32
Questions (Starred and unstarred)	198 : 22	11.42
Motions+	46 : 19	2.67
Resolutions	55 : 16	3.18
Discussions	274 : 05	15.78
Other Matters *	434 :21	25.00

Source: Lok Sabha Debates

+Adjournment Motions, Motions under rules 191 & 342 and Confidence Motions
*Debate on President's Address, Statements by Ministers, matters of urgent public importance raised after Question Hour, etc.

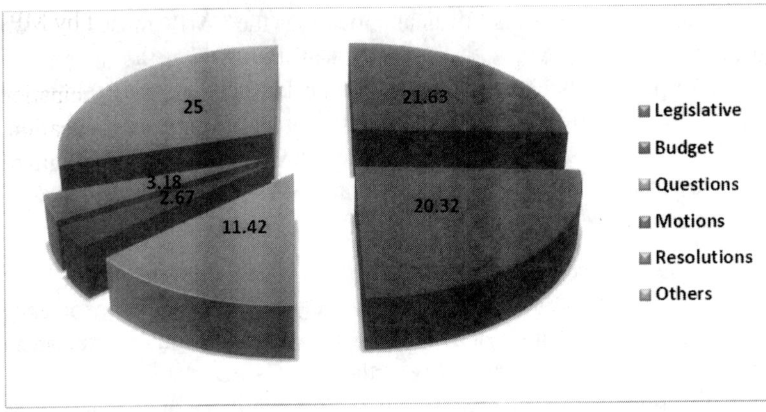

Time spent in Different Types of Business in the Fourteenth Lok Sabha

Further, the time spent on legislations and budgetary discussions has declined even more significantly[7], while the time spent on Resolutions, Motions, and Special Mentions has increased. Nearly 20 percent of the time of the 14th Lok Sabha was spent on Motions, Resolutions and other discussions which allowed members to raise local issues. The number of legislations passed by the Lok Sabha, however have remained almost the same from 13th to the 16th Lok Sabha.[8]

The reasons for the decline are many including paucity of time, wastage of time on account of walkouts and adjournments, preponderance of generalist members, etc (Manisha & Deb (ed), 2009). It may be noticed that the decline in the time spent on legislative matters and the increase in the time spent on Zero Hour coincides with the rise of State Parties. Is there a relationship between the nature of representation of the State party MPs and time spent on different types of parliamentary business? What is the opinion of the electors and MPs on what should be represented and how?

Interview with supporters of State Parties revealed that nearly 71 percent of the respondents were of the opinion that State party MPs should not merely concentrate on discussion of national issues, but focus on deliberations on local issues as well.

Table 5.3: Should MP's concern themselves primarily with national issues?

		Frequency	*Percent*
Valid	Yes	24	28.6
	No	60	71.4
	Total	**84**	**100.0**

State party supporters are unanimous that their MPs must focus on local issues. This they say "is on account of the fact that the State party MPs are specifically chosen to represent local issues". As the State Party MPs, they understood local issues better, are more approachable and had better contacts with local electorate, they are thus better equipped to represent local issues feel the electorate. MPs, too do not disagree on this matter.

It would be pertinent then to ask if the State Party members have made any cognizable contribution to the legislative functioning, as they seem to show greater interest in non-legislative activity and representation of local issues. What then is reality of their legislative performance? Also, is it different from that of national parties, which would make their representation distinct?

Let us begin by examining the extent of participation of State party MPs in the 14th Lok Sabha, followed by an in-depth analysis of the nature of participation with specific reference to State Parties.

Table 5.4: Participation of MP's in Parliamentary Proceedings of 14th Lok Sabha

	Debates		*Pvt Bills*		*Questions**		*Attendance*	
	SP	*NP*	*State*	*National*	*State*	*National*	*State*	*National*
Total No of members	**173**	**365**	**173**	**365**	**173**	**365**	**173**	**365**
						28,940		
Average	**34.6**	**28.95**	**0.48**	**0.66**	**191.8**	**171.8**	**69%**	**71%**
South Average	**31.8**	27.45	**0.4**	0.55	**147.8**	129.46	**67%**	70%
North Average	**28.3**	31.8	**0.6**	1.28	**143.8**	205.7	**68%**	70%
East Average	**43.08**	30.96	**0.17**	0.33	**198.51**	136.28	**72%**	74%
West Average	**28**	25.8	**1.58**	0.5	**414**	221.69	**64%**	69%

* Includes both Starred and Unstarred and supplementary questions
Source: Tabulated from data collected from Lok Sabha Debates.

It appears from the data of the 14th Lok Sabha that MPs of State Parties are active participants in the proceedings of the Lok Sabha, both on their own account as well as in comparison to the MPs of National parties. The parliamentary attendance of members of State Parties in the 14th Lok Sabha is as high as 69% (average) as against 71% of the national party MPs. The lowest being 18 percent for an AITC member and highest being 80% by MNF MPs. On a positive note, the high attendance of the MPs and the large number of questions raised in the House indicates their trust in the sanctity of the parliamentary institution. It is apparent that the State party members show keen interest in parliamentary work, unlike what is the popular perception, about their lack of interest in parliamentary work. However, there are certain caveats to these propositions that need to be highlighted.

First, attendance of the member may not coincide with the actual participation in parliamentary work. It is possible that a large number of members are either silent spectators or, as an MP pointed out,[9] involved in political networking within the precincts of the House, once they have signed the attendance records. It may also suggest that though members recognize the utility of parliamentary institution and its proceedings in challenging the government's position, they may not necessarily be interested to engage the government in the process. All the members of Parliament who were interviewed insisted upon the "importance of parliament" and its role in democracy. However, the empty benches during important proceedings indicate to the contrary. Often, it is easier to spot MPs in the Parliament canteen, library or lobbies.

Table 5.5: Party Wise Participation of MPs in Parliamentary Business

Party	*No. of Members*	*Debates*	*Private Members' Bills*	*Questions*	*Attendance in Parliament*
AGP	2	136	0	521	65%
AIFB	3	51	0	931	74%
AITC	2	32	0	0	18%
BJD	11	667	4	290	72%
DMK	16	266	16	1204	63%
J&KNC	2	38	0	353	65%
J&KPDP	1	14	0	8	48%
JD(S)	3	185	3	710	59%
JD(U)	9	234	1	1424	82%
JMM	6	80	0	907	46%
KEC	2	201	0	512	70%
LJSP	3	47	0	235	73%
MDMK	4	136	0	254	63%
MNF	1	10	0	8	89%
NPF	1	17	2	7	77%
PMK	6	243	6	1097	78%
RJD	25	828	2	3071	74%
RLD	3	76	1	448	55%
RSP	3	65	0	191	67%
SAD	8	116	0	275	61%
SDF	1	12	0	75	82%
SP	38	1253	31	6333	69%
SHS	14	337	12	4927	65%
TDP	6	197	0	1304	75%

Source: PRS legislative Wing.

As far as participation in House debates are concerned, MPs of the 14th Lok Sabha have shown considerable interested in Debates. A State party MP has participated on an average 34 times in the Debates during his/her term of five years, compared to 28 times by national party MPs.

The State Party MPs have also shown keen interest in procedures like the Question Hour. This is evident from the large number of questions raised by the MPs of State Parties on the floor of the House, compared to their participation in the debates. Nearly 28,000 questions were raised by MPs of State Parties, averaging about 38 questions every year in their term of five years. The MPs of State Parties are more interested in raising questions compared to that of the national parties.

Both during the legislative Debates and Question Hour, MPs of the older and well established parties have played a more active role in the House. The familiarity of the MPs of older parties with House procedures and their ease in dealing with the technicalities of the parliamentary procedures contributes to their greater interest. In addition, the larger State Parties have long term goals. They represent a greater cross-section of people and more number of issues. Hence, their interest in representation and the dividends that accrues there from is greater.

Private Members Bills and Resolutions: It appears from this data that Private Members' Bills and Resolutions do not find much favour amongst the members of State Parties. Private members' Bills have been initiated only by established and larger State Parties. Once again, the only exception to this rule is the AIFB, which has large number of MPs participating in discussing Private members bills notwithstanding its small membership.

It may be concluded from the above data that the State party MPs are as efficient as the MPs of national parties in terms of their performance on the floor of the House. However, their performance is not drastically superior from that of the MPs of national parties. In terms of their performance, the State Parties are found as efficient, or as inefficient as that of national parties. There seems to be no marked difference between the two.

Table 5.6: Zone-wise performance of State Party MPs

	No. of MPs	*Debates*	*Private Members Bills (nos.)*	*Questions*	*Attendance*
East	64	40 (2037)	6	214 (10196)	68.2
West	14	28.1 (337)	19	414 (4927)	63.5

(Contd...)

North	84	34.8 (2542)	34	164.2 (11986)	70.7
South	38	41.1 (1234)	15	173.3 (5199)	68.0
North East	3	33.6 (101)	2	139.3 (418)	79.3

Source: Lok Sabha Debates

Zone wise segregation of data relating to the performance of State party MPs indicates that State party MPs from the South (Andhra Pradesh, Tamil Nadu, Kerala, Karnataka, Puducherry and Lakshadweep) are most efficient in participating in debates (1234 times) with an average participation of 41.9 per MP. The MPs of the east are close behind (2037 times) with an average of 40. The MPs of State Parties of the North East and North participated less number of times compared to others (33.6 and 34.8).

As far as participation in the Question Hour is concerned,the MPs of Shiv Sena (SHS) from Maharashtra were ahead of their counterparts in other political parties and zones. Their participation was more than double that of their counterparts of any other region. Almost all members of the party participated actively in the Question Hour. Two MPs of Shiv Sena namely, Anandrao Adsule and Shivaji Patil raised over 1200 questions during the life of the 14th Lok Sabha, thus increasing the average number of questions raised by SHS MPs to 414. MPs of State Parties of east including those of AITC, BJD and RJD were the most active among the other zones, excluding the West. The MPs of north and south were almost equal in terms of their participation in the Question Hour. The MPs of the north-east zone raised the least number of questions during the 14th Lok Sabha.

MPs interest in engaging the House through questions is on account of the "informality" that is associated with the Question Hour and the opportunity that it offers to State party MPs in raising both national issues and those that relate to the constituencies that they represent. However, it may be mentioned here that the present data includes all the questions raised by members of the Parliament (Starred and Unstarred). It is, therefore, possible that a large number of members of State Parties submitted questions, which may not have been really discussed in the Lok Sabha. Hence, though the MPs may have shown interest in this form of parliamentary participation, the actual process of engaging the government and democratic deliberation may not have occurred.

The State party MPs of north-east and north showed greatest presence in terms of attendance (79 and 70 percent), while that of the west had least attendance in the Fourteenth Lok Sabha. This indicates that attendance alone cannot be considered as the criteria to determine the performance of MPs of State Parties.

Overall it would appear that while MPs of from the south showed greater interest in participating in the Debates of the House, State party MPs of the West were more interested in participation through Question Hour, while MPs of the North East and north were present in House, though they participated less frequently in the proceedings of the House.

Participation by Groups

Table 5.7: Participation in Parliamentary Business; Women MPs of State Parties

Women Members	*Total Participation in Debates*	*Average*	*Total No of Questions Raised*	*Average Questions*	*Average Attendance*
14	264	20.3 Median 20	1048	80.6 Median 21	56 Median 69 %

Source: Lok Sabha Debates
Author Compilation

Median of Women's Participation in the Proceedings of Lok Sabha

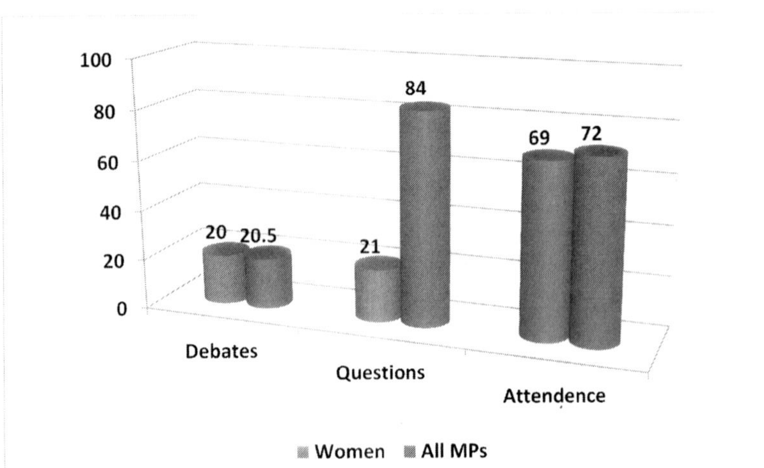

The participation of women members of State Parties appears to be less than that of men in the 14th Lok Sabha. Both in terms of their participation in legislative activities like debates and Question Hour, as well as their attendance in parliament, women MPs of State Parties were less active than their male counterparts. However, among all the proceedings of the House, it would appear that women MPs of State Parties preferred to intervene in Debates rather than in the Question Hour or other proceedings of the House.

Of the 14 women members belonging to State Parties, three women members raised no questions during the 14th Lok Sabha and four women members participated less than ten times in debates, while four of them had less than 50 percent attendance in the parliament. Most women members from the State Parties who participated in parliamentary proceedings, particularly in parliamentary debates, were leaders of their parties like Mamata Banerjee and Mehbooba Mufti or established parliamentarians with experience of more than one Lok Sabha terms.

State Party MPs from Marginalised Groups

Table 5.8: Participation in Parliamentary Business; SC MPs of State Parties

SC Members	*Total Participation in Debates*	*Average*	*Total No of Questions Raised*	*Average Questions*	*Average Attendance*
26	**1173**	**46.9**	**4040**	**237**	**79**

Of the 12 MPs from the Scheduled Castes (SC) and Scheduled Tribes (S)T categories, only 33 belonged to State Parties. The SC, ST MPs constituted 19% of the MPs of State Parties and nearly 23% of the membership of the Lok Sabha. It may therefore be deduced the SC/ST MPs were lesser in State Parties than that of national parties.

There were 26 MPs of State Parties who were elected from Scheduled Caste Constituencies. Of them the largest number belonged to the SP (seven MPs) followed by RJD with four MPs, SAD and BJD with three MPs each. Other parties with SC members in the Lok Sabha included the SHS, TDP, LJSP, PMK, MDMK, and JD(S). The participation and attendance of MPs of this category was far higher than that of either other State Parties or national parties. Thus, the attendance of SC members of 14th Lok Sabha was 79% as against 69 % of State Parties and 71% of National parties. Only one MP of SP had less than 60% attendance. Most members of this group had attendance between 80%and 95%, a high standard for any group.

Similarly, they participated very actively in Question Hour with 47 questions on an average from each MP, as against 34 of State Parties and 29 of National parties. One MP did not participate in Debates of the House. Most SC MPs participated between 15 to 60 times in the debates of the Lok Sabha.

Similarly, the number of questions that they raised together in the five year period was 4040 with nearly 237 questions per person, which would roughly mean an average of nine question in each year and three questions each session. Only two SC MPs of State Parties did not raise any question. However, these MPs participated in the Debates of the House. Seven members (26%) raised more than 200 questions and nine members (34%) raised between 50 and 200 questions.

Two SC members even proposed Private members bill in the Lok Sabha and participated in its discussion.

Table 5.9: Participation by Scheduled Tribe (ST) MPs in

ST Members	*Total Participation in Debates*	*Average*	*Total No of Questions Raised*	*Average Questions*	*Average Attendance*
7	104	14.8	1128	161	60

Source: Tabulated fro Data from Lok Sabha Secretariat

There were about seven ST MP's from State Parties in the Lok Sabha, three of them were from JMM and one each from MNF, NPF, RSP and JD (U). ST MPs' constituted four percent of the members sent by State Parties to the Lok Sabha. Like SCs, more ST members were elected from the national parties than from the State Parties.

The performance of ST members of State Parties was much below the average, both in terms of their attendance and their participation in legislative business. As can be seen from the Table, their average attendance was 60%, nearly 10% below the national average, while the number of questions raised by them was 161, a little less than that of national parties. Their participation in debates was nearly half of average of 34 of State Parties.

Session-wise Analysis of Participation

A bird's eye view however does not give us an idea of the nature and extent of participation of State party MPs in the legislative business of the House. The actual participation of members in a session may vary depending upon a number of factors such as the bill/issues debated in the House, the Ministers, the political climate of the nation, etc. These may vary from session to session of the parliament.

Secondly, while rules of procedure of the Lok Sabha allow participation of MPs in all the proceedings in their individual capacity, some of these procedures are used more frequently by members of the opposition to perform their function of seeking information, supervising the government, holding it accountable and censuring it. Thus, for instance, the Questions Hour, Short

Duration Discussions, etc. allows members the opportunity to elicit information from the government. No Confidence Motion, Adjournment Motion and Private Members Resolutions enable it to censure the government. Hence, a limited but detailed analysis would help in understanding the manner in which these MPs participate on the House proceedings.

Their contribution to the efficiency of the Lok Sabha may be assessed in terms of participation of the MPs in each of the proceedings in select session of Lok Sabha, such as

- Legislative Debates
- Question Hour
- Calling Attention Motion
- Private Members Resolution
- Discussions on Matters of Urgent Public Importance

The following sessions are considered for the purpose:

1. Monsoon Session of Lok Sabha, 2004: 5th July to 23rd July, and 16th August to 26th August, 2004
2. Budget Session of Lok Sabha, 2005: 25 February to 24 March, and 18th April to 13 May
3. Winter Session of Lok Sabha, 2006: 22 No vember to 19th December, 2006
4. Budget Session of Lok Sabha, 2007: 23 February - 21st March and 26 April to 22 May, 2007
5. Monsoon Session of Lok Sabha, 2008 - 21st July- 22 July, 17th October- 24 October, 10 December - 23 December, 2009
6. Budget Session of Lok Sabha 2009: 22 February to 26 February, 2009

Table 5.10: Performance of State Parties in Select Lok Sabha Sessions (2004-2009)

Nature of Participation	***Participants (Number)***
Starred Questions	591
Supplementary questions	100
Participation in Bill discussion	424
Raising Matters of Public Importance	179
Calling Attention Motion	57
Resolutions	74
Special Mention	510
Matters under Rule 377	410
Parliamentary committee/presentation of report	96
Budget (General/Railways)	440

Source: Lok Sabha Secretariat.

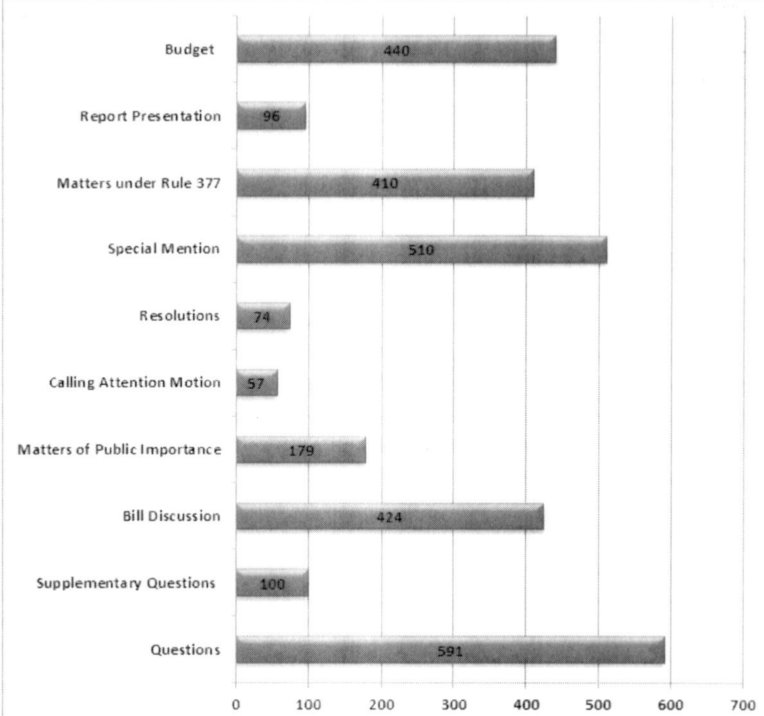

State Parties MPs Participation in Parliamentary Business

Table 5.11: Session-Wise Participation of State Party MP's in the Lok Sabha

All State Parties- Select Sessions, 2004-2009						
	2004	***2005***	***2006***	***2007***	***2008***	***2009***
Total Members of state parties	173	173	173	173	173	173
Total participation by All State party MP's	476	649	488	512	389	213
Starred Questions	116	165	87	133	60	30
Supplementary Questions	11	34	16	17	13	9
No. of members who participated in Question Hour	29	33	29	34	22	10
Participation in discussion during Bill discussion	45	121	108	38	70	42
No. Of members who participated						
Raising Matters of Public Importance	52	38	45	7	33	4
Calling Attention Motion	10	18	20	5	0	4
Resolutions	7	40	5	7	10	5
No. Of members who participated						
Special Mention	71	114	113	92	87	33
No. Of members who participated	33	21	41	41	41	16
Matters under Rule 377	64	115	70	90	37	42
No. Of members who participated						
parliamentary committee / presentation of report	8	27	17	21	27	9
No. Of members who participated						
Budget (General/Railways)	86	133	36	107	25	42
No. Of members who participated						

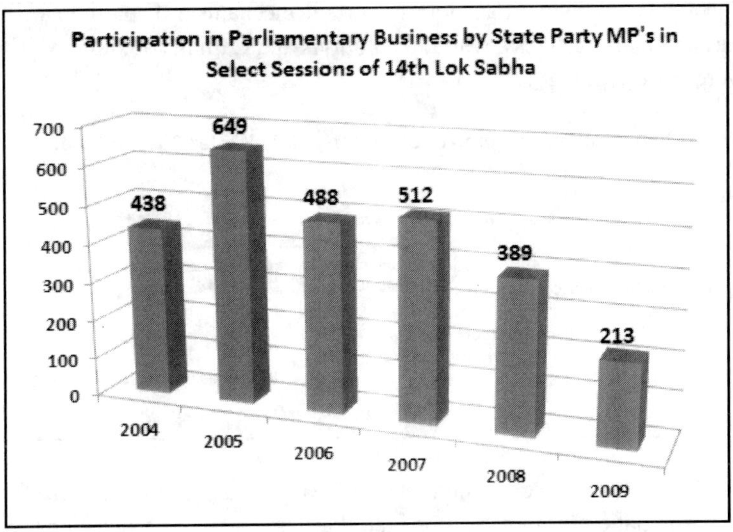

The data in Table 5.11 indicates that the participation of members of State Parties in the proceedings of the House increased as the House moved from infancy to maturity. Members showed less interest in parliamentary proceeding in the early sessions of the House. Aas the House moved towards completion of its term. Maximum interest is shown by members in the middle years and as the House progressed towards maturity.

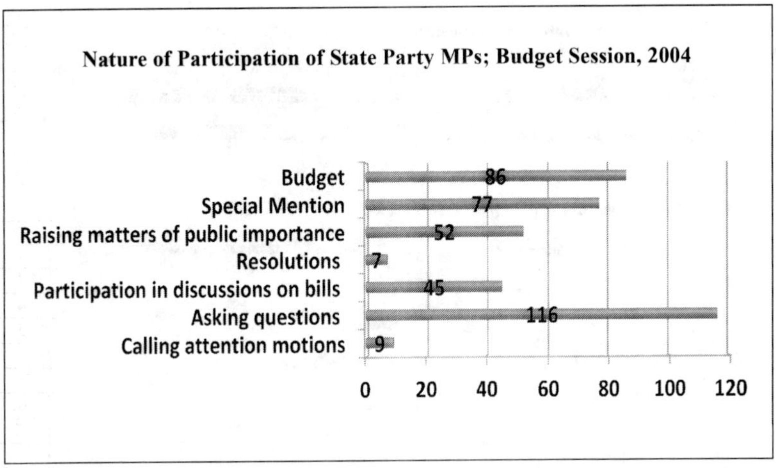

Thus, the data shows that in the Budget session of 2004, the maximum participation was in the Question Hour with about 116 questions being asked by members of different State Parties. Budgetary discussions and

Special Mentions were also an important mechanism of participation in parliamentary business, while Resolutions and Calling Attention Motions were least popular.

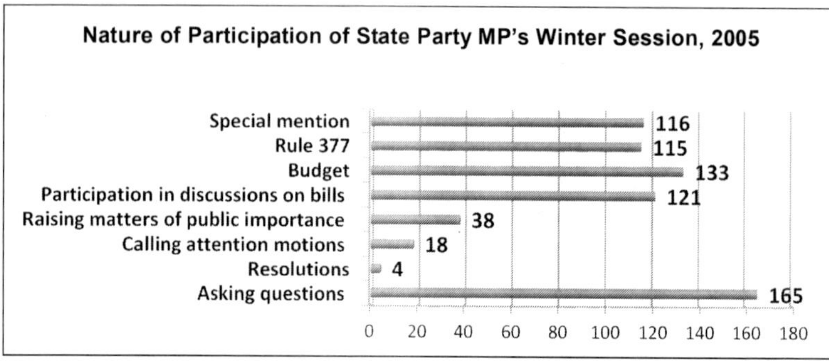

In the 2005 winter session, Question Hour was the most preferred way of participation by members of State Parties. Nearly 165 questions were raised by MPs of State Parties, averaging more than one question for every MP. Equally popular was participation in budgetary discussions. Legislative discussion, or discussions on bills and discussions under Rule 377 and Special Mentions were used frequently by MPs of State Parties in this session. Unlike in 2004, in 2005, the interest of MPs in procedures that allowed them scope of raising issues of local importance gained importance. Calling Attention Motions were not particularly used by MPs of State Parties.

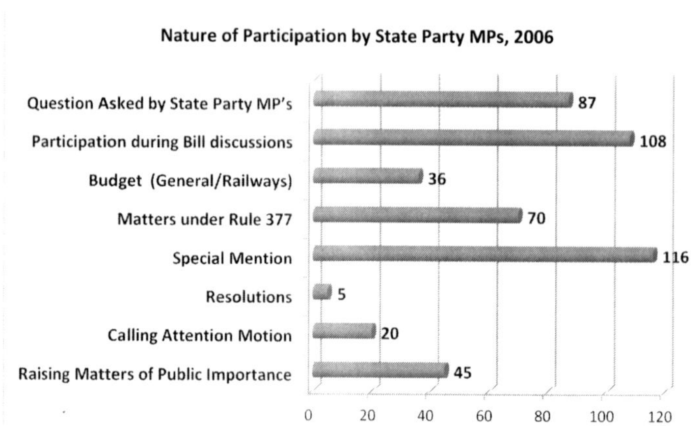

In the 2006 Budget session, participation in Legislative discussion overshadowed both Question Hour and Rule 377, while there was a increase in number of Resolutions discussed in this session, they continued to be the least preferred mode of particpation. State party MPs' interest in discussion under Rule 377 and Special Mention contined to be significant even in 2006 like 2005.

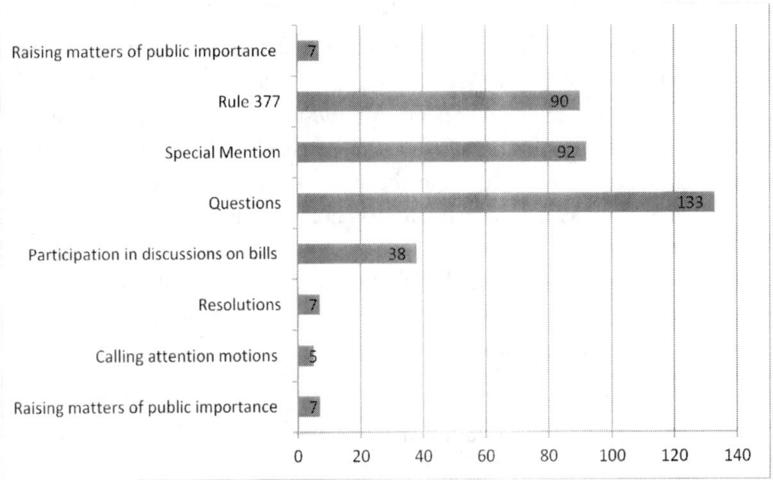

Nature of Participation of State Party MPs, 2007

Like all the other previous sessions, State party MPs found many opportunities to participate in Legislative discussions. However, in this session, their interest in discussions under Rule 377 was greater and almost equal to Special Mentions. As in the previous sessions, the members' interest in Calling Attention motions and Resolutions continued to be low. Interestingly, the members' interest in budgetary discussions which was high in 2004 and 2005 declined in 2006 and 2007.

Nature of Participation of State Party MPs, 2008

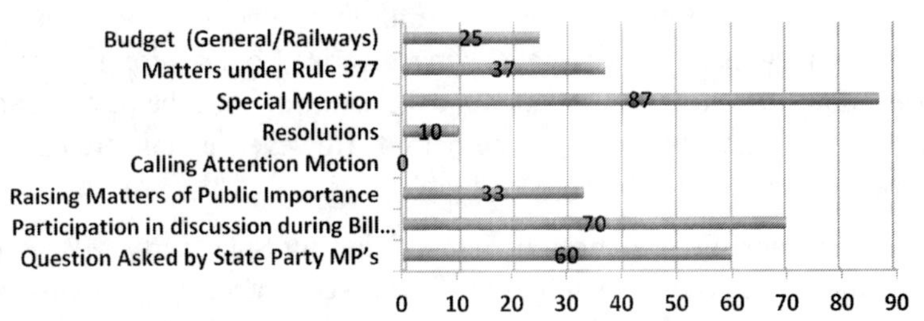

In 2008, MPs of State Parties showed interest in legislative participation. While Special Mentions were preferred and Question Hour were also frequently used by the members. Similarly, MPs used Rule 377 and Rule 55 for raising matters of public importance almost with equal frequency.

The data shows that among all the legislative procedures that were available to MPs of Lok Sabha, MPs of State Parties used Legislative and Rule 377, Question Hour and Special Mentions most frequently. Resolutions both private and government were the occasionally preferred means of engaging the government. Together, the number of interventions made through Rule 377, Special Mentions, was almost equal and some times more than the interventions made through budgetary and legislative discussions and Question Hour. Considering that the maximum time in the legislature is devoted towards legislations followed by Question Hour, the utilisation of time for other business indicates the popularity of these mechanisms.

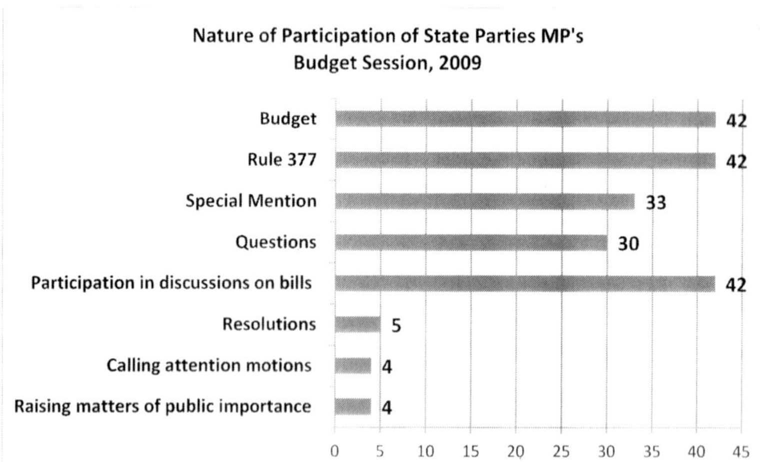

The trend that seems to emerge from the above data indicates that though the number of interventions made varies from session to session depending on the total time allotted and the nature of issues being discussed and the political dynamics of the period. However, certain trends are apparent, not withstanding other variables.

First, maximum number of intervention by State party MPs is in legislative discussions. Members also show keen interest in participating in budgetary discussions. In view of the fact that the 14th Lok Sabha spent nearly a third of its time in legislations and almost the same percentage of time in financial discussion, this trend does not appear to be out of place. Given the fact that maximum time was allotted and spent on these issues in the Lok Sabha, it is inevitable that there was greater participation of MPs both of the State and national parties on these matters. However, it needs to be borne in mind that a large number of MPs of the State Parties were a part of the opposition and not the government. Hence, their interest in legislative discussion indicates their desire to intervene in law making process effectively. It would appear that MPs consider legislative discussions both accessible and effective method of legislative participation.

Apart from legislative and financial discussions, members have also showed keen interest in discussions under Rule 377 and Special Mentions. Interestingly, State party MPs' interest in Calling Attention Motions, Resolutions, Special Mentions and Discussions under Rule 377 remains unchanged irrespective of the age of the House, time spent, nature of issues discussed and the political context of the session. This indicates the interest of members of State Parties to use less formal means to raise issues that concern them. Further, these procedures allow members to raise any matters of concern, irrespective of the issues being discussed.

Two methods which are considered important in controlling the government, namely, the Question Hour and Calling Attention Motions were however, not preferred by the members of State Parties in the sessions under consideration. Not more than 7-10 members participated in the Question Hour in every session. In particular, the Calling Attention Motion found least interest amongst the members of State Parties.

Some region-wise variation is evident in the above data. Members of south and west participated more in parliamentary proceedings. Members of established larger State Parties participated more than that of smaller parties. This may be explained in terms of the familiarity of the members to parliamentary procedures and the experience that they have. Further the allocation of time to larger established parties is also more.

In view of the fact that the MPs of State Parties are keen in participating in legislative discussions, a detailed analysis of their participation in legislative debates is considered relevant.

Socio-economic Profile and Level of Participation: Are there linkages?

The interest of the MPs in legislative participation could be related to number of factors such as the age of the members, (it is often assumed that younger members are more enthusiastic than older members), experience, and occupation.

Table 5.12: Relating Age of State Party MPs to Participation in Parliamentary Business

	No. of MPs	*Debates*	*Pvt Members Bills (nos)*	*Questions*	*Attendance*
25-35	10	11.85 (83)	8	214.7 (1503)	60.4
36-45	36	24.7 (818)	13	174.27 (5751)	63.3
46-55	64	50.6 (2782)	39	209.4 (11517)	70.9
56-65	41	30.4 (912)	10	220.4 (6611)	68.7
66 and Above	19	23.3 (273)	1	171.6 (2745)	68.5

Source: Lok Sabha Debates. Figures are average of total. Figures in bracket are total numbers.

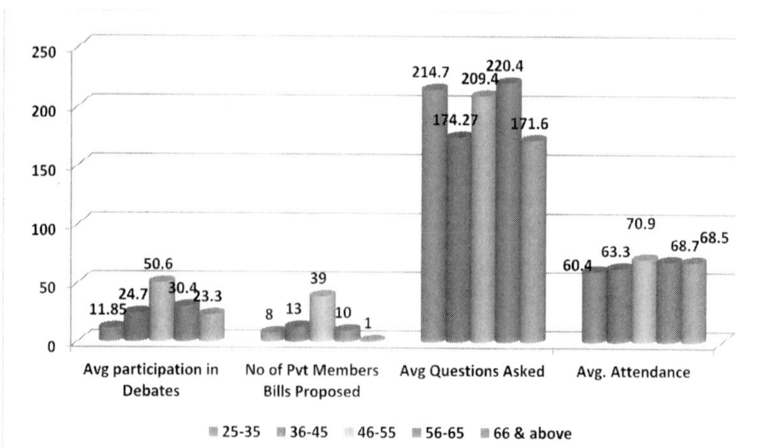

State Parties Participation in Bill Discussion.

The MPs in the middle age group (46-55 and 56 to 65 years) are most active in participating in the debates, while the MPs of younger age group of 25-35 are least active. The number of Private Members Bills proposed is also the highest among the MPs of the age group 46-55, while the least active is the older group above 65 years of age. When we look at the number of questions raised, older members of the middle aged group of MPs (56-65 years) are most active. Interestingly however, the younger MPs of the 14th Lok Sabha also showed keen interest in participation in the Question Hour. The attendance is highest amongst the middle age group and lowest amongst the younger MPs of State Parties in the age group of 25-35.

Table 5.13: Relating Education of State Party MPs to Participation in Parliamentary Business

	No. of MPs	*Participation in Debates*	*Pvt Members Bills (nos)*	*Participation in Questions*	*Attendance (Average)*
Post Graduate	59	43.75	44	176.22 (8495)	72.3
Graduates	79	35.95 (2243)	15	204 (1307)	68.6
Under Graduates	15	25.2 (328)	12	290.4 (3776)	54.0
Matric	9	18.5 167	0	196.0 (1770)	58.4
Under Matric	4	30.2 (5)	0	256 768	78.3

Source: Lok Sabha Debates.

*Figures indicate mean; Figures in bracket indicate total number

An analysis on the basis of education indicates co-relation between the level of education and the level of performance of the MPs. In general, higher the level of education the greater is the participation of the State party MPs in the proceedings of the House in the 14th Lok Sabha. Thus, for instance, the average participation in debates is highest amongst the post-graduates (44) and lowest amongst the under-matriculates (30.2) with gradual progression. Similarly, the most number of Private Members' Bills have also been introduced by post-graduates (44) followed by graduates (15) and undergraduates (12). Matriculates and under-matriculates took no initiative in this regard. In terms of attendance, post-graduates and graduates have greater attendance than under-graduates and matriculates.

Table 5.14: Median of Participation in Terms of Education

	No. of MPs	*No. of MPs on whom Data is available*	*MPs with above Median participation in Debates Median*	*MPs with above Median participation in Questions Median for all MPs 84*	*No. of MPs with Attendance above the average*
Post Graduate	57	48	25 (52.1%) Median 20 24 (50%) Median 20.5	26 (54.1) Median 84 22 (45.8%) Median 75.5	30 (62.5%)
Graduates	79	66	37 (56.01) Median 20 33 (50%) Median 27.5	34 (51.5) Median 84 33 (50.0%) Median 103.5	37 (56.0%)

(Contd...)

Under Graduates	15	12	6 (50%) Median 20 7 (50.1%) Median 14	7 (58.3) Median 84 7/12 (58.3) Median 78.5	3 (33.33%)
Matric	9	9	4 (33.3) Median 20 6 (66.66) Median 0	4 (44.44) Median 84 3 (33.33) Median 79	4 (44.44%)
Under Matric	4	3	2 (66.66) Median 20 1 (33.3) Median 19	2 (66.66) Median 84 2 (66.66) Median 156	2 (50%)

Source: Lok Sabha Debates.

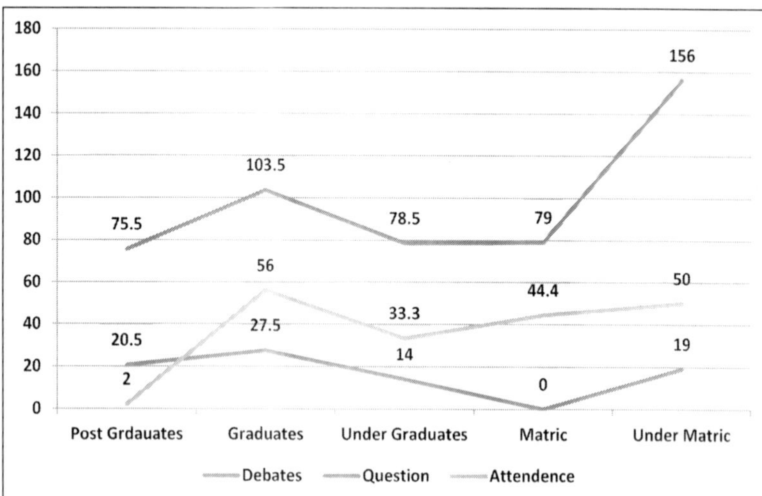

State Party MPs in Fourteenth Lok Sabha: Relating Education to Participation

However, there were two notable exceptions; first, the number of questions raised was highest by the under-graduates and under-matriculates. Similarly, the average attendance of the under-matriculates was higher than that of post-graduates (78.3). Whether this indicates the use of less formal procedures like the Question Hour by the marginalised groups needs to be ascertained.

Higher the Level of Education Greater the Interest in Legislative Debates: The proportion of graduates and post-graduates who have contributed to debates is higher than that of under-graduates, matriculates and under- matriculates. Thus, for instance, the median for participation in debates for post-graduates stands at 20.5 and 27.5, while for matriculates and under- matriculates, it stands at 14, 0 and 19 respectively. The median participation in debates for all MPs, irrespective of educational qualification, stands at 20.5. Thus, while the participation of post-graduates and graduates stands at or above the mean, the average for under-graduate, matriculate and under-matriculate members stand below the all-India average, which stands at 84.

Intermediate Level of Education, Greater Participation in Question Hour: The Question Hour however shows a different picture. Here the graduates and matriculates have a better mean scores than post-graduates, under-graduates and matriculates. The mean scores of post-graduates, under-graduates and matriculates is less than the mean of all state party MPs irrespective of educational qualification

Table 5.15: Relating Occupation of State Party MPs to Participation in Parliamentary Business

	No. of MPs	*Debates*	*Pvt Members Bills (nos)*	*Questions*	*Attendance*
Lawyers	11	57.44 (517)	1	376.1 (3385)	80.9
Agriculture	65	36.2 (1995)	65	175.6 (9657)	66.2
Social work	25	39.2 (746)	25	139 (2682)	64.0
Teacher	9	23.5 (141)	0	224.5 (1347)	73.2
Business	14	19.0 (229)	2	152 (1825)	66.8

Source: Lok Sabha Debates.

There is no clear pattern in the participation of State party MPs from the point of view of their occupation. However, certain trends are noticeable. Of all the occupational groups, lawyers seem to be most active. Thus, their parliamentary attendance is as high as 81%. The number of questions raised State Party MPs with legal background as well as their participation in debates of the House is the highest amongst all occupation groups. The median scores of their participation in debates stands at 47, which is the highest amongst all occupational groups, followed by businessmen and teachers at 28 and 27 respectively. Their participation in the Question Hour as well as their attendance is also high (307). However, they do not show keen interest in initiating Private Members Bills.

Teachers who constitute a small section of the State party membership of the fourteenth Lok Sabha show considerable interest in raising questions. The median scores of teachers in the Question Hour it stands at 392 which is the highest among all occupation groups. Their average attendance too is a high 73.2%. However, their participation in legislative debates is not as high as that of lawyers (131 times, average 26.2 percent, Median score 27).

Social workers' participation in debates is next to that of the lawyers and second highest amongst all occupational groups in terms of the average number of participation in debates. However, their median scores 2`1for participation in the debates is 14 indicating that a few among this occupational group are very active, while a large number of them had lower levels of participation. They raised as many as 25 private members' bills. However, their participation in the Question Hour is lowest (139.0). The median score for it was also amongst the lowest. Their attendance is also only about 64% against the average attendance of 69% of all state party MPs and 71% of national party MPs.

Table 5.16: Median of Participation in Terms of Occupation

	No. of MPs	*No Of MPs on whom Data is available*	*MPs with above Median participation in Debates Median*	*MPs with above Median participation in Questions*	*MPs with Above Attendance*
Lawyers	11	11	9 Median 20 10 Median 47	6 Median 84 5 Median 307	Median 72 9 Median 82
Agriculture	65	57	24 28 Median 12	29 18 Median 77	33 Median 71
Social work	26	19	7 11 Median 14	10 5 Median 89	12 Median 75%
Teacher	9	7	4 4 Median 27	4 3 Median 392.5	5 Median 73.5
Business	15	15	8 7 Median 28	8 7 Median 101	7 Median 66
Total			74		

*Amongst all MPs; + Amongst all MPs with similar qualification

Average attendance for Social Workers 66, 14 have above that, data is available for 21/26

Average attendance for Advocates 81% 3 have above it, data is available for 10/11

Average attendance for Agriculturist is 67, 36 Mps have above it, data is avialble for 60/65

Average attendance for Agriculturist is 81%, 5/9 Lawyer Mps are above it, data is available for 9

Average attendance for Teacher is 78%, 3 are above it, data is available for 7

Average attendance for Businessmen is 78%, 6 are above it, data is availed for 15

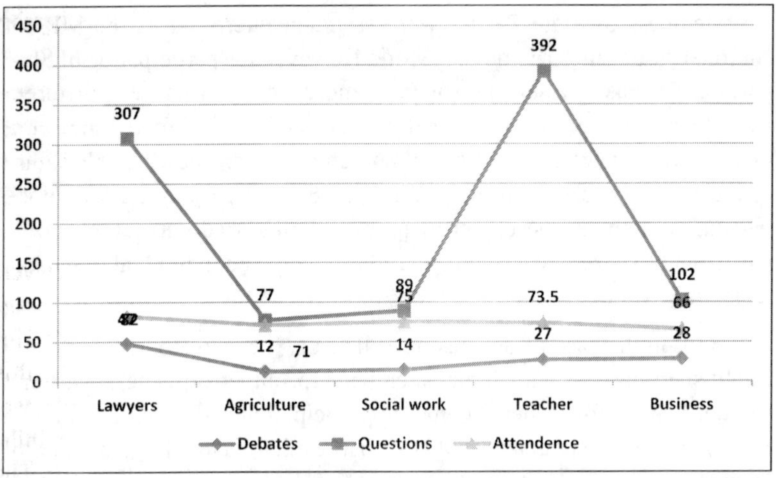

State Party MPs in Fourteenth Lok Sabha: Relating Occupation to Participation

Agriculturists, who constitute the biggest occupational group in the 14th Lok Sabha, appear to be less interested in the business of the house. Their contribution in raising questions and participation in debates is amongst the lowest in the 14th Lok Sabha. However, they show greatest interest in raising private members' bills.

The above data indicates that though it may not be conclusively said that the occupational background of State party MPs significantly impacts his/her parliamentary performance, it would be possible to deduce that different occupational groups prefer different methods of intervention. While lawyers appear to be the most active category among all occupational groups, Teachers and businessmen prefer to participate through debates. MPs who belong to the Social Workers category include those who take keen interest as well as those who are not interested in parliamentary activity. Agriculturists and social workers appear to be leastactive as far as legislative work in the 14th Lok Sabha is concerned. However, such members attend Parliament regularly and show more interest in the Question Hour than in any other proceedings of the House.

Overall it may be generalised that MPs who were middle age (age group of 46-55 years) better educated, were lawyers and teachers; males; and SC were active in the Parliament. The party and the region to which an MP belonged also play an important role in the legislative participation. Parties of the eastern region, with greater legislative presence, and ideology based parties.

Members of State Parties were as much interested as the MPs of National parties in parliamentary work. However, the participation of State party MPs was neither significantly more nor qualitatively different from that of the MPs of National parties. Within the broad framework of participation, there are certain subtends, which indicate the nature of legislative processes in India. While all State Parties participate in the legislative process, the extent of participation varied depending on the parliamentary size, the parliamentary leadership and individual interest in legislative work.

Both in the case of debates on Bills and Question Hour, the old and established parties, with larger membership outperform the newer and smaller State Parties when it comes to participation in debates and holding the government accountable. MPs of parties that have a large number of members, or have a long established political history, show greater interest in parliamentary work. Thus, for instance, MPs of State Parties such as the BJD, DMK, SP, RJD and SHS and JD (U) have not only better average attendance but also raise a large number of questions. Their participation in parliamentary debates is also better than State Parties which have smaller number of members. The only exception to this is that of the AIFB whose members have shown considerable interest in parliamentary work despite their small numbers.

Ideology driven parties such as SHS, AIFB are more oriented towards legislative participation. Also the young and inexperienced MPs cutting across party lines have shown keen interest in participation in legislative process mainly through Question Hour. Finally, the overall interest of MPs of State Parties in Private Members' bills across all categories is low.

However, notwithstanding these positive indications, not more than 10% MP's of State Parties have ever participated in the sessions of the 14th Lok Sabha, while this 10% may vary from year to year. The participation of MPs across party lines in legislative activity could not be considered as satisfactory.

While the members of Parliament have many avenues for participation, members of State Parties preferred to participate more in 377 and Special Mention than in Debates and Question Hour. This may be on account of a host of factors such as "informal nature of discussion during such procedure, greater flexibility, involvement of less time and preparation, etc." However, the importance of the fact that such procedures involved minimal effort in terms of time and effort and allowed members to represent local issues and thereby be recognised by peers and constituents, accounted for the popularity of such procedures.

A marked difference in the use of parliamentary procedures, by different categories of Lok Sabha members was also evident. Interventions through Legislative debates were more frequent amongst senior leaders of State Parties or those who had experience of participating in legislative proceedings. Further, older MPs, post-graduates, graduates, lawyers, teachers and women prefer to use debates as the preferred tool of participation.

The second level leadership of the State Parties, those with lesser educational qualifications, social workers, teachers, agriculturists, SC MPs of State Parties was more inclined towards the use of Question Hour. Such members also prefer to use Zero Hour, Special Mentions and Discussions under Rule 377 as a method of legislative participation. The participation of MPs of State Parties in Question Hour is determined by their own experience and the strength of the party in the Lok Sabha..

Legislative participation is thus determined not just by the personal interest and party ideology, but also a host of other factors. While none of these factors may be statistically significant, their role in shaping the method of intervention chosen by the members may not be wished away altogether. Thus, the age and experience of the member in parliamentary activities, the area of specialisation of members, the nature of their profession, which may or may not demand scrutiny of issues, the extent of marginalisation of group all go on to shape the legislative behaviour of the MPs.

While there can be no doubt about the fact that the level of participation of an MP, irrespective of his/her party identity, is shaped by his/her own personality and the party organisation, the level of education, training and experience ultimately adds up to the extent that the MP's participation. Further, it may also be noted that apart from the level/extent of participation, the nature of participation in terms of the issues raised and the groups represented would determine whether State Parties are different in conceptualizing the issues differently. It would also ascertain whether the changes in legislative efficiency could wholly or partially be attributed to the growing importance of State Parties

Notes

1. Other functions of the Parliament would include control of finance, criticism of individual ministers, providing a Cabinet and eliciting information from the government. Each of these functions, however, is covered under the three broad categories mentioned i.e. lawmaking, control of the Executive and representation.

For instance, law making would include passage of money and non money bills, allocation of resources, etc. So, financial control, then, becomes a part of the law making function. Similarly, criticism of the ministers is an essential mechanism to ensure control of the executive. Representation involves eliciting information and expressing views on matters of public concern. The parliament, while performing the representative function, elicits information from the government.

2. Articles 107-118 and 245 entrust the Parliament with law making functions. Article 107 of the constitution lays down that bills other than Money bill may be introduced in either of the Houses of Parliament and requires passage in both Houses of Parliament before it can be presented to the President for his assent. Article 108 of the Constitution lays down the procedure for the passage of the bill in the House.
3. Article 75(3) of the constitution provides for ministerial responsibility. Article 75(3) states that "The Council of Ministers shall be collectively responsible to the House of People"
4. The Parliament performs representative function by authoritatively securing information from the government through Questions, debates in the house and other such procedural devises a mentioned in rules of procedure and conduct of Business.
5. In U.S.A, the role of committees in making law is accepted. About two thirds of the total legislations that are accepted by the legislature have their origin in the executive department. For details refer to Skidmore Max. J. and Carter Tripp Marshall, (1992, *An Introduction to the American Constitution* (Affliated New Delhi: East West Press)
6. Life span of the Lok Sabha, in years. For instance the Sixth Lok Sabha spent 1753 business hours in its entire life span of 29 months. The average time spent by the Sixth Lok Sabha (annually) in discussing legislations was 1753 hours divided by 29 and them multiplied by 12, that is, 725 hours.
7. The number of legislations enacted has declined from 316 to 248 respectively in the second and 14th Lok Sabha, of which 205 and 173 legislations respectively were of financial nature. The time spent on questions has also declined from fifteen percent of total legislative time to ten per cent. This indicates a decline in efficiency of the Lok Sabha as a legislative body.
8. The number of legislations passed have been 332, 337 and 331 in 14th, 15th and 6th Lok Sabha Interview with an MP of the 14th Lok Sabha on 2.12. 2014, New Delhi

Chapter - 6

What do State Parties Represent and How?

In a parliamentary democracy, the legislature's collective functions such as legislation, controlling the executive and representation are performed by members belonging to different political dispensations. While the onus of supervising executive action rests on the opposition, members of all political parties use the legislative time and space to register their presence and give voice to those who have elected them. The role of State Parties Members of Parliament (MPs) in this context is of singular importance. This is on account of the fact that the context in which State Parties have emerged and continue to exist is different from the national political parties. As mentioned earlier, the emergence and popularity of State Parties is associated with the 'rise of regionalism' and growing demand for autonomy by the States in the 1980's that led to the mushrooming of regional political parties (Kumar: 2000)

The failure of the national parties to accommodate the diversity of local interests led to the gradual opening of spaces, which were occupied by State Parties. As Amit Prakash (2013) points out, unlike in the first three or four decades after independence, the national parties found themselves challenged in their ability to engage with local issues. This resulted in the emergence of 'articulate and aggressive regional identities'. Such has been the thrust on regional issues that even national political parties have engaged themselves with articulation of regional identities. Thus, for instance, the question of Maharashtra identity and '*Gujarat Asmita*' has not only been articulated by local units of national parties like the INC and the BJP but, has been whole heartedly embraced by them. Moreover, in the post-independence period the national parties have failed to offer a broad national vision that would either subsume or embrace all local issues. This has given State Parties an opportunity to raise local issues and offers to represent them not just in the state legislature, but also in the national parliament. The popularity of at least some of the State Parties is on account of this. The mobilisation strategies of State Parties, therefore focus on representation of local interests and group identities.

The increasing presence of State Parties leaves in the Parliament little doubt about the importance of State Parties in representational democracy of India. However, there are some important questions relating to the nature of representation by State Parties, which may be identified. What do members of State Parties represent in the national legislature? Does representation of 'local' occur at the level of national legislature also? Within the framework of parliamentary democracy and in the Parliament, what are the procedures used by MPs of State Parties and why? Do MPs represent issues that concerns the social groups, whom they claim to represent and the party manifesto?

This chapter attempts to answer these questions on the basis of analysis parliamentary performance of MPs of State Parties. The first section of the chapter looks into the Party Manifesto as a communicative tool that examines the agenda that parties outline for representation. The second section of the chapter qualitatively examines the main parliamentary procedures; Legislative Debates; Question Hour; Calling Attention Motion; Discussions under Rule 377; Special Mention and Resolutions to understand what are concerns that MPs represent and how they represent them. The analysis takes into account the nature of interventions made by MPs, issues raised, the language and seriousness of discussion to understand how State party MPs juggle their multiple role as representative of functional and territorial constituencies as well as that of parties to which they belong.

Party Manifesto: A Reflection of Issues Proposed to be Represented

Election Manifestos of political parties may be regarded as a communicative tool. It aims at increasing the support to the party as well as to explain the aims, plans and programmes of the party to the electorate. Hence, all political parties prepare electoral manifestos, which sets out their strategic direction and outlines of prospective legislation, if they win the elections and form the government. Legislative proposals which are featured in the manifesto of a party are often regarded as having superior legitimacy to other measures, which a governing party may introduce for consideration in the legislature. It spells out the consensus agenda that is acceptable to all the special interest groups (Wahlang, 2010). Evidently, the more powerful a special interest group is within the party, the more the likelihood of its specific issues finding mention in the manifesto and the stronger the language of commitment to them (Rao, 2014).

While the formulation of party manifesto may be influenced by several factors, including those of the long term goals of the party, its support base, ideology and leadership nevertheless it gives a broad idea of the issues that the parties are concerned with. Since the electoral support base of the State Parties is confined to a particular State or region, they are under no obligation to adopt a national stand or national perspective. On the other hand, their continued survival would depend on their ability to represent the local people at the national level. The manifestos of State Parties circumscribe the scope of the promises that local politicians can make in their election campaigns. More importantly, the recognition of and a stated commitment to resolve long standing local issues, serves to consolidate and retain the support of local politicians.

A study of the party manifesto of all the major State Parties indicates that a majority of the State Parties raise national issues, but in manners that are different from each other. State Parties, excepting J&KNC and J&KPDP are concerned primarily with state level, constituency issues. National parties on the other hand address issues like defense, foreign policy, infrastructure, transport, foreign investment norms, models for growth and development, power, oil and gas, social security, etc.

The manifestos of State Parties are indicative of the support base of the party as perceived by the party leadership. By and large, the State Parties seek to address the following broad groups:

- Agriculturists
- Women and Youth
- Dalits, marginalised, and minorities, particularly Muslims
- Unemployed

There is little distinction between State Parties in this respect. All State Parties and even national parties address these groups. However, the audience for national parties and their manifestos are the influencers on whom the urban voters depend to make their choices - editors, anchors, political commentators, security analysts, industry and a teeming litter of expert commentators.

The party platform of the State Parties, across regions shows that they broadly address the following issues:

- Waiving loans/ low interest loans to farmers
- Employment generation/creation of jobs/ employment of youth
- Promotion of Industries, agriculture, development of infrastructure,
- Increase in expenditure on education, health /health insurance and old age pensions

- Supply of laptops, colour televisions, and rice either free, or at a subsidized price, free school/college education, unemployment benefits etc.
- Ensuring justice to women/ minorities/Dalits.

State Parties employ two main instruments; subsidies to the social/ economic groups and policy initiatives. Many of the State Parties' manifestoes promise to offer subsidies or compensation to farmers for loss of crops due to natural calamities etc. Such huge subsidies and freebies and have been severely criticized. However, State Parties have defended their right to announce such measures on the grounds that it is their "prerogative to announce plans and programmes and make promises in a democracy (Balaji, 2013). In its July 5, 2013 verdict, the Supreme Court has validated the right of parties and ruled that "promises of freebies made by political parties in their manifestos would not come under "corrupt practices" and "electoral offences" under the Representation of the People Act, 1951"

In addition to these, each State party has issues that are specific to the region and concerns of the constituency that it seeks to represent. For instance, the SAD had promises to set up special courts to punish those involved in the 1984 anti-Sikh riots; the NPF declared its aim to find a peaceful solution to the Indo-Naga political issue; the PDP promised at rolling back Article 377 of the Constitution. Interestingly political parties, especially those from the Border States, often have clearly stated positions on bilateral relations with their neighbours. Thus, for instance, the TMC, the J&KNC and the AIADMK have clearly stated positions on relations with Bangladesh, Pakistan and Sri Lanka, though these may not always be stated in the manifesto itself

The issues raised in the election manifestos of State Parties leaves shows that they have limited national aspirations. Many State Parties are almost silent on national issues, or regard the 'state/ regional level issue to be of national importance.' But, do the representatives air these in legislative institutions? Let us look at issues that concern the electorate.

Peoples' Perception on Important Issues

In a study conducted by Lokniti-CSDS, nearly seven thousand respondents across the country were asked about the most important problem faced by them. Nearly 20% of the respondents referred to availability of drinking water as the most important issue faced by them. This was closely followed by unemployment (16%), price rise (10.5%), electricity (9%) and poverty (8%) as the other major problems.

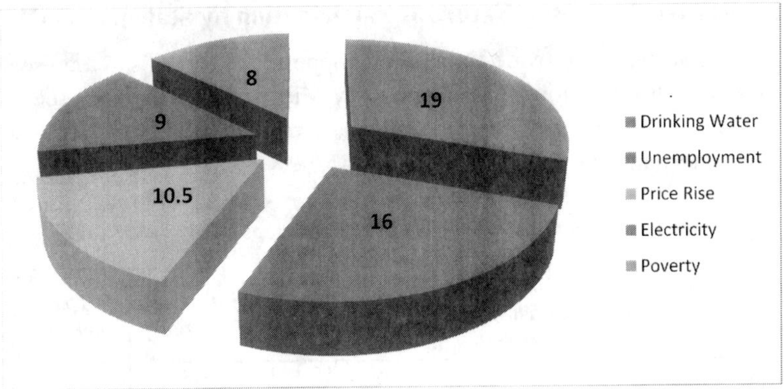

Source: NES, 2004

Important Issues before Voters

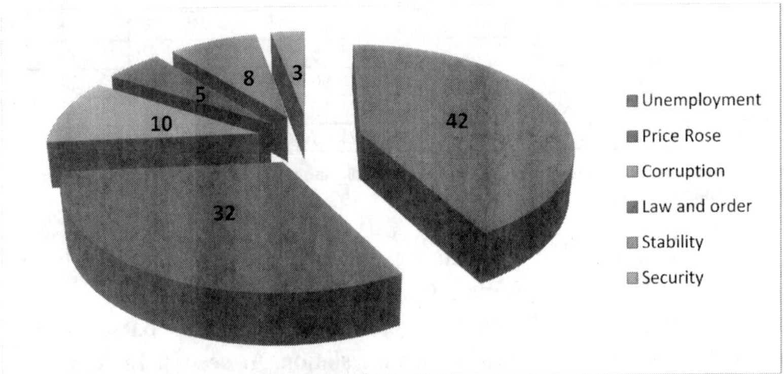

Source: India Today (August 30th 2004), New Delhi; N=17,885.

Important Issues before Voters

Before the general elections in 2004, *India Today* magazine conducted a survey covering 17,885 respondents, who were asked to list the most important problem that they faced. Similar questions were asked in surveys held in 1998 and 1999 too.

All these data sources indicate that poverty, unemployment, price rise and corruption are regarded as the most important issues since 1996 across party lines. That these issues dominate the political landscape of the country is also evident from the fact that political manifestos of all the political parties mention them. Such issues have constituted the "electoral plank" of political parties, across the spectrum. The regional political parties too, attempt to tackle these issues through a series of measures mentioned in their election manifestoes.

Legislative Debates & Nature of Participation by State party MPs

Legislative debates provide an important opportunity for MPs to represent their constituency. How do the State party MPs participate in the process and what are the issues raised by them? Are they related to what the electorate wants them to represent?

Table 6.1: Time Spent on Legislative Discussions in 14th Lok Sabha

Lok Sabha	*Bills passed*	*Time Spent in legislative Activity Hrs-Mins*	*% of Total Time Spent*	*Avg. time /bill Hrs-Mins*	*Bill passed annually*
5th	487	1121-52	27.55	2-18	83
6th	136	412-28	23.51	3-01	56
7th	336	797-48	23.99	2-22	70
8th	346	806-59	25.05	2-20	72
9th	63	122-37	16.18	1-57	50
10th	284	560-03	22.16	1-58	58
11th	64	128-15	15.66	2-00	42
12th	60	95-25	16.60	1-35	55
13th	302	493-79	25.30	1-34	60
14th	261	375-40	21.63	1-36	40

Source: Parliament of India, Fifth to Fourteenth Lok Sabha: A Study (Lok Sabha Secretariat, New Delhi, 1977, 1979, 1985, 1991, 1992, 1997, 1999, 2000, 2004, 2009).

As was seen in the earlier chapter too, over the years, there has been a gradual decline in the legislative efficiency of the Lok Sabha. This inefficiency is reflected both in the number of legislations passed as well as the time spent on discussing each legislation. As seen in Table: 6.1 the total number of bills passed by the Lok Sabha has declined from 487 in 1977 to 261 in 2004. The total time spent has also declined from 1121 hours to 375 hours, while the average time spent on bills has decreased from 2.18 hours to 1.36 hours.

The decline in interest in legislative debates can be traced back to the ninth Lok Sabha in 1989. This period coincides with the emergence of coalition politics and growing importance of State Parties. It is important to examine whether the State party MPs have led to this decline in legislative efficiency. If so, do the State party MPs abjure from legislative debates because it does not give them an opportunity to carry out the nature of representation that they wish to carry and which is expected of them by their parties and voters? In this context, it is interesting to note that majority (70.2) of people who supported State Parties considered law making an important function of the legislators. Further, they also indicated that the legislative role is an important factor in electoral choice.

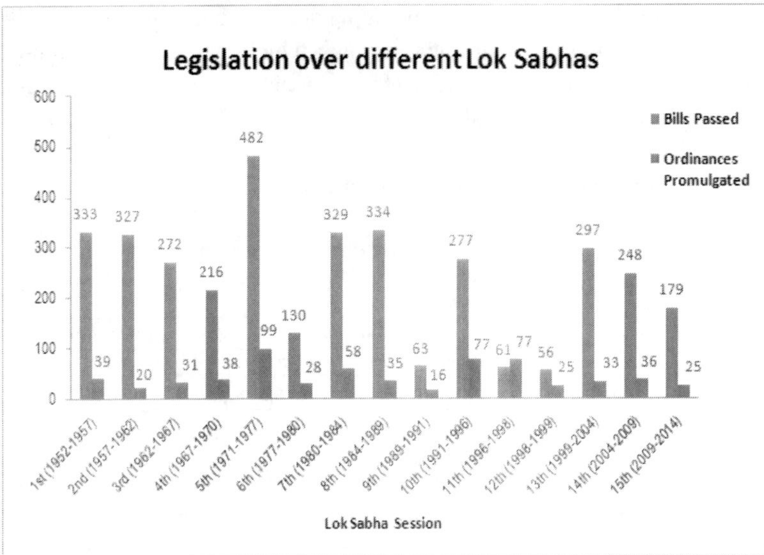

Table 6.2: Do you know that MPs also participate in making laws? Do you consider this as an important function?

	Number	*Percent*
Yes	59	70.2
No	21	25.0
No Answer	4	4.8
Total	**84**	**100.0**

Table 6.3 Does the MPs participation in parliamentary debates factor in your assessment of the performance of the MP or in voting?

	Frequency	*Percent*
Yes	59	70.2
No	13	15.5
No Answer	12	14.3
Total	**84**	**100.0**

At the same time, most people also felt that legislators must concentrate on local issues rather than on larger national issues, irrespective of the level of the government "in view of the fact that the legislators are chosen locally." The balancing act of representing ambiguous and sometimes hyper local issues at a national forum on the basis of a party manifesto, which provides broad guidelines, is a challenging task. It requires interpreting the mandate, choosing the instrument through which it is to be represented and engaging on the floor of the House, which is multi functional and deals with complex technical issues.

MPs Participation in Discussions on Bills

Table 6.4: National and State Parties MPs Participation in Legislative Debates

	Debates	*State Parties*		*National Parties*	
		Number	*Percent*	*Number*	*Percent*
Low	0	15	8.6	30	8.2
	1 to 5	29	16	67	18.3
	6 to 10	13	7.5	36	9.9
	11- 15	11	6.3	43	11.8
	16- 20	7	4.0	27	7.4
Moderate	21-25	7	4.0	13	3.5
	26-30	16	9.2	13	3.5
	30-35	14	8.0	13	3.5
	45-50	11	6.3	14	3.8
High	51-60	6	5.2	11	3.0
	61-70	5	5.1	10	2.7
	71-80	3	4.0	4	2.1
	81-90	2	1.7	9	2.7
	91-99	2	1.7	5	1.4
Very High	100-160	8	4.6	15	4.1
	200 and above	*4*	*2.3*	*Nil*	*0*

Source: Tabulated from Lok Sabha Debates.

Table 6.4 shows that members of State Parties show greater interest in legislative business of the House than national parties. While nearly two fifth of the members of State Parties have low level of participation in debates, 28 have moderate level of participation, 16 percent have high and six percent have very high level of participation in the fourteenth Lok Sabha. Thus, the percentage of MPs who have lower level of participation is lower in State Parties, indicating their greater interest to participate in legislative debaters.

Table 6.5: Members with No Participation in Discussion on Bills

Name	*Total Members*	*Members with no Participation in Debates*	*Percent*
National Parties	366	30	8.1
State Parties	173	17	9.8
Independents	6	1	16.6

As seen in Table 6.5, though the percentage of MPs with no participation in discussion of Bills in State Parties is slightly higher than that of national parties, it was also seen that four of the five top performing MPs of Lok Sabha- Bhartruhari Mahtab, Ram Kripal Yadav, Ramji Lal Suman, Rasa Singh Rawat, Shailendra Kumar- belong to State Parties. Further, session-wise analysis of the data indicates that in all, not more than 10-18 members of the 173 members of State Parties participated in Legislative debates in a particular session of approximately about 30 days.

Table 6.6: Participation in Legislative Debates of Select Sessions of 14th Lok Sabha

Session	*No of MPs of State parties who Participated*	*No of times MPs of State Parties Participated*
2004	20	45
2005	27	121
2006	35	108
2007	19	38
2008	32	70
2009	17	42

Source: Lok Sabha Debates.

The number of times that MPs from the State Parties participated in Bill (legislative) discussions ranges from 42-121. On an average, a single MP from a State party participates between two to three times during such discussions. A caveat may be added here, not all MPs participated in

Table 6.7: Nature of Participation by State Party MPs in Select Sessions

Year	*Total No. Of Bills*	*No of MPs who participated*	*State Party MPs who participated*	*Amendments*	*Bills to which Provisions were added*	*Language of discussion*
2004	9	18	2	17		English
2005	43	190	19	18	19	English
2006	29	232	15	10	17	English
2007	34	33	10	11	15	English and Hindi
2008	18	68	18	17	9	English and Hindi
2009	27	79	14	9	12	English and Hindi

Source: Tabulated from Select Lok Sabha Debates.

discussion on Bills, hence, the number of times an active MP participates is actually much greater than the average.

A study of select session of Parliament every year of the fourteenth Lok Sabha reveals that members of State Parties were occasional participants in legislative debates (see Table 6.7). Notwithstanding this, the data does not conclusively prove the relative inefficiency of State Parties, though it indicates that State party MPs include both those who are very active and those who are relatively inactive during legislative debates with a tilt toward the former. This debunks the commonly held view that State Parties are in some ways responsible for inefficiency of the Parliament and have contributed to the decline of the Parliament as a law making body. This leads us to the next question. When State party MPs participate in the proceedings of the Houses what do they represent in terms of the nature of issues; the nature of interjections, language of discussion assumes significance. It indicates both the level of interest of active and moderately active members, as well as the nature of issues raised by such MPs.

Assuming Different Roles during Discussion on Bills

A qualitative analysis of the debates during Bill discussions (see list of Tables) revealed that MPs adopted certain distinctive roles during legislative debates. The most prominent among them were their roles as supporters or opponents of government policy. While the decision to support or oppose the government was pre-determined depending on whether the party was a part of the ruling coalition or opposition, the manner of support was noteworthy.

Support for Government Policy and Suggestions for Improvement: The support of some of the MPs of State Parties to the government was in the form of support for the policies initiated by them. Such support was based on merits of the issue and facts that the draft Bills contained. The participants of such debates were from State Parties of ruling coalition. However, sometimes MPs of State Parties also supported the policy despite their alliance with the main opposition party. Thus, for instance, Prasanna Acharya (BJD) speaking on High Court Judges Salaries Amendment Bill 2008, spoke against introducing an Ordinance on the subject. However, he suggested the need for filling up vacancies in subordinate courts and on the need for evening courts in all states. Ramdas Atawale of RPI while supporting the same Bill suggested that salaries of judges be further increased in order to ensure their satisfaction. He also demanded that Schedued Castes (SC), Scheduled Tribes (ST) Judges must also be included in these ranks, and the number of judges must be increased. He wanted a Supreme Court bench in Mumbai. In another debate, P.C. Thomas (Kerala Congress) made useful and precise suggestions during the debate on National Capital Territory Laws (Special Provision) Bill, 2009. He also suggested that farm houses encroaching upon small farmers' rights need to be tackled. Cheaper accommodation could be provided to migrants coming in to Delhi and memorials could be built for statesmen in Delhi to honour them. These instances indicate the manner in which MPs offer suggestions, while extending support to the government.

Support for Coalition and Leadership: State Party MPs used legislative debates to strengthen their partnership with the government. Thus, there was an undeniable thrust on the correctness of the government policy, which was not always based on the facts. MPs also used legislative debates to display support to the leaders of their own party and the government. Thus for instance Rajiv Ranjan Yadav of the RJD (a part of the ruling coalition) spoke strongly in support of the UPA and Sonia Gandhi, during a discussion on the Maternity Benefit Bill, 2008. Yadav also used the debate as an opportunity to hint at the support base of the ruling coalition, suggesting that they (ruling coalition, UPA) were drawn from the villages of India, unlike the NDA (opposition coalition) who supported capitalists. Such discussions were laced with criticisms of policies of governments and sharp exchange of words leading to commotions were usual.

Critiquing the Government: Legislative debates were used as an opportunity by MPs of opposition parties, both national and State, to critique the government. Such critique was both of the particular provisions of the Bill, as well as those of the policies of the government at large. While the former were more pointed criticisms, the latter were more frequent and were general or vague in nature. Braja Kishor Tripathi of the BJD speaking on High Court Judges Salaries Amendment Bill 2008 strongly criticized the Bill and stated that the Bill's object was merely to negate all Supreme Court and High Court orders and directives in this regard. The previous Act of 2006 was termed "void and illegal" by the participant. He criticized the government for lack of vision to do anything and inordinate delays without specifying the two.

Critiquing the Opposition: Interestingly MPs used the debates as an opportunity not just to critique the government or its policies, but also the opposition. This showed the differences among the State Parties. Rajiv Ranjan Yadav of RJD, which was in alliance with the government, blamed the NDA (opposition coalition and previous government) for not working enough in the National Capital Region (NCR) of Delhi during their government. MPs of State Parties, who were part of ruling coalition, criticized opposition. In another debate, he said that the laws made should be so strong that the judiciary need not intervene for the common man (ambiguous).

Simultaneous Representation of Nation/State/Constituency: The nature of participation of State Parties MPs and the constituency they represented were not very different from that of the national parties. While the State party MPs do occasionally raised issues that were of local significance, they usually adopted a national perspective, citing instances of their previous achievements. Thus, A Krishnasamy (DMK) while speaking about the need for enhancement of maternity benefit for women also spoke about the steps taken by his State (Tamil Nadu) for the welfare of women workers of unorganised sector and those below the poverty line. Mohan Rawale of SHS focused on the terrorism aspect of money-laundering during his intervention in the Prevention of Money Laundering Bill, 2008. While most of his speech focused on the Mumbai Terror attacks of 2008, he suggested that the police be specially trained to deal with terrorists. He also requested that the IPS officer Shashank Shinde be awarded *Ashok Chakra*. Ramji Lal Suman of SP speaking on Central Universities (Amendment Bill) 2009 felt that chancellors from among the SC and ST must also be considered for appointment to highest offices. He opined that Patna University should be given the status of Central University. Suman, was performed, as representatives of the marginalised, as a MP of SP from Uttar Pradesh.

Demand for Resources/Funds: While supporting or opposing the government initiated Bills, the MPs used the opportunity to make demands for their constituency. Thus, Ram Kripal Yadav of RJD speaking on Central Universities (Amendment Bill) 2009 spelt out the need for a central university in Bihar. He also observed that there should be recruitment and career placement cells in every college (raising issue of unemployment) and availability of loans for poor students (representative of poor). He demanded central university status to Patna University.

The perspective adopted by the MPs also depended on the session in which they were participating. In the budget session of the Lok Sabha and during budgetary discussions members adopt a more local perspective. Herein, the demand for allocation of resources for the constituency also increased considerably. Demand for allocation of resources tops the list of issues raised by MPs of State Parties. In discussion on Bills the MPs represented gropu or social identity.

Leaders in Limelight

The participants from State Parties were either leaders of established parties or senior members of the parties. Thus, for instance, Lalu Prasad Yadav of RJD, Ram Kripal Yadav of SP, Ramji Lal Suman (SP), Brij Kishore Tripathi, Ashok Kumar Mehta and M. Ramdoss, were frequent participants in discussions on Bills. In the sessions under consideration, no first time member of a State party participated in the discussion. Members who participated in such discussion were mostly middle aged (45-65) educated, with professional qualification and with a fair command over language. They were prominent MPs of their respective parties and had considerable experience.

Interestingly in the legislative (Bill) debates under consideration, there was greater participation from the MPs of State Parties in the North. RJD and SP members were often at the forefront of debates, though members of SHS and AITC and DMK also participated. The participation of State party MPs were often during clause by clause discussion of the Bills and the participation of members of State Parties led to acrimonious debates and frequent interruptions. All such bills, in which State party MPs participated were mostly amended and new clauses were inserted. The participation was in favour of financial demands, development of infrastructure, rights of the minorities, tribals etc., where members of State Parties tried to 'represent the interest of certain groups'.

The language of discussion also changed depending on who participated. It was English during discussions of financial nature. However State party MPs from parties of the North such as SP and RJD almost always spoke in Hindi during their participation. There was often humor or lighter moments during legislative discussions. The discussions were more serious or acrimonious, with party lines clearly visible during discussion on financial matters. Some of the significant features of these debates may be highlighted

- Not more than 10% of State Parties participated in Legislative (Bill) dicussions
- Nearly 10% members never participated in discussions of Bills
- Those who participated were usually established members of their party
- MPs of north were better represented in legislative debates
- Participants in debates usually had a high level of education with professional qualifications

- State party MPs spoke on national issues and adopted a national perspective during debates on Bills
- Language of discussion was English and Hindi
- Debates in which State party MPs participated were often acrimonious with several interruptions. Party lines were clearly evident during discussions

Participation in Question Hour: Developing A National Perspective

The Question Hour is without doubt one of the most important procedural devices available to the House to raise issues of importance, seek information and hold the government accountable. It is also the most frequently watched by the media and the voters and most widely reported in the media. Members of the Parliament recognize its significance in the determining the nature of political discourse and participate in it.

Table 6.8: Participation of State Party MPs in Question Hour in Select Sessions

Session	*No of MPs of State Parties who Participated*	*Questions Raised*	*Supplementary Questions*
2004	29	116	11
2005	33	165	34
2006	29	87	16
2007	34	133	17
2008	22	60	13
2009	10	30	9

Source: Tabulated from Lok Sabha Debates, 2004-2009.

A study of the Question Hour revels that nearly 26 -30 of the 173, constitution one-tenth of the MPs participated in every session of approximately thirty days. This would mean that on an average at least one state party member rises during a Question Hour in the Parliament every day. The number of question raised by them varied from 30-165, averaging about 99 question in every session or about 2-3 questions every day. That is to say, that at least one member of a State party raised at least two questions every working day of the Lok Sabha. Previous studies of Lok Sabha, such as those of PRS legislative Research (2009) have revealed that about 7-10 questions were raised by Lok Sabha members each day. Nearly half of the questions raised in the Lok Sabha were by MPs of State Parties.

Despite the overall healthy rate of participation of State party MPs in the Lok Sabha, some shortcomings need to be highlighted. First, active members participated on regular basis, while non-active members seldom raised a query. Barring a few regular members, who attend the House religiously and also participated in the proceedings, there is a sizable number who have remained largely apathetic to the proceedings. At least 51 members of the 14th Lok Sabha did not ask a single question. The list includes Leader of Opposition LK Advani and Congress president Sonia Gandhi. Other prominent leaders who did ask any question are Atal Bihari Vajpayee, Mamta Banerjee, HD Deve Gowda, Ajit Singh, Govinda, Dharmendra, Kalyan Singh and Jagdish Tytler. These leaders spoke during discussions on Bills. Some leaders were active participants too. During the 14th Lok Sabha, L.K. Advani participated in 71 debates, 8 Special Mentions and four government Bills. Likewise, Sonia Gandhi participated in four debates and one government Bill.

Table 6.9: Extent of Participation of Members of State Party MP's in Question Hour

	No Questions	***MP's***	***Percent***
Low	1-10	22	12.7
	13-20	19	11
	21-30	8	4.6
	35-50	6	3.4
Moderate	51-100	5	2.9
	100-150	12	6.9
	150-250	11	6.8
	250-350	14	8.0
High	350-500	12	6.9
	500-1000	14	8.0
	100-1300	**5**	**2.9**

Source: Tabulated from Lok Sabha Debates, 2004-2009.

Given the fact that the MPs of the State Parties constitute only a fifth of the membership of the Lok Sabha, their participation in the Question Hour of the Lok Sabha is significant, and is more than that of national parties. However, every question was not accompanied by supplementary questions. The number of supplementary questions raised was rather low, though the rules of procedure of Lok Sabha allow for two supplementary questions. MPs often lost this opportunity of cross examination, as is evident from the data.

Table 6.10: Number of Questions Asked by MP's of Different State Parties; 2004-2009(Select Sessions)

Name of State Parties	*2004*	*2005*	*2006*	*2007*	*2008*	*2009*
J&KNC	1	2	4	3	0	0
AIFB	1	1	3	3	2	2
RSP	1	0	3	5	1	0
DMK	1	1	12	21	21	6
PMK	2	9	17	21	12	9
AGP	2	1	18	13	20	2
SP	2	25	64	44	28	23
BJD	0	9	64	51	50	33
SAD	0	8	4	10	5	0
TDP	0	7	6	13	7	4
JMM	7	3	8	2	0	0
KEC	0	7	23	34	19	22
AITC	0	6	0	1	3	0
SHS	0	4	17	16	16	15
LJSP	2	3	0	0	0	0
JD(U)	0	0	10	12	0	0
JD(S)	0	9	15	11	7	0
SDF	0	0	3	1	0	0
RSP	0	0	3	5	1	0
MDMK	0	0	0	9	5	10
MNF	0	0	0	1	0	0
J&KPDP	0	0	0	1	0	0

Source: Tabulated from Lok Sabha Debates, 2004-2009.

The party-wise disaggregation of data relating to Question Hour reveals that older and more established regional party members play a more active role during the Question Hour. The highest participation came from BJD, followed by Kerala Congress and SP. Parties such as DMK, PMK, and SHS also participated actively during the Question Hour, though their participation is otherwise much less.

Some regional variations are also observed in the manner of participation in the Question Hour. MPs from State Parties of South India participated more frequently in the Question Hour than any other region. This is followed by parties of North and west. In the East, other than the BJD, other regional parties did not participate as effectively in Question Hour, as that of other parties. However, notwithstanding the differences, it is evident that MPs of State Parties are as much interested in the Question Hour, as those of the national parties.

The difference between starred questions and unstarred questions was of significance in this analysis. Only 19% starred questions were orally answered in the Lok Sabha. Starred questions are usually followed by supplementary questions from other MPs. Of the total 1100 starred questions admitted in the Lok Sabha in 2009, only 266 (24%) were called out in the House; the remaining questions could not be called out due to the paucity of time. Of the 266 question, the inquiring MP was not present in the House for 57 questions. Thus, only 209 (19% of admitted questions) were orally answered. A similar pattern can be observed in the previous years. Interestingly, the percentage of admitted questions that received oral answers was higher in 2009 than in the previous five years.

Nature of Questions Raised During Select Sessions

Nature of issues raised	*National*	*State*	*Constituency*	*International*
2004-2009	454	15	1	60

Source: Tabulated from Lok Sabha Debates, 2004-2009.

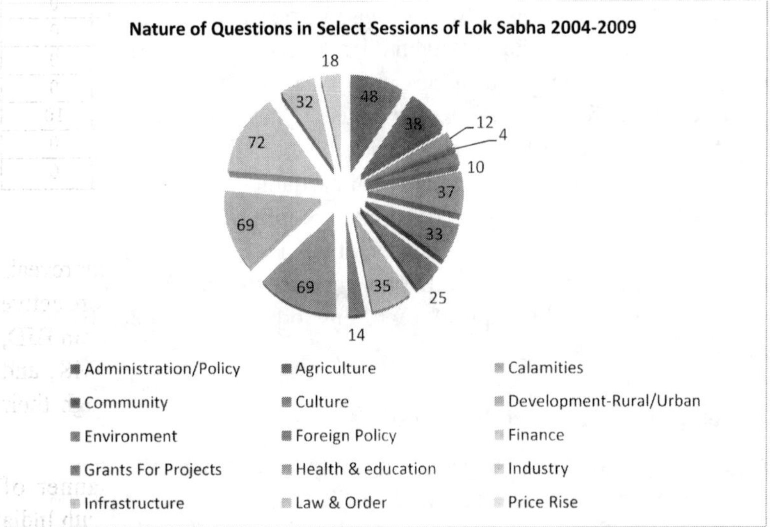

While some issues such as price rise and atrocities on minorities and backward classes, rural development (including agricultural credit, use of agricultural land for non-agricultural purposes, subsidy on fertilizers) were old, others dealt with newer issues such as water pollution, environmental degradation, viability of renewable energy resources, functioning of private airlines, etc. Development of infrastructure, industries, health and education related matters were the most frequently questioned issues by the State party representatives in the 14th Lok Sabha. Since development of infrastructure and industries is closely related to building of State capacities to deal with problems of livelihood, MPs of State Parties seemed to assess the needs of the electorate and voice to them trough the Question Hour.

Administrative issues, agriculture, finance and issues of urban and rural development also figured prominently in the questions raised by MPs of State Parties. The emphasis on administrative issues is of particular importance because it shows the problems faced by State party MPs as representatives of federal units. Here MPs were representing state administration at the national level and were acting as bridge between the two. As one member of the Parliament pointed out "MPs of Parliament are caught between the dilemmas of representing the constituency and the state at the national level."

Price rise and law and order, which figured prominently in the list of concerns of the electorate, did not figure prominently in the Question Hour. This is interesting in view of the fact that price rise has often been a major electoral issue. Structured discussions on price rise were usually taken up under Rule 193 in the Lok Sabha. Under these rules, a Short duration discussion can be initiated on any subject. However, these rules do not provide for any formal voting in the House.[1] Similarly corruption too, did not figure prominently in the Question Hour. Environment received considerable attention from members of parliament. Questions relating to marginalisation/discrimination of certain sections of the electorate too did not figure prominently in the Question Hour. This is surprising given that the popular perception of State Parties are as representatives of caste and ethnic identities. The support for them too comes largely from the marginalised

Developing a National Perspective?

MPs of State Parties raise larger number of question that may be considered national rather than local in orientation. This is interesting in view of the fact that most State Parties have limited geographical expanse. They do not always have clearly stated public positions on national issues. Their election manifestoes' too do not indicate their stand on a host of issues on the national scale. However, as members of national legislature, State Parties' MPs adopt a more national orientation.

Some sub-trends in this broader perspective become noteworthy. Firstly questions relating to some subjects are raised with a national orientation, while others are necessarily local. Thus, for instance issues relating to law and order, agriculture, natural calamities assume a more national orientation.

On the other hand, demands for funds and grant of new projects often attempt to amalgamate State concerns with that of constituency concerns. Similarly all foreign policy questions and those relating to security have an international orientation.

Majority of the questions, aimed at criticizing the policies of the government, while holding it accountable for the lacunae in governance and policy implementation, come from regional parties that are in the opposition. However, instances of controlling the executive by criticizing its policies were not limited to one session of the Lok Sabha, or only those studied in detail. Almost all the sessions studied had similar deliberations. Earlier studies (PRS: 2004) show that since the Tenth Lok Sabha, there has been a significant increase in the questions of this nature. Even where the members have sought to correct imbalances in policy decisions with a view to extracting concessions for their respective constituencies, their speeches have been laced with scathing criticism of the government. The tendency seems to have increased in 11th and the 12th Lok Sabhas.

Apart from questions that are explicitly aimed at ensuring government's accountability, the members of the Lok Sabha also used the Question Hour to perform representative functions. The questions assumed one or all of the three forms:

- Airing the Grievances of the constituency
- Securing concessions for the constituents
- Correcting imbalances in the distribution of resources that may have occurred on account of party politics

It was evident from the study that MPs often, raised issues relating to the State from which they were elected. Similarly, occupation of the members also influenced the nature of questions raised. Most members who proposed agriculture-related questions represented the concerns of the agriculturalists of their constituencies. In the sample chosen for study, women members are found to have raised issues relating to health, family planning, education etc. Party lines were rather blurred in such discussions and women members made an attempt to portray themselves as their representatives. This underlines the importance of mirror representation in the Indian context. Interviews with MPs also shows that they were encouraged to ask questions in the area of their expertise by the party. As Sushma Swaraj, leader of the opposition in the 15th Lok Sabha pointed out, the party plays no role in the choice of questions asked by the members. Ultimately the Question Hours reflects the preferences of individual MPs, who chose to act as representatives of the State, Party, Constituency or voter groups.

During the Question Hour, the predominant language used during the Question Hour was English, though there was use of Hindi also. The members of the "Hindi Belt" spoke in Hindi, and those from the east, west or south of the country spoke mostly in English. Thus, while Bills provided MPs an opportunity to put forth general views, Question Hour required members to be more specific in their interjections. This found reflection in both the language and the nature of interjections made.

In the 14th Lok Sabha, the seriousness of the debates varied with the issues discussed. When the house deliberated on financial issues, or when the Prime Minister was present during discussion serious deliberations took place. Members seemed to attempt to seek clarification from the Minister, criticized government policies, and demanded to know policy choices and implications with respect to their constituencies. The questions were usually precise and the answers were to the point. Discussions on agriculture, irrigation, etc. appeared to be carried out in an emotionally charged atmosphere. Such discussions lacked precision. Most of the opposition members gave long speeches relating to the background of the question, before asking the question. Many interruptions were because of the impatience of the ruling party MPs with such long speeches. The debates on domestic issues were characterised by greater criticism of government policies and inefficiency of its programmes. On matters of foreign policy there appeared to be greater consensus among members.

The Question Hour was frequently interrupted and the Lok Sabha debates recorded nearly 40 interruptions on an average during a single day in the study period. The members of the opposition staged walkout twice in the study period of thirty days. The Speaker had to adjourn the House on more than one occasion owing to unruly behavior of the members. Interruptions in the House during the Question Hour took place due to one or more of the following reasons:

- Dissatisfactory or inadequate response by the concerned Minister;
- Absence of the concerned Minister during the debate in the House;
- Failure of a member to raise questions effectively;
- Attempts of a member to shower accolades on his/ her party and criticize others;
- Extraneous factors, such as weakness of the government, doubts regarding its continuance; and
- Decision of the Speaker to disallow a member from speaking

In a nut shell, it appears that the MPs of State Parties show interest in Question Hour both in terms of the number of questions raised as well as participation in discussions. Their interest is at par with that of the MPs of national parties. Secondly, participation of MPs of State Parties is based on individual zeal and enthusiasm. While almost all the state party members participated in the Question Hour, majority of them raised between one and 20 questions during their term as MPs of Lok Sabha. There are however a group of enthusiastic and dedicated members, who considered their parliamentary role extremely important. They raised a large number of questions (starred and unstarred) during the Question Hour. The purpose of such questions was to seek information from the government rather than representation, though the two cannot be separated from each other. Thirdly, participation of MPs of State Parties in the Question Hour is also determined by their own experience and the strength of the party in the Lok Sabha. As mentioned, old and established parties, with larger membership outperform the newer and smaller State Parties when it comes to holding the government accountable through Question Hour. Membership of national legislative institutions seems to have a salutary effect on MPs of State Parties. Irrespective of their geographical and socio-economic support base, MPs of State Parties largely adopt a national perspective during Question Hour. Most questions raised by them have a national perspective though often the demands for the State and the constituencies are interlaced with national twist to local issues.

Fifth, the perspective of the State party MPs is also shaped by three factors: first, the demands of the electorate; second, the nature of issues being raised and the political situation. On the first count it would appear from the data that MPs of State Parties are almost in sync with the electorate. The MPs appear to take into account the broader demands of the electorate, though the nature of the institution and procedures available prevent them from raising local and sub-local issues. On a large number of issues such as those relating to agriculture, industrialisation, development of infrastructure of the state, the party MPs adopt a national perspective without losing sight of their local responsibilities.

On a large number of issues MPs of State Parties go beyond merely representing their constituency. Thus, for instance, the large number of questions raised by them relating to environment, foreign policy, sports indicates that State party MPs consider themselves as the care-takers of "public good" on behalf of the electorate. Given the fact that the electorate may not necessarily have either information to form opinion, or a clear opinion of some of the issues, the role of State party MPs in this regard is of significance. Data indicates that State party MPs once elected to the national parliament, do not necessarily regard themselves as the representatives of the State, or the community that may have contributed to their election. While this may be a positive trend, it raises questions about the representative character of the state party MPs vis-a-vis that of national parties.

Discussions under Rule 377 & Special Mentions & Resolutions: Opportunities of Representing Local ?

Discussion under Rule 377 of the Rules of Procedure provides members of the Lok Sabha an opportunity to debate on issues which cannot be raised either under the Question Hour, Calling Attention Motion, Resolution or Short Duration Discussion. These discussions allow members, with the permission of the Speaker, to raise and debate unlisted matters. There is no written procedural requirement. Discussions under Rule 377 are of recent origin and began to be used regularly from the sixth Lok Sabha onwards. Since then they have gained in popularity. A written reply to the issue raised may be given by the concerned Minister.

A study of discussion under rule 377 reveals that MPs of smaller State and regional political parties make greater use of this facility than the MPs of larger national parties. In the sessions that were under consideration between 26 and 52 percent of the issues raised under this procedural mechanism were raised by MPs of State Parties. This procedure was also used by a larger number of MPs compared to that of Question Hour and legislative debates. Thus, for instance, almost 60 members of State Parties in the Budget session of 2005 used this procedural device. Further, some members used this procedure more than once in the same session. Thus, Ashok Kumar Mehta, raised 21 issues under Rule 377 in 2009.

Table 6.12: Discussions Under Rule 377

Lok Sabha	*No of Matter*	*Time Hrs- Mins*	*% of time*
Fifth Lok Sabha	N.A	N.A	N.A
Sixth Lok Sabha	829	43.56	2.51
Seventh Lok Sabha	3134	103.22	3.19
Eighth Lok Sabha	3205	79.32	2.46
Ninth Lok Sabha	3490	16.15	2.14
Tenth Lok Sabha	2603	46.17	1.83
Eleventh Lok Sabha	628	16.09	1.98
Twelfth Lok Sabha	667	11.12	2.06
Thirteenth Lok Sabha	2964	NA	NA
Fourteenth Lok Sabha	3485	21.39	1.19

Source: Parliament of India, Sixth to Fourteenth Lok Sabha: A Study, (Lok Sabha Secretariat, New Delhi, 1971 1977, 1979, 1985, 1991, 1992, 1997, 2000, 2004, 2009).

Table 6.13: Discussions under Rule 377 in Select Sessions (2004-2009)

Dates	*Session*	*Total Number of Matters raised under Rule 377*	*Total No of matters raised by State party MPs*	*% of total*	*MPs Participants from State parties*
5/7/2004 to 26/82004	Monsoon	220	64	29	50
25/22005 to 3/5/2005	Budget	365	115	31.5	63
22/11/2006 to 9/12/2006	Winter	264	70	26.5	47
23/2/2007 to 17/5/2007	Budget	324	90	27.7	46
17/8/2008 to 25/12/2008	Monsoon	129	37	28.7	23
12.02.2009 to 26.02.2009	Budget	80	42	52.5	18

Source: Tabulated from Lok Sabha Debates, 2004-2009.

A majority of the issues raised during these discussions related to allocation of resources to special interest groups or constituents that the MPs represented. However, these questions do not deal with main issues that concern the electorate such as drinking water, unemployment, price rise etc. Interestingly, a majority of them dealt with development of infrastructure such as railways lines, airports and schools, research centers etc. in the constituency that a MP represents. A representative sample of such constituency related discussions under rule 377 is mentioned below.

- Setting up a domestic airport in Ramanathapuram Parliamentary Constituency, Tamil Nadu (Bhanvani Rajenthiran, DMK)
- Need to provide better amenities at Hardwar railway station, Uttaranchal.[2,3] (Rajendra Kumar Badi, SP)
- Need to Develop Vellore Airport and make it Operational.[4](K.M., Kader Mohiddin, DMK)
- Need to allocate more funds for speeding up gauge conversion work on Naupada-Gunupur railway section in Waltair Division of East-Coast Railway[5] (Yerran Naidu, Vishakhapatnam, TDP)
- Need to release funds for enabling early completion of the gauge conversion work on Naupada-Gunupur railway line in Andhra Pradesh.[6] (Yerran Naidu, TDP)
- Need to release funds for early commencement of work on Maharajganj – Mashrak rail line.[7] (Prabhunath Singh, JD(U)
- Need to open a Kendriya Vidyalaya at Maharajganj, District Siwan, Bihar.[8] (Prabhunath Singh, JD(U)

- Need to set up a food processing center with cold storage facility in Chamarajanagara Parliamentary Constituency, Karnataka.[9] (M. Shivanna, JD(S)
- Need to set up a Bulk Milk Centre at Chamarajanagara, Karnataka for the benefit of milk producers in the region.[10] (M. Shivanna, Chamrajnagar, JD(S)
- Need for four-laning of road between Delhi and Hardwar with a view to boost tourism.[11] (Badi, Shri Rajendra Kumar, SC)
- Need to provide stoppage of important trains at Roorkee railway station, Uttarakhand.[12] (Badi, Shri Rajendra Kumar, SC)
- Need to start 'budget airline services' from Chennai to UAE for the benefit of NRIs from Tamil Nadu.[13] (Kader Mohideen, DMK)

  Need to conduct a survey for laying a new railway line linking Arni town in Vellore Parliamentary Constituency, Tamil Nadu.[14] (Kader Mohideen, DMK)
- Need to run a passenger train in the morning hours between Patna and Islampur.[15] (Ramswaroop Tadav, JD(U)
- Need to set up new telephone exchanges in Saran and Siwan districts of Bihar.[16] (Prabhunath Singh (JD(U)
- Need to start construction of National Highway No. 85 (Hajipur to Gopalganj via Chhapra-Siwan) and National Highway No. 101 (Chhapra to Muhammadpur via Baniapur) in Bihar.[17] (Prabhunath Singh (JD(U)
- Need to set up a LPG bottling plant at Mashrakh, District Saran, Bihar.[18] (Prabhunath Singh (JD(U)
- Need to open a LPG bottling plant of H.P.C.L. in Mashrakh, district Saran, Bihar.[19] (Prabhunath Singh (JD(U)

Some of the discussions during the procedure related to development of agricultural infrastructure. However, these were far fewer than those related to railways. A few examples of such demands llustrate the nature of discussions.

- Provide irrigation facilities and evolving comprehensive Agricultural Development Scheme in Ramanathapuram Parliamentary Constituency, Tamil Nadu.[20] (Bhavani Rajenthiran, DMK)
- Need to take over the Irrigation Research Institute at Hardwar, Uttarakhand by the Central Government.[21] (Rajendra Kumar Badi, SP)

- Need to release additional stock of fertilizer to Andhra Pradesh to meet its shortage in the State.[22] (M. Jagannath, TDP)
- Need to allot Iron Ore Deposits in State of Chhattisgarh or Odisha for the use of Vishakhapatnam Steel Plant, Andhra Pradesh.[23] (Yerran Naidu, TDP)
- Need to strengthen the rain-fed river embankments in Hardwar Parliamentary Constituency, Uttarakhand.[24] (Badi, Shri Rajendra Kumar, SC)
- Need to permit cashew growers of Andhra Pradesh to continue with the existing technology of roasting seed through drum roasting system.[25] (M. Jagannath, TDP)

A large number of discussions under 377 went beyond the constituency and were related to state from which the MP was elected.

- Need to set up an office of Army Recruitment Board at Allahabad, Uttar Pradesh.[26] (Shri Ateeq - UP/ Phulpur)
- Need to provide employment to the local people of Nallathur, district Kanchipuram, Tamil Nadu in the new project of Madras Atomic Power Station.[27] (Kader Mohideen, DMK)
- Need to sanction Rs. 370 crores as Central assistance for drought relief operations in Andhra Pradesh.[28] M. Jagannath, TDP
- Need to issue directions to the Government of Andhra Pradesh to Reduce VAT levied on tea from 12.5 per cent to 4 per cent.[29] (M. Jagannath, TDP)
- Need to clear the proposal of the Government of Karnataka for implementation of Metro Project in Bangalore.[30] (M. Shivanna, JD(S)
- Need to allocate additional funds for early completion of ongoing power projects in Karnataka.[31] (M.Shivanna, JD(S)

A large number of discussions under 377 related to agriculture. In fact, a large number of MPs of State Parties were agriculturists elected from areas that were predominantly agricultural. Such members used the opportunity to represent the farming community. However, the issues raised were very general and were often of the constituency of the MP concerned. Moreover, most of them were in the nature of demand for subsidy for the farmers. A few examples may be mentioned here:

- Need to take suitable measures to safeguard the interests of farmers in Andhra Pradesh.[32] (M.Jagannath, TDP)

- Need to procure the cotton from cotton-growers of Andhra Pradesh facing distress due to suspension of cotton-purchase by Cotton Corporation of India.[33] (Yerran Naidu, TDP)
- Need to sanction adequate funds for providing relief to the coconut growers in Karnataka affected by coconut disease 'NWSI PEEDE'.[34] (M.Shivanna, JD(S)
- Need to take steps to ameliorate the plight of power-loom weavers of Karimnagar district, Andhra Pradesh facing unemployment due to crisis in power loom industry.[35] (Yerran Naidu, TDP)
- Need to take steps to ameliorate the plight of paddy growers.[36] (Yerran Naidu, TDP)

Apart from agriculturists, the MPs of State Parties also used the procedure to raise large number of issues relating to the marginalised communities particularly, SCs and ST. However, most of such issues raised were very general in nature and related to two main themes; inclusion of communities in the list of SC/ST so as to ensure that they enjoyed the benefits of reservation, and mention of the condition of the marginalised groups. Interestingly a few members developed specialisation in this respect and were often seen raising similar concerns. A list of questions raised by Yerran Naidu and M. Jagannatha of TDP in this respect is interesting. It reveals a serious attempt to'act as representative' of a constituency that is the key support base of the MP.

- Need to include *Vadabalija, Jalari, KandraPalli* communities of South India in the list of ST Category[37] (Yerran Naidu, TDP)
- Need to include fishermen community of Andhra Pradesh in the list of ST.[38,39] (Yerran Naidu, TDP)
- Need for timely release of adequate funds for providing scholarships to SC/ST/OBC students of Andhra Pradesh.[40] (Yerran Naidu, TDP)
- Need to amend the Constitution to enable uniform distribution of the benefits of reservations to all sub-castes of Scheduled Castes, particularly in Andhra Pradesh.[41] (M. Jagannath, TDP)
- Need to expedite 'Usha Mehra' Commission Report on categorisation of Scheduled Castes in Andhra Pradesh.[42] (M. Jagannath, TDP)
- Need to take action against the persons involved in desecration of the statue of Dr. B.R. Ambedkar in Mahboobnagar district of Andhra Pradesh.[43] (M. Jagannath, TDP)

- Need to take steps to check atrocities on Dalits and set up a separate Ministry for the welfare of Backward Caste people.[44] (M. Jagannath, TDP)
- Need to bring Legislation for providing job reservations for deprived classes in Private Sector.[45] (M. Jagannath, TDP)

Discussions relating to health, environment and rise in the prices of certain commodities also found mention during the procedure:

- Need to check construction activities in hilly area at Bandipur, Karnataka to protect flora and fauna of the region.[46]
- Need to take steps for desilting of Barna river in Phulpur, U.P.[47]
- Need to sanction a Central project for checking water-logging and de-siltation of rivers in Bihar particularly Chhapra and Siwan districts.[48]
- Need to check the spread of Chikungunya disease in Karnataka.[49]
- Need to formulate a plan to check water logging and siltation in rivers flowing through Chhapra& Siwan districts of Bihar.[50]
- Need to look into the health related problems of people living in rural areas of Srikakulam district, Andhra Pradesh.[51]
- Need to take suitable measures to check the spread of AIDS in the country.[52]
- Need to check increasing price of cement.[53]
- Need to review the increase in excise duty on hand-made Beedi.[54]
- Need to check the rising prices of Steel.[55]

MPs of Southern and North Eastern states often raised issues relating to preserving the language of their states. Thus for instance both TDP MPs of Andhra Pradesh and JD(S) MPs from Karnataka raised similar issues relating to Telugu and Kannada Languages.

- Need to accord the status of a 'Classical' language to Telugu.[56]
- Need to accord the status of classical language to Kannada.[57]
- Need to conduct Common Entrance Test in vernacular language for appointment in Defence Forces.

Urban MPs occasionally raised urban concerns, too. However, this was rare.

- Need to provide Rs. 1000 Crore to develop five satellite towns around Bangalore in Karnataka.[58]
- Need to encourage setting up of Chip manufacturing units in Bangalore, Karnataka.[59]

- Need to regularize the services of temporary workers in Bangalore and other parts of the country.[60]
- Regarding professional courses perused by students.[61]

Discussions under 377 were used by members to represent constituency level concern at the national levels. The issues raised ranged from demand for allocation of resources, atrocities on SCs, STs, preservation of native languages to more pressing demands of health, employment and education. The focus was on highlighting the need for building State capacities and providing opportunities for redistributive growth and developments. A few highlights of discussion under 377 could be underlined. The issues raised under Rule 377 related to demand for allocation of projects, development of infrastructure, etc. Connectivity through road, railway or airport was a major issues that was raised by various MPs. Apart from infrastructural development, marginalised and farming communities concerns found significant place in the discussions under Rule 377. However, issues such as access to food, shelter, education, safe and free drinking water were completely missing.

An interesting discussion in the study period was the demand of the State party MPs, particularly those belonging to South, to preserve their State language and to grant it the status of a 'classical language'. The demand was serious and passionate- a good example of linguistic identity being an important concern of MPs of State Parties. The State Parties, the study showed used all opportunities to represent identity concerns in the Parliament, whenever opportunities were available to them.

There were a few instances when some MPs raised issues relating to national security, too. Usually, MPs raise local issues during discussions under 377. But, some MPs of the fourteenth House raised issues of border disputes between the neighboring states and asked the government to implement the recommendations of a study undertaken by the committee's setup by the Parliament, indicating the unlimited possibilities of discussions under Rule 377.

It is clear that the MPs of State Parties make good use of Rule 377. The informal nature of the mechanism and the familiarity of the MPs with this informal procedure contributed to its use. The popularity of this procedure was because it allowed members to raise constituency-level concerns without much procedural formalities. Hence, not only were a large number of issues raised by State party MPs, but many of them participated in it as well.

The case of Discussions under 377 shows that the parliamentary procedure are successfully used by MPs, if it allows MPs to showcase local matters with which they are familiar and have long association. Since, a large number of MPs in Lok Sabha were from State Parties, this procedure gave them an opportunity to gain valuable parliamentary experience in representing the local at the national level, before participating in discussions on Bills or Question Hour, which requires knowledge of both the procedure and the subject matter. 377 is a good training ground for State party MPs for greater House participation. It is therefore not surprising that discussions under Rule 377 is one of the most popular parliamentary procedures among members of State Parties.

Attempting Federal Redistribution through Calling Attention Motion

The Calling Attention Motion is an Indian innovation in parliamentary procedures. The Calling Attention Motion allows a member of the Lok Sabha to draw the attention of a Minister to any matter of public importance. The Minister is bound to reply to such a motion either immediately, or within a short duration of time prescribed by the Speaker. The motion does not allow for any debate on the issue. The urgency of the matter determines the inclusion or otherwise of the matter in the Calling Attention Motion. The Calling Attention Motion has emerged as one of the most popular devicesfor censuring the government, while representing constituency concerns. Over the years there has been a gradual increase in the interest of the members in this procedure.

Rules of Procedures and Conduct of Business indicate that not more than one Calling Attention Motion can be taken up on a given day. However, if at the end of the session there are more than one notice of motion on matters of great importance, the Speaker is empowered to permit heir discussion. Accordingly, a very small fraction of legislative time is spent for the purpose. However, over the years the importance of Calling Attention Motion has declined and it is used as a device to obtain information and critique government's handling of a given situation.

Table 6.14: Calling Attention Motion: Notices Admitted & Time Spent

Lok Sabha	*Notices Admitted*	*Time Spent*	*% of total time Spent*
5th	4343	215-37	5.29
6th	1481	87-54	0.6
7th	4390	318	9.58
8th	1251	123-58	3.75

(Contd...)

9th	175	21-01	2.79
10th	144	10-27	0.37
11th	63	6-51	0.80
12th	33	5-36	1.08
14th	317	62-42	

Source: Parliament of India, Sixth to Twelfth Lok Sabha: A Study, (Lok Sabha Secretariat, New Delhi, 1971, 1977, 1979, 1985, 1991, 1992, 1997, 2000, 2004, 2009).

In the 14th Lok Sabha, 317 Calling Attention Motions were admitted and discussed by the House. Of these, 136 motions were in the six sessions of the fourteenth Lok Sabha that were selected for detailed study. Nearly 40 percent of motions moved during the period of sample study, were by members of State Parties, mostly of the opposition coalition. The remaining were largely by the BJP and the left political parties including the CPI and CPI (M). In the six sessions of the Lok Sabha that are under consideration, 38 MPs of State Parties participated nearly 54 times for nearly 26 hours. However, only 20 percent of the MPs of State Parties moved Calling Attention Motions and only 31 percent participated in the discussions.

Most issues discussed under Calling Attention Motion may be considered to be of national importance. However, members of State Parties adopted a way wherein they were in a position to raise issues relating to their constituency. A glance at the nature of issues discussed in the sample study clearly indicates this.

Tabl 6.15: Nature of Issues Raised under Calling Attemtion Motion by State Party MPs

National	*State/Constituency*
• fall in rubber prices • abolishing right to strike of workers • falling rate of employees' provident fund • need to develop sports and its infrastructure • non-performing assets in public sector • consequences of merging IISCO and SAIL • situation arising out of non-implementation of wage settlement • female feticide • global warming in India • working of the three organs of the government • pending of court cases	• accident site at Bettiah colliery, • floods and cyclone in Andhra, • Hydel projects in Andhra • Plight of beedi workers in • closure of several tea gardens in West Bengal • need to include Bhojpuri in the 8th schedule

Further, most of the discussions had financial implications or repercussions and could be categorised as financial or economic. Though they did not demand grants or allocation of resources, they were in the nature of urging the government to act by way of providing relief. A large number of issues relating to workers found place in the discussions. Thus for instance, H.D. Devegowda of JD(S) called the attention of the Minister of Commerce and Industry to the need to increase per barn quota for tobacco and to supply fertilizers at subsidized rates.[62] Similarly M.P. Veerendra Kumar called for a comprehensive package to help the Coffee Sector in the country particularly the small growers in Kerala, Karnataka and Tamil Nadu.[63] S.K. Khardevelanurged the Government to bring an Act paving way for the reservation for Scheduled Castes, Scheduled Tribes and OBCs.

But for a few motions, there was no substantive discussion during these Calling Attention Motions. Most often the members made demands. The Motion was followed by a statement by the Minister or participation of the minister, taking cognizance of the matter and enumerating measures taken by the government to alleviate the situation. The members were almost always satisfied with such explanation and no disruption of the proceedings took place.

The debates during Calling Attention Motions were raucous and frequent arguments by members of all parties. Party lines were amply evident. They were also characterised by large number of interruptions. In the study period, there were over 300 interruptions during Calling Attention Motion discussions. These interruptions varied from a few seconds to resultant adjournment of the House itself. Most such interruptions were due to the differences between the ruling party and opposition party members, the former supporting the government and the latter opposing it. Another reason for interruption was on account of political differences between State and National party members, especially if the former is in power in the state and the latter in the opposition.

Resolution: Declining Importance and Loss of Interest

In the Fourteenth Lok Sabha, 21 motions were discussed either fully or partly. Of these, five of them were of BJP, 4 of CPI and three each of AGP and RJD i.e., nearly 28 percent of the Private Members Resolutions were moved by Members of State Parties. Nearly 33 hours amounting to 2 percent of the floor time was spent in discussing private members' Resolutions. The issues discussed ranged from food security, compulsory education of children, correcting regional imbalances occurring due to political differences, reserving seats for women members in parliament, providing financial assistance, etc.

- Amendment of 1st and 2nd schedule of the Tariff Act in relation to state of Bihar,
- Approval of proclamation by Presidents Rule in Goa,
- Seeking to amend 2nd schedule of Customs Tariff Act,
- Seeking to amend first schedule of Central Excise Tariff Act.

These debates were characterised by bi partisanship. During the debates on all such matters, the opposition was united and tried to force the government to accept it. In the Fourteenth Lok Sabha, majority of these Resolutions were of public interest and there was no party bias evident.

Discussions on Resolutions have lost significance because of inadequate support from the ruling parties in a parliamentary democracy, where almost all legislations are introduced or supported by the government. This leave little room for Private Members to introduce Bills or Resolutions. In the fourteenth Lok Sabha, the government did not support any private members Resolutions despite its merit. This was also the case in earlier Lok Sabha's Whenever Resolutions were adopted in the past, it was done with substantial alterations, so much so that it became a government Resolution. Moreover, the ministers do not take part in debates on Private Members' Resolutions and at times the opposition had to address empty treasury benches, and on some occasions, the House had to be adjourned for lack of quorum during these discussions. The lack of time of the House has also proved to be a significant dampener and has prevented the opposition from introducing Bills and Resolutions. Only two and half hours every week is set aside for private members' business.

Introducing Private members Resolution is time consuming process with little possibility of fruitful outcome. The Resolutions have to have national character, or serve an all India purpose. Hence, State party MPs abjure from participating in them.

Raising Concerns without Discussion: Growing Popularity of Special Mention?

Under the Rules of the Parliament, members are allowed to make Special Mentions in the House. Members are required to give notice for raising a matter under this Rule to the Secretary General. Notice for Special Mention should be given by 17 hours prior to the day on which it is sought to be made by the Member.[64] Under this rule, a Member can raise only one 'matter' during a week and total number of Special Mentions to be admitted for a day shall not exceed seven. Notices not selected during the week lapse at the end of the week and to revive it the Member will have to give fresh notice.[65]

Normally, Ministers do not make statements or react to these matters raised on the floor of the two Houses. However, if a Minister so desires, he may make a statement on the subject with the permission of the presiding Officer.[66] The main advantage of this device is to bring to the notice of the House and the Government the matters and happenings of urgent public importance which take place in or outside the country and have a bearing on our national interests and about which Members are agitated and for which Members may not get an early opportunity to raise these under any other Rule of the House.[67]

Table 6.16: Use of Special Mention by MPs of State Parties in 14th Lok Sabha

Political Parties	*Number of Mp's*	*Number of time Special Mention Used*
AGP	2	40
AIFB	4	5
BJD	12	63
DMK	16	20
J&KNC	2	2
J&KPDP	1	0
JD(S)	3	26
JD(U)	10	18
JMM	6	13
KEC	2	50
LJSP	3	1
MDMK	4	16
MNF	1	0
NPF	1	0
PMK	6	14
RJD	25	72
RLD	3	0
RSP	3	0
SAD	8	10
SDF	1	1
SP	40	117
SS	14	21
TDP	6	17
AITC	1	4
TOTAL	**174**	**510**

Source: Lok Sabha Debate, 2004-2009.

Special Mentions have become an important means of participating in parliamentary proceedings. Large numbers of MPs, both from the ruling and opposition parties, us device. In the fourteenth Lok Sabha, nearly 3187 matters were raised under this procedure. This would also mean that almost an equal number of MPs participated in this procedure. While a party-wise desegregation of data with regard to Special Mention is not available, a study of the select sessions of Lok Sabha indicates the popularity of this procedure. In the six sessions of the Lok Sabha that were studied, nearly 203 members of State Parties participated. Together, they raised 431 issues in the six sessions. One third of the total Special Mentions made were by members of State Parties. Of all the State Parties that participated in this mechanism, MPs of larger parties such as SP, RJD and BJD participated more than their counterparts in other State Parties.

Since the procedure involved merely raising the issue, there were no discussions. Members were mostly precise, since the speaker did not allow members to speak for long. Members read out from written speeches, occasionally deviating. Where strong party differences existed, proceedings were frequently interrupted. Sometimes the Speaker referred the matter to the Minister concerned. The subject matter of the discussion was usually local and pertained to the state from where the MP was elected. A few examples may be cited:

- Need to Grant Special Status to Bihar.
- Need to include Bhojpuri language in the Eighth Schedule of the Constitution.
- Diversion of funds allocated for Mehsana-Taranga broad-gauge railway line in Gujarat.
- Need to open a Central University in Mau district, Uttar Pradesh.

During discussions under Special Mention also reveals that MPs of State Parties assumed the following roles.

Representatives of Caste/ Religious groups: MPs of State Parties often represented the marginalised and minority groups during Special Mentions, especially if they themselves belonged to one. A few examples may be cited:

- Yerran Naidu (Andhra Pradesh, TDP): "Hence, I urge the Government, through you, Sir, to look into it (reservation for OBC in promotions) and ensure that agitation should not bring out equality but natural justice should be given to the OBCs. (*Interruptions*) by providing reservation in promotion of Government jobs"[68]

- Francis George (Idukki Kerala, KEC): "The Forum of Dalit Christians held a Parliament March demanding the implementation of the Ranganath Misra Commission Report and I would request the Government to immediately go through the Report, accept the recommendations and grant the reservation status to millions of Dalit Muslims and Christians in the country and do not deprive them this right. ..."[69]
- Adv. Suresh Kurup (Kerala): "VHP has called for a *bandh* on Christmas Day. ... Now they have called for a *bandh* on Christmas Day. ... (*Interruptions*) There should be condemnation of this by the whole House. ... (*Interruptions*)[70]

Federal and Party Representatives: MPs of State Parties also used the opportunity to raise State concerns. In all such discussions a party line was also visible. As mentioned earlier, such debates also led to altercation between members along party lines and most interruptions that took place during Special Mentions were when such issues were raised.

Shri C. Kuppuswamy (Madras North): Mr. Chairman, Sir, I would like to draw the attention of this House to the continued killing of innocent Tamil civilians by Sri Lankan Army.There are also unprovoked firings on Indian fishermen by Sri Lankan Navy which should be stopped forthwith. Our leader and Chief Minister of Tamil Nadu, Dr. Kalaignar urged to stop the bombardment and hostilities in North Sri Lanka and to initiate the process for political settlement. Urgent steps should be taken to rush relief materials to the displaced persons and to save the suffering Tamils in Sri Lanka.[71]

Shri P. Mohan (Madurai): Hon'ble Speaker, Sir, I would like to draw the attention of this august House to the fact that Mullai Periyar Dam ....Experts have thoroughly studied the structure of the dam and have certified that it is still going strong and can store water upto its maximum capacity, i.e., 152 feet.... the Supreme Court have also accepted the views of the experts in the field of architecture and have issued a favourable order that the height of the dam can be increased upto 142 feet. Recently, the Chief Minister of Kerala, Shri V.S. Achutanandan visited Tamilnadu and called on the Chief Minister of Tamilnadu, Shri M. Karunanidhi and it has been decided that both Tamilnadu and Kerala will sit and deliberate and sort out the issue amicably taking care to benefit both the States. When the States involved have themselves decided to settle it amicably through bilateral talks, it is needless to raise it on the floor of this... Hence, I would like to draw the attention of this august House that we must not unnecessarily take up the issue here. It would be better as decided by the Chief Ministers of Kerala and Tamilnadu to settle it among them amicably to benefit the people of both the States. The just demand from the people of Tamilnadu is not a new one; it has always been there and even Supreme Court has given its verdict that the height can be increased from 136 feet. to 142 feet. So, let there not be any opposition to this on any ground other than the benefit of the people and meeting of the irrigational needs.[72]

Representing Occupational Groups: A large number of State party MPs represented the concerns of dominant occupational groups, particularly agriculturists and industrialists. Special Mentions relating agriculture, industry, mining and manufacturing were therefore most visible. A few examples where MPs represented occupational groups are cited below.

- Francis George (Idukki, Kerala, KEC): Various spices, especially pepper, are allowed to be imported free of import duty by the Spices Oleoresin Industry for value addition and re-export. Sir, the retention period for value addition and re-export of this imported goods was 90 days. Actually, 75 per cent of the spices used by the industry for value addition are imported and so, there is not much benefit for the farmers from this industry. I would request the Government, the Commerce Ministry, not to allow any extension and to strictly restrict the period of value added spice products to 90 days. That is my request and I hope that the Government will consider it favourably to help the spice farmers so that they will get reasonably good price for their products.[73]
- Charanjit Singh Dhillon (Ludhiana): I want to highlight the plight of the disabled ex-servicemen of the emergency wing. Injustice is being meted out to them. The Army rules provide for equal facilities to the 'Regular Commissioned Officers' and the 'Emergency Commissioned Officers'. During war times, the enemy bullets do not distinguish between 'Regular Commissioned Officers' and 'Emergency Commissioned Officers'. However, the injured or dead 'Regular Commissioned Officers' are provided all facilities by the Army whereas the 'Emergency Commissioned Officers' are denied these facilities and left to fend for themselves.[74]

Representing Local Issues: MPs of State Parties raised mostly local issues relating to the locality from where they were elected. Many of these issues could be categorised as largely urban in character.

- Suman Mahato: Sir, I, through this house, draw your attention to poor power supply in Jharkhand. As a result of this, industrial units in the area are on the verge of shut down. Students are facing difficulties in studying and there is a serious problem of supplying drinking water. I appeal to the government, through this house to take immediate steps to improve electricity supply in the region.[75]

- C. Kuppuswamy (Madras North): Hon. Speaker, Sir, we have received information just now about the gruesome fire accident at Lord Krishna & Saraswati Nursery School in Kumbakonam in Tamil Nadu. More than 100 students have died and injured because of this fire accident. I want to know whether the Government has got any information about this fire accident. I also want to know as to what action the Government would take to avoid recurrence of such fire accidents in future. What relief measures the Government has proposed to initiate?[76]
- Sharanjit Singh Dhillon (Ludhiana): I want to draw the attention of the Central Government towards the Baddowal ammunition depot located in my constituency. Baddowal ammunition depot was established at a distance of 12 Kms from Ludhiana. However, as the population of the city increased and the city expanded, Baddowal ammunition depot became a part of Ludhiana and today, it is located in the heart of the city. As such, now, the population living around this ammunition depot faces constant danger from it…..The lives and properties of forty lakh people of Ludhiana living around this ammunition depot are in grave danger. If a fire breaks out here, there will be large-scale death and devastation…..the people of Ludhiana have demanded that the Baddowal ammunition depot should be shifted and relocated somewhere else. I would also like to inform you, sir, that the rate of land around this depot is a whopping Rs. 2 crore per acre whereas the rate of land anywhere else needed to relocate this ammunition depot will be only Rs. 10 lakhs per acre. Hence, I urge upon the Government to accede to the genuine demand of the people of Ludhiana and shift the Baddowal ammunition depot somewhere else at the earliest so that the lives of the 40 lakh people of Ludhiana are saved.[77]

The nature of issues raised during Special Mention was such that members made appeals to the government. They could be categorised as broad constructive suggestions. Two examples of such Special Mentions are cited below

- Mamata Banerjee (AITC, West Bengal): I would appeal to this House to bring a new legislation for land acquisition. The Land

Acquisition Act, 1894 is a draconian law... First of all, I want you to scrap this Land Acquisition Act and bring a new amendment so that the State Governments cannot misuse this law for individual or private purposes.....I want to give you two or three suggestions. Scrap this Land Acquisition Act immediately; cancel SEZ policy and set up a new policy, which involves farmers also.[78]

- Mamata Banerjee: Starvation deaths are increasing in different parts of the country and especially in the tribal-dominated areas of West Bengal, namely, Amlashol in Jhargram sub-division Belpahari and Sakraial in Jhargram sub-division, Purulia, Burdwan sub-division and Bagmundi and also in some parts of Bankura and in Duars in the tea-garden area also. More than 1000 people died due to hunger..... I would request the Government to protect the people below the poverty line, especially the Scheduled Castes, the Scheduled Tribes and the minorities. I request the Government to send an official team immediately to visit these areas.[79]

Critiquing the Government: Occasionally MPs of State Parties critiqued the government while making a suggestion. One such example is cited below. Though raised by a left member, a large number of state party MPs associated themselves with this Special Mention.

Basudeb Acharya: ".....the existing airports of Hyderabad and Bengaluru should not be closed down. The ESMA, which has been imposed by the Government, should be withdrawn and the Ministry should start negotiating with the unions for settlement of the issue and for redressal of the issue. The Government should reverse its decision to close down the existing airports of Hyderabad and Bengaluru.[80]

A qualitative analysis of discussions under Special Mention lead to the following conclusions:

Issues raised under Special Mention were largely local in nature. However, the articulation of issues often had an urban bias. The discussions during Special Mentions could reasonably be categorised as urban, since they appeared to be urban and technical interpretation of rural/local/constituency level issues. During all such discussions MPs also raised matters of national and international importance. However, the irrespective of whether the cleavage was along the lines of urban or rural, local, regional or national, State party MPs usually acted as 'representatives of the States' during Special Mentions. Its therefore not surprising that the ideology based parties made better use of this procedure. Thus, SHS MPs or AIFB members were seen to be more active than members of other parties.

Interestingly, each MP spoke on a matter on which he/she had developed specialisation over a period of time. Thus more experienced MPs, better educated MPs, older MPs and those with educational specialisation or associated with occupational participated more in these discussions. Generally, discussions under this procedure were held in a bipartisan environment and members across party lines spoke on a variety of issues .On matters in which the media or the public had strong opinions, or those which were controversial, a political stand and party bias was evident. Such discussions were also characterised by arguments and interruptions.

State Party MPs represented their socio- economic or occupational constituencies during these discussions. Members of minority communities and marginalised groups spoke in favor of such groups. In particular, it was observed that SC MPs were very active and raised issues relating to their social constituency while using this procedure. However, Women and ST MPs were not very active. Concerns of the rural population were clubbed with those of agriculturists and marginalised groups

All the suggestions that were made during these discussions were broad and devoid of specific details though they were constructive in nature. They were more in the nature of pointers to the government rather than specific inputs. This could be on account of nature of the procedure itself and limitations of time.Conversely, the need to be precise allowed for greater participation in this procedure, as it served the purpose of both representation and parliamentary efficiency.

Since the procedure allowed merely mention of issues, there were no substantial debates during Special Mentions. Hence, State party MPs found it convenient to raise broad constituency-level issues. Senior leaders of State Parties used this procedure occasionally. In all newly elected or less experienced members of State party MPs used this procedure to represent primarily local interest without little investment of time and energy.

State Party MPs participation in Parliamentary Business: Success of Federal and Democratic system?

A qualitative analysis of the deliberations of the 14th Lok Sabha gives an understanding of the qualitative nature of participation by State party MPs.

As is evident from the preceding discussion, State party MPs participated in all the proceedings of the House. However, their participation in Question Hour, Special Mentions and Discussion under 377 was more than in other procedures, not just in terms of number but also in terms of nature of issues raised and the extent of intervention.

New MPs, those from marginalised groups, Indian language speaking MPs looking for recognition, often participated through Special Mention, Resolutions and discussions under 377 which saw not only a large number of issues being raised, but a large participation in it as well. The popularity of such procedural devices may be attributed to the informality associated with it. Such deliberations were mere statements (mostly constructive) and the MPs used them to make broad suggestions without going into specifics as well as low investment that went into it in terms of time and effort. Further, such procedures did not lead to controversy, serious charges or criticisms and therefore the government was also open to them. Discussions during these procedures are amicable and no animosities - ideological or otherwise-were evident even when controversial issues were under consideration. The fact that these procedures have no boundaries either in terms of territory, or of interest (MP often raise constituency related issues), account for their popularity. Most importantly, the need of the MPs to represent the interests of the largest cross section to ensure re election and return to power contributes to participating in these proceedings which allows them the reputation of being "representative", "active" and interested" without any of the pitfalls and pains associated with it .

Though, raising matters of national and international importance was also not altogether absent. State party MPs made full use of these procedures to 'act as representatives'. They raised issues that were of fundamental importance from the point of identity, occupation and territory during these procedures. It may not be incorrect to conclude that these procedures have become primary instruments of participation for average members of State Parties. They are in fact today the heart of legislative process in India.

The popularity of such procedures, however, has transformed the Parliament from a deliberative institution and as a body that exercises uncompromising scrutiny over the activities of the government. The changing composition of the Lok Sabha, where there is greater presence of middle aged, educated but generalists members has also contributed to this kind of prioritizing of business. The State Parties have singularly contributed to this trend. "The lack of expertise that is needed to deal with complicated law making process" has contributed to such prioritisation across party lines.

What has also emerged from this study is that political parties invest little in training their members in the art of constructive deliberation, legislative scrutiny and oversight. Left to their own devices less experienced MPs of State Parties from have used those parliamentary procedures that allow them to register their presence as "representative" without seriously engaging in it.

Equally, what emerges from this study is that success of the parliamentary procedure in India depends on the possibility of the procedure to allow a member to voice sub-national level concerns to which an MP can relate and which they wish to represent because of the impact it has on their long term political career. A more robust functioning of Parliament would therefore require strengthening these. But, there is a cost attached to it and that is already evident in the decline of interest in Law making and scrutiny functions.

What is also interesting is that the membership of the national legislative institution seems to have a salutary effect on MPs of State Parties, notwithstanding their geographical and socio-economic support base; MPs of State Parties largely adopt a national perspective during the course of parliamentary business. Once elected to the national parliament, they do not necessarily regard themselves as the representatives of the State or the community that may have contributed to their election.

The perspective of the State party MPs on parliamentary participation is shaped by the three factors; first the demands of the electorate, second, the nature of issue being raised and the political situation. On a large number of issues, such as those relating to agriculture, setting up of industries, development of infrastructure, the State party MPs adopt a national perspective without losing sight of their local responsibilities. On others, MPs of State Parties go beyond merely representing their constituency. The large number of questions raised by them relating to environment, foreign policy, sports indicates that the state party MPs regard themselves as delegates interpreting the "public good" on behalf of the electorate. Given the fact that the electorate may not necessarily have either information to form opinion or a clear opinion of some of the issues, the role of State party MPs in this regard is of significance.

There can be little doubt about the fact that members of all political parties adopt a national, urban, gendered perspective of representation in the Lok Sabha. This is contrary to both the popularly held view as well as the expectations of the people that representatives of State Parties are more likely to adopt 'local' view. Whether this is on account of nationalisation of State Parties or localisation of State Parties can be a subject matter of debate.

There also appears to be little or no linkages between party manifesto, party ideology and legislative participation. State party MPs appear to act more like 'delegates' or spokespersons of the party. In performing these functions they are limited by their own social and economic background. Their own educational qualifications, places of residence, caste, and gender contribute in shaping their legislative participation. Thus, often it was observed that State party MPs adopted urban perspectives, or urban interpretation of rural problems undermining their attempts to act as representatives.

There may be two different approaches to view these developments. In the first place, such representation could be perceived as weakening the State Parties that emerged on regional sentiments and sub-national identities. They defeat the very purpose and objective for which they emerged and may ultimately lead to their collapse. It may also be interpreted as strengthening the political institutions at the central level which were conceived as instruments of national consensus building. It is possible to argue that the nature of national political institutions create conditions that are conducive for developing national perspectives and national consensus. The myriad State Parties, notwithstanding their origin, ideology, objectives and support base submerge their interest creating what may be termed as "national interest." In this, we search for success of both Indian federalism and Indian democracy.

References

Kumara, Pushpa, (2009). The Changing Nature of Party System in Chandhoke, Neera Priyadarshi, Praveen (eds), *Contemporary India*, New Delhi, Pearson, p. 267.

Prakash, Amit, (2013), Regionalism, Politics of Autonomy and Smaller States in Mehra Ajay (eds) Emerging Trends in Indian Politics, the 15th Lok Sabha Elections, p. 190.

Wahlang, Allanson. (2010), Analysis of Election Manifesto of Major Political Parties in India, 21st January, 2010, *Dalit and Tribe*, www. dalitandtribe.wordpress.com/2010/01/21/analysis-of-election-manifestos-of-major-political-parties-in-india/

Rao Sarraju Narasinga,(2014,) *Lok Sabha Elections 2014: The Anatomy of the Election Manifesto*, DNA, Mumbai,ww.dnaindia.com/analysis/standpoint-lok-sabha-elections-2014-the-anatomy-of-the-election-manifesto-1976723

Balaji, J. (2013) Parties Assert Right to Announce freebies in Election Manifestos, *The Hindu*, Chennai.

Kumar,Akshay (2009). Now, 'Silent' MPs irk Lok Sabha Speaker, *Hindustan Times* New Delhi, February 26, 2009http://www.hindustantimes.com/india-news/newdelhi/now-silent-mps-irk-lok-sabha-speaker/article1-383675.aspx

Notes

1. Discussions on price rise have witnessed widespread participation in the 15th Lok Sabha - 110 MPs from 26 political parties discussed the issue for 35 hours. In some recent sessions, the opposition has demanded an adjournment motion on the issue of price rise. The adjournment motion is a call to set aside the regular business of the House and take up a specific matter for discussion. Such a motion is voted upon, and if passed, is considered as censure against the government.
2. http://164.100.47.132/LssNew/psearch/Result14.aspx?dbsl=129
3. http://164.100.47.132/LssNew/psearch/Result14.aspx?dbsl=2253
4. http://164.100.47.132/LssNew/psearch/Result14.aspx?dbsl=5835
5. http://164.100.47.132/LssNew/psearch/Result14.aspx?dbsl=1864
6. http://164.100.47.132/LssNew/psearch/Result14.aspx?dbsl=1676
7. http://164.100.47.132/LssNew/psearch/Result14.aspx?dbsl=1199
8. http://164.100.47.132/LssNew/psearch/Result14.aspx?dbsl=8248
9. http://164.100.47.132/LssNew/psearch/Result14.aspx?dbsl=3202
10. http://164.100.47.132/LssNew/psearch/Result14.aspx?dbsl=3706
11. http://164.100.47.132/LssNew/psearch/Result14.aspx?dbsl=2200
12. http://164.100.47.132/LssNew/psearch/Result14.aspx?dbsl=1564
13. http://164.100.47.132/LssNew/psearch/Result14.aspx?dbsl=4221
14. http://164.100.47.132/LssNew/psearch/Result14.aspx?dbsl=4265
15. http://164.100.47.132/LssNew/psearch/Result14.aspx?dbsl=6779
16. http://164.100.47.132/LssNew/psearch/Result14.aspx?dbsl=2162
17. http://164.100.47.132/LssNew/psearch/Result14.aspx?dbsl=8562
18. http://164.100.47.132/LssNew/psearch/Result14.aspx?dbsl=7704
19. http://164.100.47.132/LssNew/psearch/Result14.aspx?dbsl=7536
20. http://164.100.47.132/LssNew/psearch/Result14.aspx?dbsl=4156
21. http://164.100.47.132/LssNew/psearch/Result14.aspx?dbsl=2253
22. http://164.100.47.132/LssNew/psearch/Result14.aspx?dbsl=3881
23. http://164.100.47.132/LssNew/psearch/Result14.aspx?dbsl=5144
24. http://164.100.47.132/LssNew/psearch/Result14.aspx?dbsl=4555
25. http://164.100.47.132/LssNew/psearch/Result14.aspx?dbsl=2609
26. http://164.100.47.132/LssNew/psearch/Result14.aspx?dbsl=468
27. http://164.100.47.132/LssNew/psearch/Result14.aspx?dbsl=5898
28. http://164.100.47.132/LssNew/psearch/Result14.aspx?dbsl=7431
29. http://164.100.47.132/LssNew/psearch/Result14.aspx?dbsl=4047

30. http://164.100.47.132/LssNew/psearch/Result14.aspx?dbsl=2511
31. http://164.100.47.132/LssNew/psearch/Result14.aspx?dbsl=2757
32. http://164.100.47.132/LssNew/psearch/Result14.aspx?dbsl=84
33. http://164.100.47.132/LssNew/psearch/Result14.aspx?dbsl=10651
34. http://164.100.47.132/LssNew/psearch/Result14.aspx?dbsl=2671
35. http://164.100.47.132/LssNew/psearch/Result14.aspx?dbsl=10360
36. http://164.100.47.132/LssNew/psearch/Result14.aspx?dbsl=8791
37. http://164.100.47.132/LssNew/psearch/Result14.aspx?dbsl=8504
38. http://164.100.47.132/LssNew/psearch/Result14.aspx?dbsl=2561
39. http://164.100.47.132/LssNew/psearch/Result14.aspx?dbsl=8504
40. http://164.100.47.132/LssNew/psearch/Result14.aspx?dbsl=5737
41. http://164.100.47.132/LssNew/psearch/Result14.aspx?dbsl=1255
42. http://164.100.47.132/LssNew/psearch/Result14.aspx?dbsl=9652
43. http://164.100.47.132/LssNew/psearch/Result14.aspx?dbsl=9959
44. http://164.100.47.132/LssNew/psearch/Result14.aspx?dbsl=2390
45. http://164.100.47.132/LssNew/psearch/Result14.aspx?dbsl=182
46. M.Shivanna, chamrajnagar, JD(U)http://164.100.47.132/LssNew/psearch/Result14.aspx?dbsl=4896
47. Ahmad, Shri Ateeq, SP, UP/ Phulpurhttp://164.100.47.132/LssNew/psearch/Result14.aspx?dbsl=80
48. Prabhunath Sigh (JD(U)http://164.100.47.132/LssNew/psearch/Result14.aspx?dbsl=9575
49. M.Shivanna, chamrajnagar, JD(U http://164.100.47.132/LssNew/psearch/Result14.aspx?dbsl=5618
50. Prabhunath Sigh (JD(U)http://164.100.47.132/LssNew/psearch/Result14.aspx?dbsl=8882
51. Yerrain Naidu, Srikakulam, Andhra Pradesh, TDP, http://164.100.47.132/LssNew/psearch/Result14.aspx?dbsl=6758
52. M.Jaganath, Andhra Pradesh, TDP http://164.100.47.132/LssNew/psearch/Result14.aspx?dbsl=860
53. Yerrain Naidu, Srikakulam, Andhra Pradesh, TDP, http://164.100.47.132/LssNew/psearch/Result14.aspx?dbsl=5176
54. Yerrain Naidu, Srikakulam, Andhra Pradesh, TDP, http://164.100.47.132/LssNew/psearch/Result14.aspx?dbsl=7384
55. Yerrain Naidu, Srikakulam, Andhra Pradesh, TDP http://164.100.47.132/LssNew/psearch/Result14.aspx?dbsl=10168
56. M.Shivanna, Chamrajnagar, Karnataka, JD(U), http://164.100.47.132/LssNew/psearch/Result14.aspx?dbsl=9361
57. M.Shivanna, Chamrajnagar, Karnataka, JD(U), http://164.100.47.132/LssNew/psearch/Result14.aspx?dbsl=6401
58. M.Shivanna, Chamrajnagar, Karnataka, JD(U), http://164.100.47.132/LssNew/psearch/Result14.aspx?dbsl=7103

59. M.Shivanna, Chamrajnagar, Karnataka, JD(U), http://164.100.47.132/LssNew/psearch/Result14.aspx?dbsl=5056
60. M.Shivanna, Chamrajnagar, Karnataka, JD(U), http://164.100.47.132/LssNew/psearch/Result14.aspx?dbsl=6148
61. M.Shivanna, Chamrajnagar, Karnataka, JD(U), http://164.100.47.132/LssNew/psearch/Result14.aspx?dbsl=8023
62. rates - http://164.100.47.132/LssNew/psearch/result14.aspx?dbsl=10182
63. http://164.100.47.132/LssNew/psearch/result14.aspx?dbsl=3226
    http://164.100.47.132/LssNew/psearch/result14.aspx?dbsl=3834
64. http://mpa.nic.in/chapter7.htm
65. http://mpa.nic.in/chapter1.htm
66. http://mpa.nic.in/chapter1.htm
67. http://mpa.nic.in/chapter1.htm
68. Lok Sabha Debates
69. On 25.2.2009 http://164.100.47.132/lssnew/psearch/result14.aspx?dbsl=11268
70. On 18.12. 2008 http://164.100.47.132/lssnew/psearch/result14.aspx?dbsl=10859
71. Shri A.K.S. Vijayan, Shrimati Bhavani Rajenthiran and Shri K.C. Pallanishamy are allowed to associate on this issue; On 22.10.2008
72. http://164.100.47.132/lssnew/psearch/result14.aspx?dbsl=6358 on 8.8.2006
73. On 22 .2.2009, http://164.100.47.132/lssnew/psearch/result14.aspx?dbsl=11245
74. Sarnjit Singh Dhillon (SAD) on 22nd June 2006 (http://164.100.47.132/lssnew/psearch/result14.aspx?dbsl=5561)
75. http://164.100.47.132/lssnew/psearch/result14.aspx?dbsl=9847, 25.8.2004
76. http://164.100.47.132/lssnew/psearch/result14.aspx?dbsl=664 on 16.7.2004
77. Lok Sabha Debates 22nd August, 2008, http://164.100.47.132/lssnew/psearch/result14.aspx?dbsl=8341
78. http://164.100.47.132/lssnew/psearch/result14.aspx?dbsl=8046 on 15.7.2007
79. http://164.100.47.132/lssnew/psearch/result14.aspx?dbsl=936, 8.12.2004
80. Dr. Babu Rao Mediam, Shri Prahlad Joshi, m04 Shri Ananth Kumar, m05 Shri Sunil Khan, m06 Shri Amitava Nandy, m07 Shri Samik Lahiri, m08 Shri Chandrakant Khaire, m09 Shri Mohan Singh, m10 Shri Gurudas Dasgupta and m11 Shri Ajoy Chakraborty are allowed to associate with this matter.
    On 13.3. 2008 64.100.47.132/lssnew/psearch/result14.aspx?dbsl=10005

Chapter - 7

Conclusion: Alternative Imagination?

State Parties are not a new phenomenon in Indian politics. The anti-Brahmin movement in the pre and early post independent India which resulted in creation of Dravidian parties such as the DMK and AIADMK in the south, and the Akali Dal which represented the Sikh community in the politics of Punjab have a long history of existence. Similarly, the movement for Telugu Pride in 1980s and the issue of Marathi identity in 1970s resulted in emergence of TDP and the SHS. However, the influence of State Parties till the 70s was confined to the states or the regions to which they belonged.

The political landscape of India changed somewhat, when the Janata Party government which was a coalition of major State Parties forayed at the national level. The Akali Dal, a prominent regional party of Punjab and the DMK of Tamil Nadu were a part of the Janata Government. This was the first time that regional parties shared power at the national level. However, the Janata experiment was short lived. It lasted for less than two years under two Prime Ministers. It was anti-Congress sentiments and the travails of emergency in 1977 that held the parties of Janata coalition together. Once the impact of the binding factor began to wane the difference between parties resurfaced and undid the coalition. Thus, the Janata experience had little impact on the national progress of State Parties.

However, the National Front government that came to power in 1989 was an important landmark in the growing prominence of regional forces. Both in terms of ideology and leadership, the National Front government was only partially regional, as the Janata Dal which formed the government was a national party, and V.P. Singh who led the government was a leader of national standing. As a former Finance Minister in the Congress government, he represented less regional and more national perspective

Even though the coalition experiments till 1996 had given way the United Front (UF) government in 1996 first underscored the centrality of

State Parties at national politics. (Palshikar: 2000). In the 11th Lok Sabha 137 MPs belonging to various regional parties were elected. Most regional parties of the time were against the BJP, while many of them were formed by disgruntled Congressmen. They formed a front comprising of non-Congress and non-BJP parties under the name of United Front. Ninety Five of the 137 MPs belonged to regional parties in the UF coalition. This, for the first time, gave rise to the impression that regional parties were occupying the 'third' space-outside of Congress and BJP poles.

Since 1996, State Parties occupied important positions in national politics till 2014, though most of the State Parties have gravitated towards the Congress or the BJP or occasionally tried to form an independent third front. India's famed 'one party dominant system'(Kotahri,1970)[1] had given way to what has been referred to as bi- nodal party system (Arora, 2012)[2], with the Congress and the BJP leading a constellation of state/regional parties. The growing popularity of the State Parties was reflected in the increasing number and influence of the parties not just at the state level but also at the national level and this trend has been shown in the table below.

Table 7.1: Performance of State and National Parties; 1989-2009

Year	*State Parties*		*National Parties*	
	Seats	*Vote Share*	*Seats*	*Vote Share*
1989	27	9.28	471	79.34
1991	51	13.08	478	80.58
1996	129	22.43	403	69.08
1998	101	18.97	387	67.98
1999	158	26.93	369	67.11
2004	159	28.90	364	62.89
2009	146	28.4	376	63.58

Source: Election Commission of India, *Statistical Report on the General Elections to the Lok Sabha*, First to the Fifteenth Lok Sabha, 1952-2009, (1990, 1991, 1996, 1998,1999, 2004, 2009, New Delhi)

As seen in Table 7. 1 the number of State Parties that contested the elections increased from 27 in the 1989 Lok Sabha to 146 in the 2009. Their vote share also increased by 20 percent while that of national parties declined by 13 percent in the period between 1989 and 2004 indicating a rise in the popularity of State Parties.

With conspicuous changes being observed, the 2004-2009 period marked the high point of parliamentary ascendency of State Parties. The fourteenth Lok Sabha had 158 MPs (maximum) members from State Parties and their vote share too stood at an all- time high of 28.9 percent. Taking into account all the by-elections to the Lok Sabha seats, 173 MPs became a part of the 14th Lok sabha. They were elected from across the country comprising all five regions of the country, with maximum representation from the North. They enjoyed support and recognition similar to that of national parties and emerged as active and prominent actors in Indian politics since then.

The success of State Parties may be attributed to a series of factors; the decline of the Congress and its failure to accommodate local interest, emergence of new political elite, democratisation of the political process, etc. However, perhaps the most important factor in the rising influence of regional parties has been their success in mobilizing the electorate. They have politicized and mobilised newer forces in Indian society, on multiple cleavages of language, religion, caste, identity, ethnicity, regional pride, development and demands of autonomy and have brought them within them folds of electoral democracy. In the process, these parties democratized Indian politics.

The Parliament has provided the State Parties a platform to represent and respond to their support base and gain national recognition, in turn paving the way for multiplying their influence and increasing their support base. It has also provided them with a unique opportunity to chart the course of the nation, redefine political and institutional representation and pave the way for further democratisation.

The growing influence of State Parties at the national level has altered the nature of Indian democracy in many ways; from a centralised, one party dominant system India with low to medium level of participation and weakly developed structures of negotiations, it has become a more decentralised, federal and multi-party coalition with high level of electoral participation. This tectonic shift in India's party system was boosted by the Economic liberalisation of 1991 which opened up the economy to foreign investments and paved the way for large scale private sector participation and gave the states a greater stake in attracting FDI. This in turn led to power flowing down, to the state level with a large number of State Parties competing for power (Mishra,2009).[3]

On the other hand, for the electorate the nature of political choice now varies from state to state. At the national level, the contest was between two coalitions, each with a large constellation of state based parties and states became the 'locale' of Indian politics and propellers of development and democratisation. Accordingly, it appeared, at least till the rise of BJP in 2014 that national politics was an aggregation of multiple state-level contests (Tillian, 2014).[4]

The growth of State Parties has altered the manner in which political decision-making takes place. Stake in national governments had given the state leaders an opportunity to influence decision-making, democratizing the political leadership and language of discourse. While detractors criticized the instability and opportunism that came to fore, it was clear that the centre point of Indian politics had shifted. Indian democracy was no longer an elite project, superimposed by a patronizing leadership. It had found its roots.

Who Supports State Parties?

But an important question remained unanswered: who were the supporters of the regional parties, why did they support them? And did the MPs of regional parties reflect the aspirations of newly politicized supporters.

Our study showed that the support base of State Parties came largely from lower castes, lower income groups and those with lower level of education. Support for State Parties declines as we moved up the social, educational and economic ladder.

The NES 2004 data indicated that nearly half of the voters (41 %) had a propensity to support regional political parties. A caste wise disaggregation of the data revealed that among those who supported regional political parties, 37 % i.e. more than a third were from OBC's. In contrast the national parties got the support of 31% of OBCs; 17% Dalits support State Parties, whereas 12 % of Muslims voters supported regional parties.

Similarly, the support for State Parties was more amongst the non-literate and the poorer sections of the society. Of those who supported regional political parties two fifths were non-literate, one-fifth had primary and one-fifth matriculate level of education.

In terms of income standard, three quarters of those who voted for regional political parties were from lower economic background as per the data. In constituencies were the state party candidates won the elections, the support group consisted of 72% from the lower income groups, 80% of less educated and 38 % of the OBCs. These are broad generalisations and do not unravel local factors that vary region to region and determine support for a party. The supporters of each regional party is unique in some ways, but a series of factors determine the nature of party competition.

1. ***The number of parties in the state***: The number of State Parties that compete in a state determine the nature of support base of a party. In some states there exist only one state party (Assam, states of North East) and therefore there is a consolidation of votes in favour of the party, while in others there exist more than one state party (Bihar, Tamil Nadu). In many such cases, like Tamilnadu where DMK, MDMK and AIADMK compete, the support base of all the regional parties was similar to each other indicating a split of votes amongst them. Herein, the personality of the candidate was a significant determinant in characterizing the support base of the parties. In some states like Bihar for instance, where many State Parties competed, each party attempted to mobilize a certain core group of voters (RJD and JDU).
2. ***Nature of Party Competition in the State***: In many states such as Kerala and Meghalaya, the parties are coalitional in nature. Hence, there is a consolidation of support in favour of the one or other coalition. The support from the marginalised group of voters went to the winning coalition. The nature support base varied in such states as compared to states which have straight contests.
3. ***Socio-Economic Composition of the State Population***: The support base of State Parties is also determined by the socio-economic and demographic profile of the states. States such as UP, Bihar and MP which have a large population belonging to traditionally marginalised groups such as OBCs and STs the support for State Parties from these groups has been greater.

   Thus, the support base of political parties is reflective of the population of the state, its level of economic development and level of educational attainment.
4. ***Ideology of Party***: In some states like Bengal and Kerala ideology is an important determinant of the support base. The socio-economically marginalised parties that have leaned to left of the centre, are often more popular than State Parties with different ideology.
5. ***Experience/Age of the Party***: Older and established parties have greater support across groups than younger State Parties. This is on account of the experience of the party and its members and their longer presence in the political scenario. Such parties are seen inspiring confidence among the voters.

We can identify certain group of parties, which share similar support base and characteristics, and they were categorised into groups below.

Group I: AGP, SP, DMK, AIADMK, PMK, MDMK, JD(U), RJD, KEC, TMC

- Mostly Splinter groups of the Congress or born out split in the ranks of the Congress Party
- Centrist ideology
- Articulates regional interests largely in terms of identity and demand for autonomy
- Support base similar to that of the Congress

Group II: JD(S), BJD, TDP

- Centrist ideology
- Articulates regional concerns in developmental terms
- Greater acceptability among the middle class
- Has support across groups

Group III: J&KPDP, J&KNC, MNF, NPF, SHS, Akali Dal

- Regional and religious ideology
- Focus more on local issues
- Have varies support base

While the parties grouped above show certain similarities, each group and each party has a distinctive support base.

Table 7.1: State Parties and their Support base

AIADMK	OBCs and SCs	lesser educated voters	Low Income category
MDMK	OBCs and SCs	intermediate level of education	***Poor***
PMK	STs and OBCs	non literates	***High Income***
AGP	BCS and STs,	moderate to high level of education	***All Income groups***
RJD	lower OBC	Educated voters (PGs) and non literates..	very low income category voters (21.2%)
SP	OBCs and SCs	non -literate and	lower income group voters.
TMC	SCs/OBCs. it is also popular amongst the upper castes	balanced, though it has slightly higher level of support from non - literates too	and lower income groupd, the high income group and urban population.
TDP	OBC &ST		low and high income groups
BJD	upper castes and the OBCs	well-educated voters.	of illiterates and the well-educated voters

(Contd...)

Category III			
Shiv Sena	Maratha caste and OBCs	moderately / less educated voters	lower and very low income groups
PDP	OBCs	moderate to high level of education	all income categories except the high income groups
NC	SC and ST,	are less educatedand those with the High income.	are less educatedand those with the High income.
MNF	SC	moderately educated voters as well as that of graduates	uniformly across income group highest coming from among the very low income group (45%).
NPF	ST	higher levels of education.	all income categories and especially for the higher income categories
SDF	OBC		low income group.
JMM	OBC, ST	non-literates, with primary level of education	very low and low income group.

Why Support State Parties?

Supporters across groups preferred State Parties to national parties on account of its perceived proximity to the people. The approachability of their candidates and their connect with the people on account of their personal contact and understanding of local issues and problems and their ability of speak the local language and understand local customs, traditions and problems contributed to developing a trust.

Voters expected state party MPs to represent their problems and seek redress. Hence, the expectations of the supporters of State Parties was more in the nature of service and functional representation as the expectation of the voters was not different from that of national parties, however the degree of expectation varied. It appeared that, State Parties had succeeded in developing a trust amongst their supporters and seemed to be better in symbolic representation, which has been described by scholars as follows:

> The representational relationship is not... one of such concrete transactions, but also one that is built on trust and confidence expressed in the support that the represented give to the representative and to which he responds by symbolic, significant gestures, in order to, in turn, generate and maintain continuing support
>
> Irrespective of level of institutional structures, voters expected state party MPs to represent them and representation was interpreted as an "activity" that ensued concrete measurable gains both in terms of 'presence' in the institutional structure as well as policy outcomes and

material gains. The voters demanded both symbolic representation and policy responsiveness. In view of this understanding the table and section below looks into the nature of representation with respect to State Parties.

Who Are State Party MPs?

Table 7.2: Socio-economic Profile of MP's of State Parties in the Fourteenth Lok Sabha

Age	*State Parties (%)*	*All India (%)*
25-45	*32.12*	25.67
46-65	*60.73*	59.43
66 and above	*12.00*	14.48
Education		
Under Graduates	*16.5*	21.17
Graduate	*46.5*	45.85
Post Graduates	*33.8*	31.12
Occupation		
Lawyers	5.7	13.6
Agriculturists	37.4	41
Social & Political workers	*14.4*	*20*

Source: Profiles of Members of Parliament.

The study found that (Table 7.2) a large majority of the MPs of State Parties were middle aged. Nearly 61 % MP's were in the age group of 46-65 years. This is almost similar to that of an all India average. Nearly three quarters of all the MPs of Lok Sabha were either graduates or postgraduates. The MP's of State Parties possessed slightly higher academic qualifications with specialisations than that of national parties, especially, the percentage of postgraduates amongst them was higher than that of national parties. This kind of high educational standards may be indicative of the dominations of leadership position by the educated elite and their desire to influence the political process, directly.

In occupational terms, nearly 37% of MP's of State Parties were agriculturists. This was lower than that of the national average which stood at 41%. A large percentage of members were also involved in social work however, nearly 65% members of State Parties were from broadly four professional groups which are lawyers, agriculturists, social and political workers.

On the other hand, the asset base of MP's of the State Parties was large, though the national parties have far richer members. Thus, majority of the 315 MPs of Lok Sabha who were Crorepatis in 2009 were from national parties. Of the 315 Crorepati MP's in 2009, 226 belonged to national parties. The State Parties had a lesser number of Crorepati MP's standing at 86. Of the total membership of national parties, 61% of MP's were Crorepatis and nearly 39.5 % of State Parties belonged to the same category. If assests were correlated of the members with their occupation, it would appear that while some of the MP's of State Parties, particularly such as those of RJD, SP derived their wealth from agriculture, others indicated business or professions at the source of their earning.

Speaking of assets, the average asset of MP's of some State Parties like BSP, SAD, BJD, TDP, DMK was far more than some of the national parties like the BJP and CPI. The education as well as the income/ asset base of members of State Parties clearly indicated that the leadership of the State Parties belong to the educationally and economic elite amongst the marginalised sections of the society. In fact, parties such as the BSP and SP which claim to espouse the cause of the Dalits in North India have far more educated and affluent members than that of the Congress. Within this broader trend however, it is possible to identify regional variations.

Representatives of State Parties of North and Hindi Heartland

State Parties of Northern India and Hindi heartland including the states of Punjab (SAD), Uttar Pradesh (SP), Bihar (RJD, LJSP) and Jharkhand (JMM) consisted of members who are older and middle aged and highly educated (79%) with specialisation in humanities (47%). Professionally majority of them are lawyers and derive their income from agriculture (46%) and related occupations. The number of social and political workers from these parties was also large. The MP's of such parties have large asset base and belong to what may be referred to as the upper middle class. These parties also consisted of a large number of members (12%) who have intermediary levels of education. Although these parties are products of democratic upsurge and assertion of the backward castes in politics, their members are moderately elite measured in terms of education. A large number of the members of these parties belong to what may be referred to as other backward castes.

Representatives of State Parties of South

The State Parties of the South consisted of members who are younger. The average level of their education though high (80%) was lower than that of the parties of East. Their MP's have varied in terms of educational specialisation. While 10/37 members were law graduates, 8 had specialised in engineering, medicine, science and commerce and 8 in humanities. These parties too had a large number of MP's with intermediate level of education (16%). They belonged to the class of business person, traders and industrialists. Nearly a fifth of them were businessmen and traders with and another one-fifth of them were lawyers, teachers, engineers. One third of them are agriculturist.

Representatives of State Parties of East and North East

The number of State party representatives from East and North East is few (BJD, AITC, AIFB, SDF, MNF and AGP). The BJD is the largest State party from the east with a considerable legislative presence. But for the BJD, AIFB and AGP almost all the parties of this region have only one member in the Lok Sabha. Hence, it is difficult to generalize about them. However, a few features of the State Parties of East and Northeast are amply evident. These parties have older members and more experienced members. They are also more educated (17/20 members) and have almost negligible presence of members with lower levels of education. They have greater presence of middle class professionals, social workers and almost no presence of businessmen. A large number of them are also teachers.

Representatives of State Party of West

There is only one part in Western India, namely the Shiv Sena which has a significant presence in the Lok Sabha. In terms of the socio-economic profile of the members the Shiv Sena shares similarity with the parties of the South, with some variations. The members of this party are younger than their southern counterparts and less educated. In all other respects, (educational specialisation, occupation and assets), they are similar to that of the southern State Parties.

The membership of State Parties indicates a regional pattern in the evolution of political process. It would appear from the data that the process of democratisation (entry of intermediary caste members with intermediate levels of education) is a little ahead in the south than from that of the north. If the representation of State Parties in the legislature is any indication of the party structure, the State Parties of north are predominantly led by intermediate caste, agricultural community, which may be categorised as middle class with high level of education and asset base. In particular, lawyers of north have particular inclination towards politics.

The parties of south and west on the other hand have evolved into institutions that provide institutional support to intermediary caste members of business community with median levels of education. The educated and social elite of middle classes have abjured from participation in the political process, given their numerical inferiority. They have however, tried to influence the political process from other institutions such as the bureaucracy.

This indicates the domination of State Parties by younger, & middle aged, educated, affluent elite. While some of them may have had backward caste origins, they neither socially nor economically marginalised. Majority of them had access to higher education and professional degree's. They were also experienced or reputed members of State Parties, making a transition from state level to national level politics, looking to influence it on their terms.

Such a development indicates three things: first, the continued domination of political institutions by educated, middle class, political elite, across party lines is indicative of the domination of the political process by the 'elite' through state politics and regional political parties. The domination of national parties by the entrenched elite made it difficult for the emerging elite to make inroads into the institutions through established political parties. But, State Parties have provided better opportunities of political recruitment for the emerging political elite.

Second, the development is indicative of a larger and more important trend in Indian politics which is the emergence of states as the epicenter of political contestation in India. The performance of the elite at the state level determines their fate at the national level. Thus, emerging political elite appear to have found entry into the system at the state level through local parties and have then made gradual transition to the national level. The transition to the national level however, has not altered the nature of representative.

State Parties and Participation in Legislative Business

An interesting question is whether MPs of State Parties, given their social and economic background perform their work in their Parliament similarly? Are there dissimilarities, if so what and why. This study showed that MPs of State Parties were as interested as MP's of national parties in parliamentary work. Their work was not qualitatively different from that of national parties. Since the procedure of Parliament is fixed, one could only think of differences in terms of time spent or nature of issues raised. Within the broader framework, the state party MPs showed greater interest in debates and in discussions under less formal discussions such as Special Mention and discussions under rule 377. However, the performance of members may be distinguished along the following lines:

Age of the Party and Experience of the Members: Both in case of Debates and Question Hour old and established State Parties, with larger membership outperformed the newer and smaller State Parties. MP's of parties that have larger number of members, or are established and have long political history showed greater interest in parliamentary work. Thus, for instance, State Parties such as the BJD, DMK, SP, RJD and SHS and JD (U) have not only better average attendance but also raise a larger number of questions. Their participation in parliamentary debates is also better than State Parties which have smaller number of members. The only exception to this is that of the AIFB whose members have shown considerable interest in parliamentary work despite their small numbers.

Party Ideology & discipline Matters: The ideology and the discipline of the party organisation seem to have had a salutary effect on the extent and nature of participation of MPs in the Lok Sabha. Our study indicates that ideology driven parties such as SHS, AIFB are more oriented towards legislative participation. Often members of such parties are regular participants in Question Hour and legislative debates.

Age & Education of the Members: Young and inexperienced MPs across party lines show keen interest in participation in legislative process mainly through Question Hour. The older and more educated members of State Parties choose legislative debates, while inexperienced and less educated members are often in search of parliamentary exposure and experience and hence they choose less formal procedures such as Special Mentions and discussions under Rule 377. On the other hand, older MPs, post graduates, graduates, lawyers, teachers and Women prefer to use Debates as the a means of intervention.

Occupation determines the choice of Legislative Procedures: Those with lesser educational qualifications, social workers, teachers, agriculturists, SC MPs of State Parties were more inclined towards the use of Question Hour. Lawyers preferred to participate through legislative debates and those with technical qualifications participated in Debates and Question Hour whereas generalist prefer to participate through less formal procedures of the House.

Personal characteristics have Role to Play: Personal characteristics of MPs have a bearing on the level of participation. The most active MPs of State Parties included those who are middle aged MPs (age group of 46-55 years)

- Better educated MPs and
- Lawyers and teachers
- male and
- SC MPs (Together)

Similarly, the nature of the party, its location, its organisational structure and leadership also played a role in determining the extent of participation. Greater interest in legislative business was generally from the following categories of parties:

- Parties of Eastern region
- Parties with greater legislative presences
- Ideology based Parties (Together)

Low level of Participation: Though the interest of state party MPs in parliamentary business is slightly more than that of national party members, not more than 10% MP's of state party MP's ever participated in the sessions of the 14th Lok Sabha, while these 10 percent varied from year to year.

Reflections on MPs Interpretation of Representation

The nature and extent of participation of state party MPs were determined by a series of factor including whether they were a part of the government or opposition, the ideology of the party, the importance that the party attached to legislative participation, the party's need for publicity, the personality, the age and the experience of the members and his/her familiarly with the issues that were being discussed.

In relation, the participation of MPs of State Parties took the following forms:

- *Support for Government Policy and Suggestions for Improvement*: The support of some of the MPs of State Parties to the government was in the form of support for the policies initiated by them. Such support was based on merits of the issue and facts that draft bills contained. The participants of such debates were State Parties of ruling coalition. However, sometimes MPs of State Parties like BJD also supported the policy despite their alliance with the main opposition party.

- *Support for Coalition Leaders/ Leadership*: MPs also used legislative debates to display support to the leaders of their own party and the government.
- *Critiquing the Opposition*: Interestingly MPs used the debates as an opportunity not just to critique the government or its policies but also the opposition. This indicated the fragmentation of the State Parties.
- *Critiquing the Government*: Legislative debates were used as an opportunity by MPs of opposition parties, both national and state to critique the government.

Based on the forms of participation the following section points out the nature of issues that were raised. The questions raised by the State Parties on the floor of the House during the 14th Lok Sabha covered a far wider gamut of subjects. While some issues such as price rise and atrocities on minorities and backward classes were old, others dealt with newer issues such as water pollution, environmental degradation, viable of renewable energy resources, functioning of private airlines, etc. The wide array of subjects addressed in the House has thus been summarised to show the trends pertaining to State Parties in the House.

Development a Prime Concern: A study of nature of discussion during legislative debates and questions that were raised by MPs of State Parties indicated that development of infrastructure, industries and health and education related issues were the most frequently issues by state party. In this context, it may be pointed out the drinking water, and unemployment were amongst the most important issues that concerned the electorate. In particular, questions relating to railways elicited attention of the MPs.

Urban Development: Administrative issues, agriculture, finance and issues of urban and rural development also figured prominently in the questions raised by MPs of State Parties.

Not Much on Price Rise and Corruption: Price rise and law and order which figured highly in the list of concerns of the electorate however, did not figure very prominently in the Question Hour. This is interesting in view of the fact that price rise has often been a major electoral issue and structured discussions on price rise are usually taken up under Rule 193 in Lok Sabha. Under these rules, a short duration discussion can be initiated on any subject. However, these rules do not provide for any formal voting in the House.[5] Similarly, issues of corruption did not figure prominently in the Question Hour.

National Issues with a Local Twist: In the first place, MP's of State Parties raised larger number of question that may be considered national rather than local in orientation. This may be interesting in view of the fact that most State Parties are limited to the states. They do not have clearly stated public positions as far as national issues are concerned. Their election manifestoes too do not indicate their stand on host of issues relating to national issues. However, as members of national legislatures, State Parties MPs adopted a more national orientation.

Some Issues are necessarily National, Others Local: Some subtends in this broader trend also become note worthy. Firstly, questions relating to some subjects were raised with a national orientation while others were necessarily local in their orientation. Issues relating to law and order, agriculture, calamities assumed a more federal orientation. On the other hand, demands for funds grant of new projects often attempted to amalgamate state concerns with that of constituency concerns. Similarly, all foreign policy questions and those relating to security had an international orientation.

Apart from questions that explicitly aimed at ensuring governmental accountability the members of the Lok Sabha also used the Question Hour to perform representative functions. The questions that aimed at representation assumed one or all of the three forms:

- Airing the Grievances of the constituency
- Securing concessions for the constituents

Correcting imbalances in the distribution of resources that may have occurred on account of party politics.

Members also represented their territorial, constituency or their occupational constituency. The MPs raised issues relating to the state from which they were elected. Similarly, occupation of the members also influenced the nature of questions asked. Most members who proposed agriculture-related questions represented the concerns of the agriculturalists of their constituencies. Women members usually spoke on issues relating to health, family planning, education etc, in the sample chosen for study. Party lines were rather blurred in such discussions and members made an attempt to portray themselves as their representatives.

The predominant language used during the Question Hour was English, though there was use of Hindi also. The members of the "Hindi Belt" spoke in Hindi and those from the east; west or south of the country spoke mostly in English.

The importance that members attached to the debates varied with the issues that were discussed. Debates on financial issues, or during the presence of the Prime Minister issues appeared to be serious deliberations on policy matters. Members seemed to attempt to seek clarification from the Minister, criticized government policies, and demanded to know policy choices and implications with respect to their constituencies. The questions were usually precise and the answers were to the point. Discussions on agriculture, irrigation, etc. appeared to be carried out in emotionally charged atmosphere but such discussions appeared to lack precision. Most of the opposition members gave long speeches relating to the background of the question before asking the question as such which led to many interruptions because of the impatience of the ruling party MPs with such long speeches. On the other hand, the debates on domestic issues were characterised by greater criticism of government policies and on matters of foreign policy there appeared to be greater consensus among members.

Interruptions and Walkouts: In the 14th Lok Sabha, the Question Hour was frequently interrupted and the Lok Sabha debates recorded nearly 40 interruptions on an average during a single day. The members of the Opposition staged walkouts twice in the study period of thirty days. The Speaker had to adjourn the House on more than one occasion owing to unruly behaviour of the members. Interruptions in the House during the Question Hour took place due to one or more of the following reasons as mentioned below:

- Dissatisfactory or inadequate response by the concerned Minister.
- Absence of the concerned Minister during the debate on the issue in the House.
- Failure of a member to raise questions effectively.
- Attempts of a member to shower accolade on his/ her party and criticize the other.
- Extraneous factors, such as weakness of the government, doubts regarding its continuance.
- Decision of the Speaker to disallow a member from speaking.

State Parties and Participation in Less Formal Discussions of the House

An interesting feature of the legislative participation of MP's of State Parties was their keenness to make use of devices such as discussions under Rule 377, Special Mentions. MP's of State Parties were found to use this device more frequently than larger national parties. New MPs, those from marginalised groups and Indian language speaking MPs looking for recognition often participated through Special Mention, Resolutions and discussions under Rule 377 which saw not only are large number of issues being raised, but a large participation in it as well. This may be on account of a host of factors such as "informal nature of discussion during such procedure, greater flexibility, involvement of less time and preparation, etc."[6]. Most importantly, the need of the MPs to represent the interests of the largest cross section to ensure re-election and return to power has contributes to participating in these proceedings which make allows them the reputation of being "representative", "active" and "interested" without any of the pitfalls and pains associated with it .

Though, raising matters of national and international importance was also not altogether absent, state party MPs made full use of these procedures to 'act as representatives'. They raised issues that were of fundamental importance from the point of identity, territory, occupation or caste during these procedures. However, it may not be incorrect to conclude that these procedures have become primary instruments of participation for average members of State Parties. They are in fact today the heart of legislative process in India

However, the fact that such procedures involved minimal effort in terms of time and effort on the part of the MPs and allowed members to represent local issues and thereby be recognised by peers and constituents accounted for the popularity of such procedures. But, most discussions under Rule 377 went beyond the constituency and were related to states from which the MP was elected. Based on this the following section highlights the key features that dominated state participation in the House.

Focus on State: The subject matter of discussion was usually local and pertained to the state from where the MP was elected. They were couched in general language and related to the larger issue of the state rather than the constituency or their specific support group. Members of State Parties used the opportunity of deliberation to establish their position as delegates of the states to which they belonged. Neither functional representation nor symbolic representation seemed to determine the approach of the MP's ***Occupational Bias***: The study found that most discussions under Rule 377 were related to agriculture. Apart from agriculturists, the MP's of State Parties also used the procedure to raise large number of issues relating to the marginalised communities particularly,

SCs and ST's. Discussions relating to health, environment and price rise in the form of inflation in the prices of certain commodities also found mention during the procedure. ***Regional Bias: MP's*** of Southern and North-Eastern states often raised issues relating to preserving the language of their state. They were also more keen on raising issues of autonomy and development.

Urban Bias: Though related to the state/constituency, the issues often had an urban bias and could reasonably be categorised as urban.

Rural – Agricultural Synonimity: In all the discussions that the MPs of State Parties participated in the issues related to rural population were always clubbed with those of agriculturists and marginalised groups.

Representing Multiple Constituencies: State Party MP's were seen representing their geographical, socio- economic or occupational constituencies. Members of minority communities, marginalised groups spoke in favor of such groups. In particular, it was observed that Scheduled Caste MP's were very active and raised issues relating to their social constituency, while using this procedure. Women and Scheduled Tribe MPs' were not very active and they did not always appear to raise gender related issues.

Representing the Party & State: MP's of State Parties also used the opportunity of informal discussion to raise federal issues. In all such discussions a party line was also visible and the stand taken by the MPs was largely determined by the party.

Representing Dominant Groups: A large number of State party MP's represented the concerns of dominant groups. Given the strong agricultural background of MPs of State Parties the interest agriculturist's found significant mention. However, what is interesting is the representation of interests of industrialist's. During informal discussions of the House, MPs of State Parties took up the cause of industrialists in general and agro industrialists in particular. These discussions were often couched in the language of development and welfare for a state.

However, suggestions that were made were broad and devoid of specifics. They were more in the nature of pointers to the government on account of the nature of the procedure. It may also be that the requirement of being short and precise allowed for greater participation in this procedure.

State Parties Functioning in Bounded Democracy?

The support for the State Parties is largely on account of their ability to focus on the local/regional issues. In addition to this a major factor that has contributed to their success is their affinity to local population, approachability of their MPs, sense of identity with such parties on the basis of issues they espouse and the language of their political discourse. However, such parties (without exception) do not appear to be sociologically representative of their support group. While a chasm between the representative and represented is not unknown, congruence between the two is indicative of institutional democratisation.

The level of democratisation of political institution, particularly the Parliament which is elected is dependent on the structure and organisation of political parties. On the other hand, parliamentary membership is reflective of the structures within the political parties. A more representative Parliament would indicate the openness of the process of political recruitment and structures of mobility based on merit and performance within the political parties. It appears from the study that notwithstanding the tremendous surge in electoral participation, the Lok Sabha continues to be the domain of the elite (variously defined as economic, caste, or class elite). The poor, tribals, women and the backward castes continue to be marginalised within the institutional structures of politics. This is reflective of the limits within which democracy exists in India.

The increasing presence of State Parties in Parliament provides a window of opportunity to expand the democratic space for institutional presence and functional representations. It creates hopes of a substantive democracy. The continued success of State Parties, whose vote share and seat share increased consistently despite the failures of administration, following the United Front experiment is a testimony to the faith reposed in them. Since 1996 the State Parties have aligned with both the government and opposition, giving them an opportunity to influence both equally. This was in a sense a historic opportunity for democratisation. However, State Parties have failed to carry forward the process of political democratisation over the years.

Several structural reasons explain this phenomenon. In the first place as the study shows, the socio-economic composition of the political elite of State Parties is not significantly different from national parties. In terms of age, education, occupation and income they are not significantly different from their counterparts in the national parties. It is found based on the study that the social background of the political elite determines the strategy, the ideology and the political programmes of political parties both within and outside institutional politics. It may be mentioned that the caste affiliation of such parties is different from national parties which has contributed to the innovative strategy of mobilisation. Overall, they appear to a 'chip from the old block' that has not radicalised the Indian democracy beyond elections.

On the other hand most State Parties are leader driven. State Parties such as DMK, AIADMK, BJD, TDP, SP and RJD are all lead by charismatic leaders. Their leaders have contributed to the electoral success of their parties. However, once successful, such leaders have not institutionalised the process of internal democracy within the party. Regional parties often function like 'family enterprises' with decision being taken by the leader or his/her close confidants who is often the members of his/her family. This has restricted the entry of new leaders and new thinking.

The ideology and the roadmap of regional parties is also determined by the leadership. The rigid internal structure of the party and party discipline along with anti-defection laws leaves little room for dissent. The second level leaders of the state party, who are often represented in the legislature, are keen on representing the ideas of the leader/ party. The representation of the concerns related to the constituency assumes secondary importance in the interest of political survival. The fate of the state party elite thus becomes "determined more by the party leadership than the electorate" that determines their continued political relevance.

Much of the shortcomings of the State Parties in legislative performance is also related to the large size of the Lok Sabha and the multitude of complex functions that is required to perform in the post-liberalisation era. This has resulted in gradual dilution of legislative and oversight function of the parliament. The qualifications that are required to contest elections ensure that the composition of the Lok Sabha is essentially that of generalists. Individual legislators, in the absence of adequate technical assistance, find it difficult to participate in the legislative process. Hence, they confine themselves to general discussions on non-technical issues as strict party discipline leaves little time and space for using the legislature as a forum for representation.

State Parties' inability to come to terms with the challenges of modern legislatures are much of their own making as of the product of any general structural changes in Indian politics, or the economy. For instance, while it is true that legislation is becoming increasingly complex and demands a set of technical skills that few parliamentarians possess, much of the inattention to legislative matters is due to their own predilections and incentive structure (Kaur, Mehta, 2006)[7] that places emphasis on symbolic representation, publicity seeking and theatrics.

To this, the role that the State Parties have conceptualised for themselves has added to the chasm. Regional parties have conceived their role as that of 'influencers of the political processes' rather than 'makers of public policy' at the national level and have exercised power accordingly. As a result, the focus of the State Parties has become non-legislative in extra parliamentary bargaining, negotiations and the like. Legislative debates, Question Hour and other instruments of accountability are seen as instruments that further the process of extra-parliamentary bargaining. At most parliamentary procedures like discussions on rule 377 and Special Mention are conceptualised as instruments that provide recognition and exposure to new and inexperienced MPs.

Further, they have failed to capitalize on the mandate given to them for expanding their spheres of operation and influence. This is evidenced by the fact that while their leaders such as J. Jayalalitha of AIADMK or Lalu Prasad of RJD have national aspirations, they had limited ambitions for the party as a whole. Regional parties in general have preferred to increase their influence through power sharing.

Therefore it is often noticed that the continued success of State Parties, is more on account of the perception that they enjoy as "local parties, representing local issues". Their acquaintance with local language, issues and problems have helped in developing a trust between all the representatives of State Parties. Also, State Parties are perceived as being more oriented towards the 'local' and working towards their development. This has helped State Parties in creating bonds of symbolic representation. But, the national parties have failed in this on account of their centralised structures and high command styles, where the candidates for all the elections are chosen by top leadership with little or no consultation with local leaders and party workers.

Legislative Hierarchy and Varying Conceptualisation of Representation

An interesting feature of the State Parties performance in the Lok Sabha is that their articulation of political issues (whether federal, local or national) within the legislature and it is determined by a host of factors such as, their position within the government- opposition continuum, the party ideology, the requirements of party leadership and their own interest. Representation of the constituent's interest is important only in so far as it contributes to remain in public memory. MPs of State Parties have been found juggling between multiple activities of representation and multiple demands of the leadership. Hence MPs are keen in utilizing procedures that give them an opportunity to appease the leadership or gain publicity.

There also appears to be little or no linkages between party manifesto, party ideology and legislative participation. Both for MPs of State Parties as well as the voters there is a clear line of demarcation between the written manifesto and the understood manifesto. The citizens' assessment and the MPs performance are both guided by the understood manifesto. What member's represent and how and when they represent is dependent on two factors like, the understood manifesto and the representative "who" undertakes the responsibility of representation.

It is possible to identify a definite hierarchy within the State Parties, on the basis of their participation in legislative business. In the first place, there are senior leaders of State Parties, who are experienced, often educated with professional background and either leaders of their party or close confidants of the party leadership. Often, parliamentary strategies of state party MP's are drawn out by them. Such members are articulate, participate regularly on issues of national importance and put forth the party's view point and political stand within the legislature. Such members participate on important legislative discussion, no confidence motions (if in opposition) and sometimes in Question Hour.

A second level of MP's articulate on local and constituency level issues. Such members are less educated /articulate than their senior counterparts, often carrying out the commands of the party leadership, with limited degree of autonomy and they participate largely in discussions that do not involve voting and stating of party position. The audience for the two categories of MPs is different. While the first group speaks to the nation about the party/leaders stands, the second group largely addresses the local electors who elect them. The first is national in its orientation, the second more local. The first wants and encourages arguments, the second is interested in immediate reach that the issue may have amongst its electorates.

Both groups of state party elite conceptualize representation differently, while the former, representation refers to the act of representing the interest or ideology that the party stands for to the larger public, the latter interprets representation in narrow sociological terms as well as an activity that brings local issues to the forefront temporarily. There is little or no match between the conceptualisation of these two ideas of representation and often take place simultaneously.

National Legislature & Local Perspective

What is also interesting is that the membership of national legislative institution seems to have a salutary effect on MPs of State Parties, notwithstanding their geographical and socio-economic support base. Therefore, MPs of State Parties largely adopt a national perspective during the course of parliamentary business. Once elected to the national parliament, they do not necessarily regard themselves as the representatives of the state or the community that may have contributed to their election. The perspective of the State party MPs towards his role is shaped by the demands of the electorate; the nature of issue being raised and the political situation.

On a large number of issues such as those relating to agriculture, setting up of industries, development of infrastructure the state party MPs adopt a national perspective without losing sight of their local responsibilities. On a large number of issues MPs of State Parties go beyond merely representing their constituency. Thus, for instance, the large number of questions raised by them relating to environment, foreign policy, sports indicates that State party MPs regard themselves as delegates interpreting the "public good" on behalf of the electorate. Given the fact that the electorate may not necessarily have either information to form opinion or a clear opinion of some of the issues, the role of state party MP's in this regard is of significance.

MP's of State Parties are akin to that of national parties in their educational and economic background, with some difference between them in terms of caste background. Often the more active members of the Parliament are those that belong to bigger and older State Parties, are leaders of their respective parliamentary party and have considerable legislative experience. Such members are also often better educated, articulate, socialised in urban or semi-urban surroundings and are able to speak either in English or Hindi on account of their familiarity with the language. The political philosophy and world view of such members are often influenced by national issues. Such members distinguish between national level political institutions and state /local level institutions as well as electioneering and institutional functioning. In view of this, such members across party lines often articulate on national issues.

Whither Now?

There may be two different approaches to these developments. In the first place, representation could be perceived as weakening of the State Parties that arose on regional sentiments and sub- national identity. They may appear to defeat the very purpose and objective for which they emerged and may ultimately lead to their collapse. It may also be strengthening of political institutions at the central level which were conceived as instruments of national consensus building. It is possible to argue that the nature of national political institutions create conditions that are conducive to developing national perspectives and national consensus. The myriad State Parties, notwithstanding their origin, ideology, objectives and support base submerge their interest creating what may be termed as "national interest."

It would appear from the study that State Parties that have often followed the principle of focused mobilisation (Palshikar: 2000), mobilizing the electorate on a single issue and a single identity do not have a single point or focused agenda for representation. While the political manifesto of the parties does provide a basis of representation for MPs, often there is little in common between what the manifesto seeks to do and what the representative does. There is in practice a difference between the written manifesto and the manifesto that is understood. The MPs are aware of the written party manifesto however, the understood manifesto is what actually guides the MP.

The dichotomy between the two often leads to tension between the representative, the represented and the observer. Thus, the transition from mobilisation to representation has not been a seamless process for State Parties. While MPs of State Parties have made attempts to interpret the mandate given to them, participate in legislative process, they have opted for issues and procedures that may give them the visibility. This has also meant that they have along with the members of national parties, resorted to the use of unparliamentary methods. What is of greater importance is that State Parties despite their large numbers and growing influence has not done anything that is either different or new. They have followed the trails of national parties, losing out on opportunities of innovation. Even on issues of central state relations or procedures that allow for representing local issues state party MPs participation has not been much different. They have raised local issues from national lenses and rural and sub-national issues from urban points of view. Their own personal background and education and economic status has often created a chasm between what they represent and what they seek to represent.

State Party MPs have also adopted such perspective to shrug the parochial tag which is often ascribed to them. Thus, members have shunned from exhaustively discussing local issues, even when there was an opportunity to do so. Notwithstanding these, the reelection of MPs of State Parties, at least till 2014 and their high approval rating in the 15th Lok Sabha indicates that there is a degree of satisfaction with the State Parties. Most respondents of the survey too held a similar opinion.

Summing Up

The success of State Parties may be attributed to structural shift in Indian politics on account of democratisation of Indian polity. The deepening of electoral democracy, partially due to strategies of mobilisation adopted by State Parties has brought the dominant, economically prosperous backward castes, within the fold of democratic process. The leadership, policies and programmes of State Parties have made them appear more accessible compared to national parties that appeared to be impermeable with their rigid structure and unchanging leadership styles.

Ironically, however, the State Parties have not been able to carry forward the process of political democratisation at the institutional level of parliamentary institutions. They have neither provided access to institutional structures to a new category of people, nor have they used the institutions effectively to further the ends that their constituents chose them to represent. State Parties have failed in their responsibility of representing both in sociological sense and in terms of representation of interest. They have confined their roles to representing the party interest, often appeasing multiple constituencies of party leadership, electorate, state, region and constituencies. In the process they have failed to use the democratic potential of the legislature which could have served as a game changer. They have in essence followed the footsteps of older and established national parties, the discontentment of which contributed to their success.

Therefore, the disjuncture between electoral democracy which has become increasingly robust and institutional democracy that is faced severe challenges has effectively limited the political choices available to the electorate.

Echoing the same concern, B.R. Ambedkar, the father of the Indian Constitution, had observed in the Constituent Assembly:

> I feel, however, good a Constitution may be, it is sure to turn out bad because those who are called to work, happen to be a bad lot...The working of the Constitution does not depend wholly upon the nature of the Constitution. The Constitution can provide only the organs of state such as the Legislature, the Executive and the Judiciary. The factors

on which the working of those organs of the state depends are the people and the political parties they will set up as their instruments to carry out their wishes and their politics. Who can say how the people of India and their parties will behave?

Though the nature of political system has changed there is fear that political dissatisfaction may lead to realignment of existing parties or emergence of newer political forces that may carry forward the process of political democratisation to the realm of institutions and policies. In this hope lies with the future of the Indian democracy.

References & Notes

Kothari Rajni, (1970) *Politics in India*, New Delhi: Orient Longman, pp. 152-167.

Arora, Balveer 2012 in *The Party System in India, Federalised and Bi-nodal,* in Mehra Ajay (ed) Party System in India and its Emerging Trajectories New Delhi: Sage.

Mishra Vandana (2009), Crisis of Indian Parties, Mainstream Weekly.

Tillin Louise (2014), Battle for Regions in India's Parliamentary Elections, Ballots and Bullets, The University of Nottingham.

Kapur, Devesh. Mehta,Pratp Bhanu (2006) The Indian Parliament as an Institution ofAccountability, UNDP Democracy, Governance and Human Rights Programme, Paper Number 23, January.

Notes

1. Kothari, Rajni. (1970) Politics in India New Delhi :Orient Longman, pp. 152-167.
2. Arora, Balveer. in the Party System in India, Federalised and Bi-nodal, in Mehra, Ajay (ed) *Party System in India and its Emerging Trajectories*, Sage, New Delhi, 2012.
3. Mishra, Vandana. (2009) Crisis of Indian Parties, *Mainstream Weekly,* Delhi.
4. Tillin, Louise. (2014) Battle for Regions in India's Parliamentary Elections, Ballots and Bullets, Nottingham: The University of Nottingham.
5. Discussions on price rise have witnessed widespread participation in the 15th Lok Sabha - 110 MPs from 26 political parties discussed the issue for 35 hours. In some recent sessions, the opposition has demanded an adjournment motion on the issue of price rise. The adjournment motion is a call to set aside the regular business of the House and take up a specific matter for discussion. Such a motion is voted upon, and if passed, is considered as censure against the government.
6. Interview with MP.
7. Devesh Kapur, Pratap Bhanu Mehta,The Indian Parliament as an Institution of Accountability, UNDP Democracy, Governance and Human Rights Programme Paper Number 23, January 2006.

Bibliography

1. *Lok Sabha, Parliament of India (1957-2009), New* Delhi: Lok Sabha Secretariat
2. Lok Sabha Secretariat, (2004-2009) *Resume of Work Done by the Lok Sabha First to Fifteenth Session*, New Delhi: Lok Sabha Secretariat.
3. Lok Sabha Secretariat, (1958-2004) *Who's Who of Lok Sabha*, New Delhi: Lok Sabha Secretariat.
4. Election Commission of India. (2004), *Statistical Report on the General Elections, to the Fourteenth Lok Sabha*, Vol. 1, National and State Abstracts, New Delhi.
5. Government of India, Ministry of Parliamentary Affairs, (2009), *Statistical Handbook of Ministry of Parliamentary Affairs*, New Delhi: Government of India.
6. Government of India, Ministry of Parliamentary Affairs. (2004), *Handbook on the Working of Ministry of Parliamentary Affairs* New Delhi: Concept Publishing.
7. Government of India, Ministry of Parliamentary Affairs. (2004) *Manual of Parliamentary Procedures in the Government of India*, New Delhi.
8. Piano Aili And Puddington Arch (Eds) (2004), *The Annual Survey Of Political Rights & Civil Liberties,* Washington DC: Freedom House
9. Arora, Balveer and Kailash, K.K. (2013), The New Party System; Federalised and Binodal, in Mehra Ajay. K. (Ed.) *Party System and India and its Emerging Trajectories*. Atlanta: Lancer Publisher.
10. Beard, Charles A. (1941), Whom Does the Congress Represent? in A.N. Christensen and E.M. Kirkpatrick (Eds.), *The People, Politics and Politician.* New York: Henry Holt and Company.
11. Beard, A. Charles and Lewis, D. John. (Eds.) (1967), Representative Government in Evolution, in Hanna F. Pitkin. *The Concept of Representation*. Berkeley: University of California Press
12. Burns. J.H. & Hart, H.L.A. (Eds.) (1996), *The Collected Works of Jeremy Bentham: An Introduction to the Principles of Morals and Legislation.* Delhi: Oxford University Press.
13. Carr, Robert,(1959) *American Democracy in Theory and Practice.* New York: Holt, Rinehart, Winston.
14. Chandhoke, Neera and Praveen Priyadarshi (Eds.) (2009), *Contemporary India: Economy, Society and Politics.* New Delhi: Longman.
15. Sheth, D.L., (2002), Caste and Class: Social Reality and Political Representations, in Ghanshyam Shah (Ed.),in *Caste and Domestic Politics in India,* Ranikhet: Permanent Black.

16. Downs, Anthony. (1952) *An Economic theory of Democracy*. New York: Harper.
17. Diamond, Larry and Gunther, Richard. (Eds.) (2001), *Political Parties and Democracy.* Baltimore and London Johns Hopkins University Press.
18. Emden, S. Cecil. (1933) *The People and the Constitution.* Oxford: Oxford University Press.
19. Ford, Henry. J. *Representative Government.* (1924) New York:, Henry Holt & Co.
20. Francine, Frankel, R and Zoya Hasan. (2000) *Transforming India: Social and Political Dynamics of Democracy.* New Delhi:, Oxford University Press.
21. Friedrich. J. Carl. (1950) *Constitutional Government and Democracy: Theory and Practice in Europe and America.* Boston Ginn and Company.
22. Omvedt, Gail. *Dalits and Democratic Revolution*, (1994) New Delhi: Sage.
23. Gosnell, Foote. Harold. (1948) *Democracy, the Threshold of Freedom.* New York: Ronald Press.
24. Grazia, Antonio. (2004) *Encyclopedia of Political Ideas.* London: Blackwell Publication.
25. Hansen, Herman Mogens. (1991) *The Athenian Democracy in the Age of Demosthenes: Structure, Principles, and Ideology* J.A. Cooks, Trans, Oxford: Blackwell Publishers.
26. Held, David. (Ed.) *(1993) Prospects of Democracy- North, South, East, West. Cambridge: UK Polity Press.*
27. Hogan, James. (1945) *Election and Representation. Oxford:* Cork University Press.
28. Morris-Jones, W.H. (1957) *India: Parliament in India*. London: Longmans Green and Co.
29. Kothari, Rajni. (1970) *Politics in India*. Delhi: little Brown and Company.
30. Kohli, Atul. K. (2009) *Democracy and Development in India: From Socialism to Pro- Business*. New Delhi: Oxford University Press.
31. Kumari, Pushpa. 'The Changing Nature of Party System' in Neera Chandhoke and Praveen Priyadarshi (Eds.), (1999) *Contemporary India: Economy, Society, Politics.* New Delhi: Pearson.
32. Luce, Robert. (1930) *Legislative Principles: The History and Theory of Lawmaking by representative government,* Boston: Houghton Milflin and Co.
33. McBain, Lee. Howard. (1927) *The Living Constitution*. New York: The Macmillan Co.
34. Weiner, Myron. (2001) "The Struggle for Equality, Caste in Indian Politics", in Atul Kohli and G.P. Hawthorn (Eds.), *The Success of India's Democracy*, Delhi: Cambridge University Press.
35. Palishkar, Suhas. (2004) The Regional Parties and Democracy: Romantic Rendezvous or Localised Legitimation? in Ajay K. Mehra, D.D. Khanna and Gert W. Kueck (Eds.) (2003), *Political Parties and Party Systems.* New Delhi: Sage.
36. Pitkin, Hanna. F. (1967) *The Concept of Representation*, Berkeley: University of California Press.

37. Stokes C, Susan, Adam Przeworski and Bernard Manin (Eds.) (1999) *Democracy, Accountability, and Representation*. Cambridge: Cambridge University Press.

38. Ranney, Austin and Kendall. W. (1956) *Political Parties, Democracy and American Party System,* New York: Harcourt Brace and Company.

39. Wolin, S. Sheldon. (1960) *Politics and Vision*, Princeton, New Jersey: Princeton University Press.

40. Strene, Simon. (1871) *Representative Government and Personal Representation,* Philadelphia: J.B. Lipponcot& Company.

41. Suri, K.C. (2010) Parties under Pressure. *Working Paper Series*. New Delhi: (2010) CSDS.

42. Roy, Ramashray and Wallace, Paul. (Eds.) (1999) *Indian Politics and the 1998 elections,* New Delhi: Sage publication.

43. Pai, Sudha. *Dalit Assertion and Unfinished Democratic Revolution: (2002), The Bahujana Samaj Party in Uttar Pradesh*, New Delhi: Sage Publications.

44. Weiner, Myron.(1957) *Party Politics in India: The Development of a Multi-Party System*, London: Oxford University Press.

45. Kumari, Pushpa. The changing Nature of Party System in Neera Chandhoke, Praveen Priyadarshi (Eds.), (2009) *Contemporary India: The Changing Nature of Party System*, New Delhi: Pearson India.

46. Prakash, Amit. Regionalism, Politics of Autonomy and Smaller states in Ajay Mehra (Ed.) (2010) *Emerging Trends in Indian Politics*, the 15th Lok Sabha Elections, New Delhi: Routledge.

47. Wahlang, Allanson.(2010) Analysis of Election Manifesto of Major Political Parties in India, in *Dalit and Tribe Worldpress.com,* (Available at www.dalitandtribe.wordpress.com/2010/01/21/analysis-of-election-manifestos-of-major-political-parties-in-india/)

48. Rao, Sarraju Narasinga. (2014) Lok Sabha Elections 2014: The Anatomy of the Election Manifesto, Wednesday, 9 April 2014, DNA, Mumbai (Available at ww.dnaindia.com/analysis/standpoint-lok-sabha-elections-2014-the-anatomy-of-the-election-manifesto-1976723)

49. Balaji J., (2013) Parties Assert Right to Announce Freebies in Election Manifestos, in *The Hindu*. Chennai.

50. Manisha, M. (2012) *Parliamentary Efficacy and Role of Opposition in India: A Comparative Study of Second and Fourteenth Lok Sabha*, Unpublished Report to Rajya Sabha, 2012.

51. *Kumar, Akshay (2006)* Now 'Silent' MPs irk Lok Sabha Speaker', *in Hindustan Times* New Delhi:, Available at http://www.hindustantimes.com/india-news/newdelhi/now-silent-mps-irk-lok-sabha-speaker/article1-383675.aspx)

52. Dhillon, Sarnjit Singh, (SAD) on 22nd June 2006 (http://164.100.47.132/lssnew/psearch/result14.aspx?dbsl=5561)

53. Jaitley, Arun. (2013). *Third Front: My Opinion (*Available atwww.arunjaitley.com, http://www.arunjaitley.com/en/my-opinion-inside.php?id=77&mode=Read&icatId=16 (Accessed on September 3, 2013)

54. Nigam, Aditya and Yogendra Yadav, (2000) 'Electoral Politics in Indian States, 1989-1999, *Economic and Political Weekly*, Mumbai: Sameeksha Trust

55. Kohli, Atul Kohli (Ed.), *(1988) India's Democracy: An Analysis of Changing State Society Relations, Princeton,* New Jerssy: Princeton University Press.

56. Sheth, D.L., Caste and Class: Social Reality and Political Representation in Ghanshyam Shah (Ed.), (2002) *Caste and Democratic Politics in India,* New Delhi: Permanent Black.

57. Panandiker, V.A. Pai and Ashis Nandy (Eds.) (1999) *Contemporary India,* New Delhi: Tata-McGraw Hill, p. 220.

58. Kapur, Devesh and Mehta, Pratap Bhanu. (2006) *The Indian Parliament as an Institution of Accountability, Democracy, Governance and Human Rights Programme, Paper Number 23*, United Nations Research Institute for Social Development, Geneva: 2006.

59. Kumar, Gopa K. (1886) *Regional Political Parties and State Politics,* New Delhi: Deep and Deep Publications.

60. Granville, Austin. (1966) *Indian Constitution: Cornerstone of a Nation* New Delhi: Oxford University Press.

61. Pai, Sudha, (1998) The Indian Party System under Transformation: Lok Sabha Elections 1998', in *Asian Survey*, vol. 38, no. 9, Berkeley: University of California Press.

62. Yadav, Yogendra. (2001) Understanding the Second Democratic Upsurge: Trends of Bahujan participation in Electoral Politics in 1990s, in Francine Frankel, Zoya Hasan, Rajeev Bhargav (Eds.), (2001) *Transforming India: Social and Political Dynamics of Democracy*, New Delhi: Oxford University Press

63. ————————, (2002) Understanding the Second Democratic Upsurge: Trends of Bahujan Participation in Electoral Politics in the 1990s, in *Transforming India: Social and Political dynamics of democracy* (Eds.) Francine Frankel and Ors., New Delhi: Oxford University Press.

64. Hasan, Zoya (Ed.) (1999) *Parties and Party Politics in India: Themes in Politics*, New Delhi: Oxford University Press.

65. Chandra, Kanchan. (2004) *Why Ethnic Parties Succeed: Patronage and Ethnic Head Counts in India,* Cambridge: CambridgeUniversity Press, Cambridge.

66. Jafferlot Christophe and Blom Hansen, Thomas (Ed.), (1998) *The BJP and the Compulsions of Politics*, New Delhi: Oxford University Press.

67. *Background Paper on the Working of the Indian Parliament and Need for Reforms*, Ministry of Law, http://lawmin.nic.in/ncrwc/finalreport/v2b3-1.htm (Accessed on 8 July 2016)

68. Mehra Ajay K.(2007) 'Indian Parliament and the "Grammar of Anarchy"', in National Social Watch Coalition (ed.), *Citizens Report on Governance and Development*, New Delhi: Sage.

69. Malhotra G.C. (Ed.), *Fifty Years of Indian Parliament*, New Delhi: Lok Sabha Secretariat, 2002.

70. Rao Gorantala. Bhaskar (2010), *Research Brief on Performance of MPs of 15th Lok Sabha*, National Social Watch, http://socialwatchindia.net/images/documents/418/Performance%20of%20MPs%20of%2015th%20Lok%20Sabha.pdf; *Citizens Report on Governance and Development*, National Social Watch, New Delhi: Sage, 2010 (Accessed on 16 July 2016)

Websites

http//www. http://www.legalreform-now.org/menu1_5.htm

Official website of election Commission of India: http://www.eci.gov.in

For Miscellaneous Statistics provided by Election Commission of India http://www.eci.gov.in/MiscStats/misc_fs.htm

For Election Results from 1977-2004:http://eci.gov.in/DataBase/DataBase_fs.htm

For a report on the working of the 14th Lok Sabha : http://www.socialwatch.org/

For handbook in the working of Ministry of parliamentary affairs : http://mpa.nic.in/handbook1/part-1.pdf

For Manual on Parliamentary procedures http://mpa.nic.in/Manual/Manual_English/Chapters.html

For annual report of Ministry of Parliamentary affairs: http://mpa.nic.in/annualre.htm

Official website of Lok Sabha: http://www.loksabha.nic.in/

For Constituent Assembly Debates : http://parliamentofindia.nic.in/ls/debates/debates.htm

For Debates in the 14th Lok sabha : http://164.100.24.208/ls/lsdeb/ls-archivedeb.htm

Appendix

Top Performing Members in Legislative Debates in 14th Lok Sabha

Name	*State*	*Party*	*Participation in Debates*
BhartruhariMahtab	Orissa	BJD	227
Ram Kripal Yadav	Bihar	RJD	230
Ramji Lal Suman	Uttar Pradesh	SP	204
Rasa Singh Rawat	Rajasthan	BJP	194
Shailendra Kumar	Uttar Pradesh	SP	340

Source: Lok Sabha Secretariat (2009-2014). Lok Sabha Debates, New Delhi.

Nature of Issued Raised During Legislative Debates(Select Sessions)

Session	*International Issues*	*National Issues*	*Local/ Constituency Level issues*
2004 Monsoon session	0	9	0
2005 Budget Session	4	33	7
2006 Winter Session	0	26	4
2007 Budget Session	0	33	2
2008 Monsoon session	0	18	0
2009 Budget Session	0	23	5

Source: Lok Sabha Secretariat (2009-2014). Lok Sabha Debates, New Delhi.

Nature of Bills Discussed; Bills Under Discussion in Select Sessions of Fourteenth Lok Sabha

Central Universities Bill, 2009	2/19/2009	22	Smt. Purandeswari (INC), S. Kharventhan (INC), J.M Aaron rashid (INC), Balasaheb V. Patil (INC), Giridhar Gamang (INC), K.C Singh Baba (INC), Prof. Chander Kumar (INC), Tejaswini Gowda (INC), Rasa Singh Rawat (BJP), Bachi Singh Rawat (BJP) Virendra Kumar (BJP), Basudeb Barman (CPI), Suvaram S. Reddy (CPI), P. Rajendran (CPI) Varkala Radhakrishnan (CPI(M)) Ram Ji Lal Suman (SP), Ram Kripal Yadav (RJD), Bhartruhari Mahtab (BJD), P.C. Thomas (Kerela Congress), Alok Kumar Mehta (RJD), K. Francis George (Kerela Congress), Sansuma K. Bwiswmuthiary (BPF)	7	English: 15 Hindi:7

(Contd...)

High Court and Supreme Court Judges (Salaries and Conditions of Service) Amendment Bill, 2008	2/19/2009	13	Prasanna Acharya (BJD), Ramdas Athawale (RPI), H.R Bharadwaj (INC), Varkala Radhakrishnan, CPI(M), Tejaswini Gowda (INC) S. Kharventhan (INC), Vijay Bahuguna (INC), Rasa Singh Rawat (BJP), Bachi Singh Rawat "Bachda" (BJP), Rewati Raman Singh (SP), Ajoy Chakraborty (CPI), P. Saathedevi (CPI), Sebastian Paul (Independent)	4	English :9 Hindi: 4
National Capital Territory of Delhi Laws (Special Provisions) Bill, 2009	2/19/2009	10	S. Jaipal Reddy (INC) Syed Shahnawaz Hussain (BJP) Sajjan Kumar (INC) Krishna Teerath (INC) Jagdish Tytler (INC) Ajay Maken (INC) Sudhangshu Seal (CPI) Rajesh Ranjan (RJD) Braja Kishore Tripathy (BJD) P.C Thomas (Kerela Congress)	4	English:5 Hindi:4
Maternity Benefit (Amendment) Bill, 2007	3/19/2008	17	Krishna Teerath (INC) Pratibha Singh (INC) Oscar Fernandes (INC) Sumitra Mahajan (BJP) Sangeeta Kumari Deo (BJP) Rupatai Patil (BJP) Kiran Maheshwari (BJP) Karuna Shukla (BJP) P. Sathidevi (CPI) Prabodh Panda (CPI) Varkala Radhakrishnan (CPI(M) Shailendra Kumar (SP) Ram Kripal Yadav (RJD) SHh. A. Krishnaswamy (DMK) Sugrib Singh (BJD) Kalpana Narhire (SS) M. Shivanna (Janata Dal Secular)	6	Hindi:8 English :7 Oriya Kannada
The Prevention of Money Laundering (Amendment) Bill, 2008	2/24/2009	11	Pawan Kumar Bansal (INC) Laxman Singh (BJP) Vijyendra Pal Singh (BJP) Suvaram S. Reddy (CPI) C.K Chandrappan (CPI) Rupchand Pal (CPI) Mohan Rawale (SS) Alok Kumar Mehta (RJD) Bhartruhari Mahtab (BJD) Braja Kishore Tripathy (BJD) Suresh Prabhakar Prabhu (SS)	5	English:8 Hindi :3

Top Performing Members in the Question Hour of 14th Lok Sabha

Name	***State***	***Party***	***No. Of Questions raised***
Anandrao Vithoba Adsul	Maharashtra	SS	1255
Braja Kishore Tripathy	Orissa	BJD	1048
Ravi Prakash Verma	Uttar Pradesh	SP	1050
Salarapatty Kuppusamy Kharventhan	Tamil Nadu	INC	1108
Shivaji Adhalrao Patil	Maharashtra	SS	1251
Sugrib Singh	Orissa	BJD	1083

Source: Lok Sabha Secretariat (2009-2014). Lok Sabha Debates, New Delhi.

Subject Wise Classification of Issues Raised by MPs of State Parties

Nature of issues raised	*2004*	*2005*	*2006*	*2007*	*2008*	*2009*
Industry/trade	18	20	11	29	3	4
Infrastructure	9	26	15	8	3	9
Agriculture related	7	10	10	9	2	o
Development -rural, urban	9	15	6	2	1	4
Health and education	15	18	14	13	3	6
Environment	6	13	5	4	4	1
Calamities-man made and natural	8	2	1	1	0	0
Grants for projects	6	5	1	1	0	1
Funds/finance	8	12	6	6	1	2
Law and order	11	6	6	3	1	3
Community marginalisation	1	3	0	0	0	0
Price rise/ Current issue	6	2	1	2	1	2
FP/Security	3	13	2	4	2	1
Culture/ sports	6	3	2	1	1	
Administration/Policy	3	17	3	20	2	3

Source: Lok Sabha Secretariat (2009-2014). Lok Sabha Debates, New Delhi.

Participation in Discussion of Resolution by MPS of State Parties (Select Sessions) of 14th Lok Sabha

Dates	*Session*		*Participation*	*No of Participants from State parties*	*Time Spent*
5/7/2004 to 26/8/2004	Monsoon		7	6	
25/2/2005 to 3/5/2005	Budget		40	22	
22/11/2006 to 9/12/2006	Winter		5	5	
23/2/2007 to 17/5/2007	Budget		5	5	
17/8/2008 to 25/12/2008	Monsoon		10	10	
12.02.2009 to 26.02.2009	Budget		5	5	
Total					

Source: Lok Sabha Secretariat (2009-2014). Lok Sabha Debates, New Delhi.

Participation of State Party MPs in Special Mentions (Select Sessions) of 14th Lok Sabha

Dates	*Session*	*No of matters raised by MPs of state Parties*	*No of participants from State Parties*
5/7/2004 to 26/82004	Monsoon	77	39
25/22005 to 3/5/2005	Budget	114	21
22/11/2006 to 9/12/2006	Winter	113	41
23/2/2007 to 17/5/2007	Budget	92	41
17/8/2008 to 25/12/2008	Monsoon	87	41
12.02.2009 to 26.02.2009	Budget	33	16

Source: Lok Sabha Secretariat (2009-2014). Lok Sabha Debates, New Delhi.

Issues Considered Important in Elections

	Basic Needs	**Corruption**	**Violence**	**Stability**	
1998	42	14	12	13	
	Poverty	***Corruption***	***Law & Order***	***Employment***	***Unity of the Country***
1996	42	16	6	24	6

Source: India Today, 4-8 Feb, 1998,N= 8938, India Today June 6-9, 1996, N=12777.

Index

Q

R

S

T